PROBATION—THE SECOND CHANCE

By the same author

ROAST BEEF AND PICKLES

A TRICK OF THE SUN

SURGEON AT ARMS
(with Daniel Paul)

Probation—The Second Chance

by

JOHN ST JOHN

VISTA BOOKS
LONDON

First published 1961 by
VISTA BOOKS
Longacre Press Ltd, 161-166 Fleet St., London E.C.4.
Printed in Great Britain by
Cox and Wyman, London, Fakenham and Reading

AUTHOR'S NOTE

'Why, precisely, do you want to write this book?' The question was scarcely unexpected but I knew that anything I could say must sound inadequate. The interview took place at the Home Office in a high-ceilinged room on the first floor, designed, one felt, to provide a suitable setting for the initialling of deportation orders and last-minute reprieves from the gallows. It was not the place nor was it the occasion for the lengthy self-analysis that alone could reveal the complex of motives and hopes that propelled me into asking for their help. Not that everyone was not being very kind. There was nothing intimidating about the lively, boyish man who presided and had asked the question, even though he was an Assistant Under-Secretary of State; the presence of the head of the Probation Division and also of its Principal Inspector, of the Home Office's Principal Information Officer and his assistant showed that my request was being taken very seriously.

I explained why I believed it would be in the interests of the Service if the public were told a little more about what it did . . . that many believed the fallacy that probation officers were only concerned with juvenile delinquents . . . that apart from textbooks the subject had been largely neglected . . . that like most writers I was interested in criminals and the law . . . Offenders who got probation disappeared from public view—unless accused later of a further offence—and I wanted to discover what happened to them, what was done to help them, and how they reacted. But the book would be impossible unless I was granted access to confidential records.

'You know, you're asking quite a lot. It's something we've never permitted before—for very obvious reasons.'

I agreed, but went on to argue that I had often heard that no one still in the Service felt able to write about his or her own cases, because they were involved in them too personally and it would amount to an unthinkable breach of trust. The officials replied that they would have to think my proposal over.

A few weeks later there was a further interview at which I submitted a more detailed outline of the book I had in mind. My request was granted. I could examine case-records, visit courts, meet probation officers and probationers, with the Home Office's backing and blessing. The terms could not have been more generous. I was invited to show them my manuscript, not so that they could censor it, but merely to allow them an opportunity to offer their comments. I was free to say what I liked—and I must emphasize that the opinions expressed in this book do not necessarily belong to anyone but myself—subject to only one, very understandable, safeguard: that I should take every reasonable step necessary to disguise the individuals in the cases I described, so that they could not be identified. By changing the circumstantial details, altering names and so on I have been very careful to do this, and the probation officers concerned have double-checked my precautions. In their important essentials, though, the cases in this book are as true as it has lain in my power to make them.

Apart from this single safeguard, the Home Office imposed no limitations whatsoever. The facilities I was granted by its Probation Division were unique, and I am very grateful for them. This book could never have been written if I had not also been able to count upon the co-operation and advice of the probation service itself and, in particular, of several individual probation officers. Unfortunately, as I am pledged not to reveal their identities, I cannot thank them by name, but I do so now collectively; and also the many other experts both in and outside the courts who have given me so much of their time and knowledge. I hope they will understand that to single out names would, in the circumstances, be invidious. There is, however, no hindrance to my expressing publicly my gratitude to the National Association of Probation Officers, nor to their excellent journal Probation *and their textbook* The Probation Service[1] *which has been my most important source of information about the technique of probation casework. I also gratefully acknowledge a very special debt to the* British Journal of Delinquency,[2] *published by the Institute for the Study and Treatment of Delinquency.*

J. St J.

[1] Edited by Joan King, Butterworth, 1958.

[2] Now the *British Journal of Criminology*, published for the I.S.T.D. by Stevens.

CONTENTS

FOREWORD

FRANK DAWTRY, M.B.E.

General Secretary, the National Association of Probation Officers

'I would like to do a useful job and, as I am very fond of children, will you please tell me how I can become a probation officer?' This is a common inquiry, one that shows how persistent is the misunderstanding about the work involved in probation. Simply being fond of children is no guarantee of an ability to help them; while probation officers do of course deal with many children, a sizeable proportion of those placed on probation are adult—and it is with adults that Mr St John is most concerned. A probation officer must indeed be able to love the whole human race, but even that is not sufficient.

Nor is it sufficient to want to do a useful job, encouraging though such a desire is in this age of mechanical but frustrating progress. 'Vocation' is a noble word, for too long used to exploit those who follow it, but vocation needs to be supported by training and practice. Those who come into probation must expect to meet new forms of frustration and disappointment, they must understand their own motives; and because many of the people they meet will be unwilling partners in the process of rehabilitation and will not have asked for the help which is being offered, every probation officer must be able to 'accept' a good deal of aggression and opposition. He, or she, must combine the desire to help with skill in understanding and with the authority of the courts. It is not a job for lightweights or simple 'do-gooders'.

Mr St John realized all this; he realized also how little it is understood and he set about a self-appointed task of interpreting, as a layman to laymen, some aspects of the life and work of the probation service. He had official permission to attend courts, to sit with probation officers, to meet offenders and share visits to their homes; the result of his research is a valuable survey both of people who find themselves in trouble and the technique used in assisting them. He helps to unravel some of the strange, mysterious reasons that can bring a person into court, to explain the apparently inexplicable.

This is no official handbook; the views and comments are the author's own. He has done a remarkably successful job in describing and conveying a section of the life of a national service which today is dealing with 60,000 people on probation, with 10,000 who have left penal institutions, and many others under supervision; which handles some 75,000 matrimonial problems a year, and makes over 100,000 inquiries each year for the guidance of the courts. The picture given in the pages that follow should help to widen understanding of what all this involves, and for this reason those who work with and in the Service will be grateful to Mr St John, whose own understanding and tolerance during the preparation of his book made him seem like one of us. I am proud enough of the probation service for this to be meant as a sincere compliment. I hope this book will be widely read.

FRANK DAWTRY

I

Laying the Odds on Terry

*

'ANOTHER let-off! What he needs is a bloody good thrashing—no blotting-paper in his trousers neither.' I was half-way across the court's vestibule and had been buttonholed by one of the 'regulars' from the public gallery. He had little time for probation, 'except for some of the nippers'. He knew: he had been coming for close on ten years, he reminded me with a nudge, though he spent his afternoons in the reading-room at the municipal library. 'That young man, he'll be back, you mark my words—as sure as there's tea in China . . . treating 'em soft never did no good . . . give 'em something they'll not forget in a hurry . . .'

I had heard it all before and escaped as soon as I could, leaving him muttering to himself. Afterwards I wished I had tried to explain all I had learned about the boy who had just left the dock—not that it would have sounded very convincing. A fortnight earlier, on the day when Terry was remanded for a report, Mr Young, the senior of the court's four probation officers, had been very uncertain. It was the mother, he told me, her self-righteousness and failure to understand the boy, that had first made him feel that Terry might deserve a chance:

'If they send Terry away, my husband—his stepfather that is—will never get over it. It's not as if he's a strong man as it is. I'm

Note.— These are not true names. Throughout this book, for reasons which appear in the author's introductory note, there has been in the case of all probationers and their families and of the probation officers concerned, a change of name; and, where necessary, of other personal description in order to avoid disclosure of indentities.

telling you, Mr Young, the shame is more than either of us can bear. I don't know how I can force myself out to do the shopping, I don't really. I just don't understand where Terry gets it from. My family's respectable, never been in trouble and nobody could have done more for him. He's only got himself to blame. It hasn't always been easy, but he's never been made to feel unwanted. He's only had to ask and he's had his own way—not that we ever spoiled him. He's never lacked a good home—and this is all the thanks we get for——'

'We quite understand, Mrs Cox,' Mr Young interrupted. 'You've told us about that already. What we've now got to think about is what's best for Terry in the immediate future, though the decision of course lies with the court. I can only make recommendations.'

'If they send him away, Mr Cox is as good as in his coffin. You tell that to the judge!'

'I should have thought,' Mr Young replied with abnormal coldness, 'that both of you have rejected the boy enough already, without your husband going to quite those lengths.' The sarcasm was usually reserved for colleagues or his case-notes—not that Terry's mother was capable of grasping what he meant. Her sallow, faintly rodent, resentful little face was twisted by an increasingly belligerent self-pity, and it was time to bring the interview to an end, particularly as the lunch adjournment would be over in another ten minutes.

When she had finally been manœuvred back into the waiting-room, Mr Young released a little more frustrated aggression by saying: 'Terry calls her "a bitchy old cow" and for once I'm inclined to agree with him.' When I first attached myself to his court, Mr Young had not spoken to me so frankly. Though I could not have been there without the Home Office's blessing and he had agreed very readily that the kind of book I had in mind could be useful, I suspected that he was more worried at my presence than he showed; but once I had managed to disperse his very reasonable doubts, there was nothing, I believe, he kept back from me. He was the first and most generous of my tutors. Like no one else, he also had the gift of communicating a reasoned optimism. The unhappiness, anger, stupidity, dirt of all kinds, and cruelty met with during a normal morning in court, the mere quantity of it all was, I found, depressing and exhausting, but Mr Young's company usually restored me and made it easier to view cases less subjectively. Occasionally, as with Terry's mother, he found relief himself in sarcasm as tart as an olive, his normal style, which was reassuring and quietly wise, making it all the more effective.

Terry meanwhile had been kept locked in the cells at the court, waiting to be taken back to the remand prison, as his case had been put back for a probation officer's report, following a plea of guilty: the offence was assisting two older men in the theft of some cases of whisky from the back of a lorry. His role had been to divert the lorry-driver's attention by asking the way to the nearest bus-stop, while his two associates removed the whisky. In their hurry one of the cases had been dropped. The crash caused the driver to look round. With one jump he was out of his cab and trying to grab them. Dropping a second case, they fled. The driver's shouts attracted a passing cyclist who eventually cornered them in a coalyard. Terry might easily have escaped: instead, he panicked and, sprinting in the opposite direction, ran into the arms of a surprised police constable.

The two main culprits received sentences of four and six months, and it was only because Terry was seventeen and it was his first known offence that he could expect to be treated more leniently, not that he was by any means what Mr Young called a 'natural' for probation. In court he had made a bad impression. I was permitted to sit with the probation officers in a kind of church pew below and to the right of the platform occupied by the magistrates, and from here I got a good view of the defendants' faces. I suspected that Terry's general act of 'not being bothered', his exaggerated shoulder-shrugs and derisive scowling smirks masked a violent anxiety. His appearance was grotesquely in character: bootlace tie, 'Italian' tapered trousers, inch-thick crêpes, his hair cut in an 'Osterley' with V-shaped sideboards. Interviewed in the cell, he was at first very surly, boasting that he was not one to be scared of taking the rap, but after twenty minutes, coaxed by Mr Young's quiet, conversational questions and several Woodbines, he became a little calmer and more natural, talked about his job in the warehouse, his ambition to qualify as a long-distance lorry-driver, and even about his parents. They would never leave him alone, he complained. They did nothing but criticize his clothes and his friends and because he had different ways of enjoying himself than whist drives and growing geraniums. What seemed to irritate him most was that they expected him to be home by ten o'clock each evening as if he was his kid brother. If the court would only give him a chance . . .

'My Dad . . . the proper one—he lives in Lancashire, not far from Blackpool it is . . . he'd be willing to have me. He'd help me make a new start. Don't think I haven't learned my lesson . . .'

My inquiry had by then reached its sixth month and several probation officers besides Mr Young had warned me that one had to suspect these stock promises. Before being sentenced, the most unredeemable offenders will make every kind of promise and resolution—and usually intend to keep them. The assessment of whether an offender may be a suitable subject for probation has to be made on more reliable evidence, though in far too many cases it is patchy, vague, and inadequate and much depends on what one can only describe loosely as the probation officer's experience and intuition. The final decision is, of course, the responsibility of the judge or the magistrates, dependent upon the type of court, but in practice the assessment by the probation officer who has been asked to consider the case carries very considerable weight.

When I first saw Terry I remember remarking to Mr Young that here in the flesh was the popular image of the juvenile delinquent, the typical participant in the crime wave, the classically disturbed family background . . . but I have chosen him as my first example for the very opposite reason :

'There is no such thing as the "typical" case,' Mr Young retorted. 'The word has no meaning. It's nonsense. Except at a superficial level, I've never had two cases alike. We're only interested in the individual.' However mean or even horrifying the crime, however unattractive or repulsive the culprit's manner or attitude, he has to be seen as being unique, accepted as a victim of forces, very often within himself, that for the moment he cannot control and which help to make him different from anyone else. At the first interviews with a potential 'client'—the jargon is instructive and in this instance I shall use it—a probation officer has to try to measure the strength of these forces and also the dormant power and ability possessed by the client to disperse them or become their master.

'Terry may be right? Perhaps he ought to go and live with his proper father? That's one of the things we've got to discover. But whoever he lives with, he is likely to find things difficult—still he'll have to wait till tomorrow'. Mr Young eyed the office clock. 'One of my alcoholics is in the waiting-room and after that I've a couple of new matrimonials.'

Perhaps the most wearing of the job's many demands is the need to be able to turn without pause, yet revictualled with fresh supplies of reassurance, sympathy and hope, from one case to another—from a juvenile delinquent to an alcoholic, followed maybe by an incestuous brother, a compulsive shoplifter, a misunderstood exhibitionist, an inadequate senile . . . for each of whom his or her personal problems usually constitute the boundaries of reality. The more cases I studied, the more officers I talked with, the more varied appeared the reasons and hopes that could lie behind the probation order. The outlooks of individual officers and courts differed, I found, within surprisingly wide limits. Strata of existence of which I was but abstractly aware also revealed themselves insistently. Intense physical misery, so often said to have disappeared under the Welfare State, is, I kept realizing, still massive and widespread.

There was Mrs Hook, for instance, mother of six, who at forty-five looked nearer sixty. Her offence was to sell two items of fancy underwear that had been sent her by mistake by the firm of dry cleaners for whom, at piece rates and at home, she did invisible mending. For ten of her fifteen years of married life her husband had been in prison and at the time of the offence he had just started another three-year stretch. For her, debts have the familiar menace of a chronic sickness. Part of the furniture is in pawn, the money-lender will not increase her loan of £10, what is left of her public assistance and family allowances will only with luck feed them all till the end of the week . . . and then the gas bill of £4 3s. 10d. rears up with its ultimate ultimatum, to prompt the desperate, unhappy impulse. No wonder Miss Lane, the woman probation officer, reports that Mrs Hook tends to have a violent temper and is not a very good manager; but she adds that she is by nature honest, has a warm heart and surrounds her family with affection. She tells Miss Lane that she always insists on the older children doing their homework, though this is extra difficult when it rains because then they have to crowd into the kitchen as the ceilings of the two upstairs rooms drip with water —the house was condemned years ago, though the landlord still wants his rent. All seven of them fit, according to sex and size, into three beds, Mrs Hook sharing with the toddler and one of the girls, aged eight, who has spent spells in hospital with a spinal disease; this child is becoming slowly stronger but she can be very querulous and still wets the bed and in her sleep clings to her mother as if her dreams were full of a menacing anxiety. The older children, too, often appear to be out of control while their father is away, though when he is at home things can also be very stormy and during his last spell of freedom he kicked his wife very badly on the shin—yet she talks of this as a happy time . . . Probation, as you can read later, not only saved Mrs Hook from prison but did something to make her life less calamitous.

There seemed to be no boundaries to the shapes and directions taken by human unhappiness and frustration. There was nothing, for example, apparently unusual about Peter who visited Mr Young once a fortnight with rigid punctuality, though I suppose you might think him withdrawn and over-polite. He had pleaded guilty to an indecent assault on an eight-year-old girl. She belonged to the couple he lodged with and at week-ends he would spend hours making furniture for her doll's house or telling her stories about his life in the Merchant Navy; her parents were grateful to him—until the little girl told them what had happened. It is his first conviction and he talks readily, almost eagerly, about himself. He has never managed to make many friends and, being an orphan, lived until he was twenty in institutions: he is not particularly bitter about his childhood, though for most of the time he shared a 'hostel-mother' with fifteen other boys and the discipline must have been very strict—he always speaks of how busy they were kept with scrubbing. The psychiatrist who is also treating him describes him as obsessional and writes that his emotional reactions and relationships with adults are very immature. It is perhaps significant that the little girl spoke of no force being used. Children were people Peter could cope with. They were easier to form a relationship with, so much more accessible.

It would be quite false, though, to give the impression that everyone who attends probation offices is distorted by private tragedy. Certainly not Valerie. Her husband is also in prison—for living on her immoral earnings—but she is never short of money and briefed an expensive lawyer for his defence. She has over fifty convictions for soliciting—before the 1959 Street Offences Act—but is on probation as a result of a quarrel in a pub with a maid of another prostitute which led to a broken finger and a bitten ear. With powerful-looking but slender hips, a grand bust, and harsh good looks, she is well-equipped by Nature for her profession and there is great warmth in her racy if vituperative gossip which gushes non-stop in a husky Tyneside accent. She even teasingly offers Miss Lane a job as her own maid, saying quite truthfully that she could pay her more than she earns as a social worker. On her good weeks Valerie herself grosses £50 to £100: on boat-race night she picks up £30 between midnight and two o'clock. She lives in the suburbs and when she first came into court she was carrying on her trade in taxis, but later she got a flat in Soho to which she travels every day like any other commuter . . .

My material was so copious and multifarious that at first I thought of using the obvious device of choosing all my cases from the same court, as this would supply a natural limitation. But when I asked myself 'which court?' the method appeared to have nothing but disadvantages: the probation cases met with at the assizes can be very different from those at the magistrates' court; in some areas the probation officers are so overworked that their methods must inevitably vary from those of their colleagues whose case-loads are lighter; no one court was likely to provide every type of case I needed. To re-create a court was after all a very secondary objective: the court-room has been written about many times before, its atmosphere, its types, even its procedure are familiar to anyone with access to a television set or who visits the films. Probation only has its formal start in the court-room; its truer setting is the office, the client's home, his place of work, the streets . . . wherever he may be helped to rebuild his life. I decided in the end to concentrate on a group of courts on the fringes of Greater London—outside the Metropolitan Magistrates' Courts Area (which differs from the Metropolitan Police Area)—and it is from these courts that all the cases in this book have been selected. Parts of my area are completely urbanized, others are subtopian; and yet others can be counted as semi-rural; it is as typical a cross-section as one is likely to discover.

At a few of these courts I became quite a familiar figure, and accompanied the probation staff on visits to clients' homes, doss-houses, mental hospitals, hostels, and prisons. The courts I had chosen provided interesting—and sometimes disturbing—differences not only in the extent to which they made use of probation but in the time they allowed their probation officers to investigate potential clients. The longer the period, the greater the likelihood that probationers are selected on a sound basis; and it was surprising to find after a lengthy trial, maybe lasting more than a day, based on the meticulous sifting and weighing of evidence, that the defendant's future would often be settled in a matter of minutes; and on evidence that was assembled hastily and was inevitably very incomplete. It may be true that people are more communicative before they hear their sentence than after it, yet on the day of the trial and in a hurried interview in the court cell they are likely to be so overwrought or humiliated or angry or full of self-pity or revengeful that it is impossible for them, or the probation officer, to see their future with anything approaching objectivity. The more efficient method, therefore, is to remand the case, either on bail or in custody as happened to Terry, for a week or more so that the full circumstances of the offence, its causes and the chances of removing them, the defendant's history and present situation, the structure of his personality, and everything else relevant to a reliable assessment can be investigated thoroughly.

In certain courts, quarter sessions for example, long enough remands are often not practicable, and in some, especially rural courts where the magistrates sit less frequently, it is the rule for all inquiries to take place before the trial, let alone before conviction; in many courts this is also the practice where it is known that the defendant will plead guilt. While this saves time and is more likely to give the probation officer the chance to make a proper assessment, there is the objection, and it is a powerful one, that to interfere with a citizen's privacy at this stage is tantamount to ignoring the presumption of innocence until guilt is established, a principle enshrined in our whole legal procedure—but it must be emphasized that the bench is not shown the report until guilt has been established, and the inquiries are not proceeded with if they are objected to by the accused or his parents.

In evaluating the offender's personality, gauging his attitude to Authority, attempting to fathom his personal relationships, the stresses of his environment, the combination and interaction of all these and other factors that might lead to a further breakdown, the probation officer needs an adventurous imagination: unless he can magic himself into the offender's skin, think his thoughts and feel his feelings, he has little hope of arriving at a viable plan for the offender's future, let alone a pattern of reform. Compared with other social workers, the probation officer is handicapped from the start in his desire to win trust and co-operation. His client is usually only too aware of the far-reaching, fateful influence of these preliminary inquiries. Nor is the probation officer able to promise that what he is told at this stage will be treated as confidential; requests for essential information such as income, employment, accommodation, debts, can lead to one being confused with the police. As well as having to allow for the anxiety that stems from the very circumstances of the interview, the probation officer's first duty may well be the invidious one of making the offender face the realities of his predicament and explaining its possible consequences. He does this kindly and helpfully but he must disabuse the offender of any ideas that he is a kind of defending counsel.

When there is sufficient time, the inquiry should reach far beyond the client himself—to the husband or wife, parents, brothers and sisters, schoolteacher, and where necessary, opinions should be sought from the doctor or psychiatrist. The people approached and the technique vary of course, but the stages in Terry's 'social diagnosis' make as good an illustration as any and are worth telling in detail. They provide to some extent a prototype for all the cases that follow.

II

Mr Young's next move was to send a letter off to the probation office in Lancashire nearest to where Terry's real father lived, asking if they could visit him and send a report on his circumstances. Would he be willing to have Terry to live with him? Did he seem at all likely to be able to handle such an awkward son with the necessary mixture of firmness and sympathy? What were the local employment circumstances? The chances of a favourable answer, at any rate according to Terry's mother, were small. The matrimonial hearth had been deserted for that 'cheap little Blackpool doll' when Terry was only three and, apart from a couple of meetings in teashops in London and a holiday spent in Lancashire with his father and the 'doll' when Terry was twelve, there had been no contact.

'He never so much as sent Terry a birthday card,' Mrs Cox complained when visited at home two days later. 'Little he's cared what I've had to put up with, though he's always sent my money regular, that I'll grant you—that is until my husband—Mr Cox I mean—had me up to the altar.'

'That's right,' Mr Cox butted in. 'From the start I looked upon Terry as my own. "What's her's mine," has always been my motto—though I don't mind admitting I feel a bit different what with the way Terry's been behaving.'

The Coxs lived in a classier road than I had imagined: semi-detacheds of mid-nineteen-thirties' vintage, with alternating pairs of Tudoresque and pebble-dash gables, double sunrise-gates and a smaller one for the tradesmen. The sitting-room was rather too full of chunky walnut-veneered furniture, Cubist-type mirrors, empty cut-glass vases and silver-plated fruit bowls: the curtains, the wallpaper, the carpet, the coverings of the immense three-piece suite were various shades of toadstool beige. I felt we were sitting in a showroom: there was not a book nor even newspaper in sight. Unlike many of Mr Young's cases, Terry certainly did not lack home comforts of the physical kind. Mr Cox was very much the self-made man, a local estate agent, specializing in reconditioned flats with exorbitant 'premiums' for fittings. Around fifty, ten years older than his wife, he was short with a little black moustache clipped almost out of existence and an overlarge double-breasted suit. He seemed as annoyed with his own son, Nigel, thirteen and at the grammar school, as he was with Terry:

'Nigel is heading the same way if you ask me—always late for everything, getting into fights at school, spends all his money on pop discs, and last week I caught him going to his mother's purse. Said he was only looking for a safety-pin—I ask you! I dealt with him good and proper, just as my guv'nor did with me, not that it'll make a jot of difference. Some days Nigel won't even go to school and we have to ring up with a pack of lies about him being sick or having a temperature: one time he locked himself all day in the lavatory, even threatened to yell out to the neighbours. It's all Terry's doing. It's Terry what puts him up to it. They're as thick as thieves those two—that's just the right word for them—thick as——'

'You wouldn't say that,' Mrs Cox interrupted crossly, 'not if you'd heard them quarrel as much as I have. It's Nigel who's always going for Terry. Remember what happened over the bicycle-pump——'

'How could I ever forget, with you always dragging it up?'

'That's what you always say . . .'

The parents became so upset with each other over the bicycle-pump that our presence was forgotten—only for a moment, but enough to show the extent of their animosity, that it was something that should certainly be included in any assessment of Terry. It would be surprising if either of the boys had escaped becoming involved emotionally in their disputes; they must have absorbed plenty of lessons in at least verbal aggression. From the way he talked, Mr Cox in particular seemed unsuited to parenthood: he was boastful about being tough and stern and how he was old-fashioned enough to believe in the cane and to be dead against mollycoddling, and the next minute he would be complaining that his nerves could not stand much more, that thanks to the rows he was now under the doctor and never slept a wink without sleeping pills. The boys never lacked anything, he declared, could go everywhere that they did, but their only repayment was ingratitude: 'The other day we arranged a nice run in the car to Brighton, slap-up lunch when we got there, the pier, the Royal Pavilion, the lot—but Terry wouldn't come, said he preferred to go down to the caff. Nigel of course had to copy him, said he'd be much happier playing with his trains at home. I ask you now! They don't know a good offer when they see one!' On the whole, though, Mr Cox struck me as being mean. It was noticeable how he kept coming back to money. Almost everything he mentioned had a price: the pound notes crackled behind every sentence.

To begin with he had been very suspicious of Mr Young, tended to confuse him with the police and resented being questioned. Mrs Cox, on the other hand, was obviously the type who believed that probation officers were a cheap form of defending counsel and blamed Mr Young for Terry still being in custody. Patiently Mr Young explained all over again that he was only interested in finding out the exact situation. They must look upon him as a neutral figure who was trying to sort things out in the interests of all of them, that he wanted their help in building up a picture of Terry against the background of his history and family.

Surprisingly, the pieces did begin to fit together. It appeared that Terry had started to steal before he was ten, though it was probably not without significance that they had once caught him throwing coins into a canal. He had been a great one for collecting things: birds' eggs, matchboxes, bus tickets—'a proper little magpie he was,' in Mrs Cox's words, 'always littering the place up. Half my time went in shovelling his mess up after him and burning it.' A difficult, 'prickly' baby and a 'proper little terror' as a toddler, he was nearly five before he was pot-trained. After his mother remarried he became more manageable, that is until Nigel was born when he showed the classical symptoms of jealousy even to the extent of hiding the baby's feeding-bottle. The kind of tantrums typical of a four-year-old persisted until he was well into his 'teens and, though recently he was mostly sullen and locked up in himself, he would suddenly give way to what they described as inexplicable and frightening tempers.

Towards the end of the interview it was even possible to feel sorry for Mr and Mrs Cox. Overshadowing their prejudices was an alarming bewilderment. It was as if they had nurtured an uncontrollable, spiteful monster, and in a way they had: for years behind those beige-netted bay-windows they had been the target for every eruption of Terry's swollen, festering resentment and, paradoxically, now that his conflict with them had been directed against society itself it was even more painful. It was simple to reconstruct the rows and hurtfulness that must have come with adolescence: their dismay when he refused to have his hair cut, their greater horror when he came back with it shaped as the 'Osterley'; their shame when neighbours mentioned that he had been seen in the doubtful café in the High Street, the one full of pin-tables and with the juke box; their fears and recriminations over his doubtful friends, his refusal to enter his stepfather's business . . . and then the fateful scribbled telephone message from the police station asking if Mr Cox would mind calling in to assist them . . . The Coxs' experience must have been similar to that of many other parents of adolescents, except the gulf seemed, and really was, so much more dangerous.

Mr Young's method had little to do with interrogation; he listened far more than he questioned, cleverly directing the conversation and easing the atmosphere so that more light was thrown on Terry's history and their feelings towards him. Much of his schoolboy naughtiness, it seemed pretty clear, came into the category of 'testing': for example at the age of ten he had hidden all night in a public park, causing his parents to call in the police to help find him: to his child's mind the fact that they had bothered, their relief and even the beating that followed his return home were gratifying and palliated his uncertainty about his stepfather's affection.

The report received from the psychiatrist at the prison in fact confirmed the conclusion that the source of Terry's difficulties was the breakdown of his mother's first marriage and the boy's failure to make a sound relationship with Mr Cox: 'This young man,' the psychiatrist wrote, 'has a surprisingly useful insight into how the failure of his relationship with his stepfather has spoiled relationships with other people, especially those in charge of him —his teachers, the foreman at the warehouse, and so on. Terry is under an impulsion to work out many of his authoritarian conflicts. He is still in an extremely unsettled state; he tends to despair and this will always go against him. My impression is that if left to his own devices he has not the capacity to avoid anti-social conflicts in negative company, but there is also in Terry a fund of accessibility on which anyone in authority can draw—greater stability could emerge from this.'

The headmaster of Terry's secondary school, whom Mr Young also visited, seemed equally prepared to emphasize characteristics which anyone who had studied the scowling Terry on the day of his trial would scarcely have suspected. His intelligence quotient was well above average and the head remembered him as an unhappy, uncertain boy who tended to stick at the bottom of the class instead of reaching his rightful place among the top ten. His chief trouble was that he could not take criticism; he had an abnormal resistance to correction or even advice from the teachers. It seemed that this could sometimes take a positive form as the head recalled an incident in which Terry had taken the lead in a justified protest against bad cooking of school dinners, but generally he seemed to have ganged up with the known trouble-makers, as if it was important to be accepted by them. He was far from being a bully.

Armed with this extra information, a further visit was paid to

Terry himself at the remand prison. A corpulent prison officer, dressed to my surprise in a kind of white linen mess-waiter's tunic and round uniform hat and displaying the inevitable bouquet of clinking keys, admitted us through tall steel inner gates at the main entrance; exchanging heavy jocularities with Mr Young, he led us across the central courtyard to a small one-storeyed building, the interview block. Here we were passed over to another prison officer who let us through another gate, which was also locked behind us, and led us along a corridor flanked by small barred cells—unexpectedly, each was tarted-up with peach or duck-egg blue paint and chintz curtains. In the end cell Terry was standing waiting for us.

Perhaps it was the prison garb—a shapeless sacklike suit that looked as if it had been boiled—but again I felt that this was a very different Terry from the derisive, brash youth I had seen at the court. He was less ready to boast about taking the rap or even with promises to go straight: he seemed now to care at a deeper level, as if he was allowing himself to recognize his anxiety as to what would happen to him, to realize that the future had to be met with more than a smirk and a shrug. Not that he was very articulate. Mr Young, I noticed, was being careful not to be reassuring about the chances of avoiding Borstal and asked several blunt questions as to how Terry ever managed to get mixed up with such a crime.

'It just sort of happened.' Mr Young pushed the Woodbines across the table and waited. 'They told me,' Terry mumbled at last, 'it'd be easy—a simple knock-off.'

'And how was it you got invited to take part?'

'Dunno really.'

'But you must have known the other two. Where did you come across them?'

'Down the caff——' Terry hesitated. 'Kind of got caught up like. It wasn't in the caff actually . . . but . . . well, 'cos of someone I knew there.'

'What kind of a person? Was he an older man?'

'No, I'm telling you. It was someone else—but what's it to you?'

Mr Young made it clear that he was not concerned with names, that he was not a policeman, that he was only trying to find out what made him commit such an offence. At this Terry almost looked sorry for him:

'I needed the nickers—what else would I be doing it for?'

Mr Young next suggested that, coming from such a well-to-do home, even if his wages did not amount to much he could hardly have been so desperately short of money. This, perhaps as was intended, provoked a revealing comeback:

'You'd be surprised. At home they take more than half of what I earn and there's not a lot left after you've paid for smokes. Most of the others—down the caff—have a lot more in their pockets. Dad—my stepfather I mean—he's always on about having plenty and yet he won't give it me. He thinks, you see, I ought to be like him, not have things easy, make my own way . . .'

Mr Cox's belief in his own personal success story and business acumen was without much doubt a major cause of Terry's sense of inferiority. One could see again how the whole family was dominated by money. From snatches of what Terry told us it seemed to provide the theme for most of the parents' squabbles: they were always rowing over some bill or other, and a dispute with Mr Cox's brother over the price of a secondhand garden-mower had worked Terry's mother into such a state that the doctor had to put her on sedatives. This upset had apparently occurred a week before the offence—though that may have merely been a coincidence.

Terry still hoped he would be allowed to go and live with his true father and when he asked if Mr Young had yet heard anything from Lancashire, he appeared more like a pathetic Fourth Former than the tough 'teenage delinquent. The more I learned about him, the less Terry seemed to be a member of that inscrutable, 'beat', frightening, exclusive, new generation, but an unhappy and very muddled, immature creature—someone who was much more familiar. Quite apart from his dislike of Mr Cox, his jealousy of Nigel was acute and possibly justified: the Coxs were as much in need of readjustment as Terry was. To leave home, to make a new start with his father did seem the best solution—until, that is, two days later when the confidential report arrived from Lancashire.

It was a thorough document that ended: 'This man is willing to have Terry to live with them—more out of a muddled sense of duty than because he wants him. He says he doubts if he would now recognize Terry if they passed in the street. Of course he is shocked at the crime but blames it on Mrs Cox who, he maintains firmly, comes of "bad stock" and is some kind of sexual maniac (I didn't go into this!). There are now four other children and the second wife, though a kindly woman, is a bit of a slattern and the place is never very clean. It's a small back-to-back house and Terry, if he came, would have to share a bed with one of the other boys. Employment prospects up here are not as good as they were and . . .'

It was the kind of invidious choice which frequently challenges probation officers. Lancashire held out scarcely less unfavourable prospects than a return to the Coxs, but should this mean that Borstal was the only answer? This would be equal to saying that Terry must be punished for having two unsatisfactory lots of parents. Of course it was doubtful if he was suitable for probation in any case, but the very fact that he had been dealt such a difficult background made him more eligible. Probation can rightly be described as the organized mercy that tempers justice.

Terry therefore had his second chance. A condition of the probation order was that he should reside for a year in an approved hostel.

'Maybe he'll be back in the dock before we've finished with him,' was Mr Young's comment. 'Borstal sometimes does wonders, but with Terry it would be more likely to confirm his grudge and uncertainty. That unpleasant mask would become rigid and permanent . . . and yet for us to accept him may mean an even greater risk—and I'm not only thinking of Terry.'

It took me some time to realize that where there is no risk at all, no likelihood of a further offence, there is no need for probation. In these cases the right sentence, short of imprisonment, is a fine or a discharge (which, unlike a charge that is dismissed, is not a complete acquittal). The probation service is already too overloaded to take on clients who have a reasonable chance of coping with their futures unaided. It cannot select a proportion of 'sound' cases for the sake of improving its ratio of successes, as if it were a sought-after grammar school selecting potential candidates for university scholarships. It is the risk that comes with each case, its inherent suspense and drama, the wager of faith placed each time on a human being, that gives the job its extraordinary attraction and interest.

2
Seen from the Bench

*

THE language and manner of the judge or magistrate issuing the probation order can have a persistent influence on the offender's attitude to his new status. In some courts the decision is mumbled so inaudibly or pronounced so briefly that the offender has little notion of what is happening to him; and, when eventually he realizes that he is not going to be locked up, it is understandable that at first he imagines he has been 'let off'. In a sense, of course, he has been, in that he is not sent to prison and that his conviction will be disregarded for the purpose of any statutory disqualification or disability, in that the essence of probation is reform without punishment; but, properly understood and applied, probation is very far from being a let-off and makes very definite demands, some of which can for certain individuals be as exacting and painful as a prison sentence. The probation order, too, may well last longer than a sentence—it can be anything between one and three years.

If over fourteen, the offender's consent has to be obtained to the probation order being made and, though in view of the alternatives this may appear like a hypocritical formality, it is important that he should know what he is letting himself in for. In a well conducted court he is left in no doubt: the purpose of the order is explained in detail and he is warned of what may happen if he is so rash as to break its stipulations. At Mr Young's court the chairman of the bench prided himself that anyone put on probation by him was not likely to forget the experience. The dressing-down took anything up to ten minutes and if there were several probation cases that morning, the court officials and visiting solicitors tended to get restless, but I am sure the process was justified. To Terry, standing to attention in the dock, it must have sounded something like this:

'We shall not keep you wondering what we are going to do with you. I expect by now you know perfectly well that we are going to give you a chance on probation. But now I have said that, *you have got to listen to me*. Do you understand?

'Don't for one moment imagine that you are being let off; still less that you are going to leave this court with a pat on the back. You are in disgrace, serious disgrace. You have thrown away a clean record, and now you have something ugly to live down. You saw what happened to the other two—four and six months in prison. If it weren't for your only being seventeen, we might have sent you there too—or anyhow taken steps to send you to Borstal. And what's more, we may do so yet! You can choose it now if you like. You have only to refuse to be put on probation. But if you agree to it, you will have to learn to stand on your own feet. That will be much harder, I can tell you, than just obeying orders in Borstal. But it will prove that you are a man. And that's what you want to be, isn't it?

'Well, I think you can be. I have been taking a good look at you—and strange as it may seem, I believe in you. We all believe you can make good, if you try. You won't have to try all alone. Your probation officer will help you—if you will back him up. But you will be on probation for two years and there will be some strict conditions, and you will have to keep them—or back here you will come! And there is not likely to be another chance if you spoil our faith in you. Do you understand that?

'Very well, then. Now listen carefully to the conditions. First of all, you will not make a nuisance of yourself to anyone; you will not commit any further offence or get into any sort of trouble with the police. Secondly, you must lead an industrious life; this means, among other things, that you will only leave or change your employment of your own accord provided your probation officer agrees that you should do so; if you should ever be out of work, you will at once do your best to find another job—and you will keep on until you are successful.

'I understand from the probation officer that there is a vacancy in one of the approved hostels and that they are prepared to receive you. You will live there for a year and obey the instructions laid down by the warden. On no account must you leave there until this court gives you permission and, even then, you can only live in a place which the probation officer approves of.

'What's more—and this is most important—you must always keep in touch with your probation officer. You must go and see him regularly at the times he tells you. If he should wish to visit you at the hostel, you must be there at the times he fixes. You will truthfully answer any question he asks about how you are behaving, what work you are doing, and so on.

'Finally, if ever you should fail to do any of these things, you will have committed what the law calls a "breach of your probation", and this bench has the power to fine you up to £10 for each separate breach—or, if we think fit, send you to prison for the present offence, for which you are now being placed on probation. This is quite apart from, additional to, any punishment you may receive, here or elsewhere, for a further offence.

'I want you to say now if you really understand these conditions? Are you willing to observe them, if a probation order is made?'

In reaching the decision to try probation the bench, as we have seen, leans very heavily for facts and guidance on the probation officer who presents his report in a form that can be quickly and easily understood, and makes tactical allowances for any quirks and prejudices that he knows from experience his magistrates or judge are liable to. Not only does he supply more information about the offender's history and background than is usually found in the police 'antecedents', but he has to summarize his assessment of the offender's character and chances in the future, arrived at during the preliminary investigation. He is wise to eschew all kinds of jargon—talk of 'schizoid syndromes' and 'social ecology' merely alienates the bench's sympathy—and to stick to information that has some bearing on the actual offence. Whether or not a specific recommendation for or against probation appears in the report depends on local protocol but in all the courts I attended it was customary for it to conclude with a respectful, circumlocutory phrase such as: 'If your worships should see fit to consider taking a certain course, we shall be prepared to assist in any way we can.' The dividing-line between expressing an opinion about an offender and making a recommendation is clearly narrow. In an address to the Magistrates' Association Lord Goddard, the late Lord Chief Justice, certainly encouraged probation officers not to be overcautious: '. . . if you are asking a probation officer for his opinion, surely it is right that he should state his opinion quite frankly to you, and if he thinks from his knowledge of the boy or man that prison is the only thing . . . why in Heaven's name should he not be allowed to mention it? . . . the decision is yours; you are at perfect liberty to accept or disregard his opinion . . .'

Probation officers attached to courts that tend to ignore their advice, or do not allow sufficient time for the preliminary investigation, usually complain that the bench 'in its wisdom' frequently foists onto them cases that are hopelessly unsuitable. Where investigations are the rule, quite a considerable proportion—I have heard it put as high as 50 per cent—do not lead to probation, either because the bench disagrees with the probation officer's recommendation or, more likely, because the investigation shows that the offender is not suitable. It has to be remembered, too, that a court has the power to ask probation officers to inquire into the circumstances of the offender even when probation is not envisaged, so as to assist it in arriving at the best method of dealing with the case. It is undoubtedly true to say that most probation officers err in favour of giving the offender the benefit of their doubts but, however charitable, they are not likely to saddle themselves willingly with offenders who for anything up to three years are almost certain to remain unco-operative and waste time that could be devoted to more promising cases.

Whatever some of their clients may like to pretend to themselves, a few months' work in a probation office will cure any tendency to be made into a sucker. Basil, for example, when he first appeared in court seemed an obvious case for probation. There were no previous convictions and he seemed to be a well integrated, polite young man who was genuinely unable to understand what had made him commit the offence—the theft of some Chinese vases from an antique shop. The investigation, however, made things look rather different. The shop was owned by an elderly man with a cataract over one eye and Basil had deliberately taken advantage of this disability when removing the vases —in fact the crime was carefully planned and he had arranged for his landlady's daughter to come into the shop independently and to ask to see some Venetian glass in order to divert the old man's attention. Further inquiries showed that Basil had not had a job for at least six months but, despite this, had been showing signs of unaccustomed and inexplicable affluence, had bought several new suits and a hi-fi record-player, and had spent a holiday in Paris. He was also known to go around with three unprepossessing young men each of whom had a police record. When questioned about all this, Basil had suddenly become very aggressive, entangled himself in a further set of lies, and finally demanded to know what the fuss was about anyway, as wasn't he going to be put on probation? Instead Basil got fifteen months.

It would be false and inaccurate to suggest that many probation officers expect their charges to be humbly repentant, but arrogant complacency probably tops the list of discouraging qualities. This was also the trouble with Charles. A middle-aged bank clerk, with a clean record, he found himself in the dock for starting a fight with his brother-in-law who ended in hospital with a lacerated cheek and a fractured arm. It appeared to be a sudden outburst of temper, an isolated offence, brought about by a dispute over the ownership of an arm-chair that had once belonged to Charles's mother-in-law.

'What I'd like someone to explain,' Charles asked the probation officer petulantly, 'is what all this has to do with you—or anyone else for that matter. All you people make too much fuss. This is, after all, a family matter and if a man can't protect his family in his own way, in his own house, I don't know what's coming over the old country.'

But Charles also was a humbug. It did not take the probation officer long to discover that he had often before used violence against his wife and even against two of the children, that he was living with another woman in some style while his wife and family went in need of essentials. The truth was that the brother-in-law had for a long time been sending his sister money and trying to protect her, though none of this had come out in court. Instead of probation, which was being seriously considered in view of his good record, Charles was sent down for twelve months.

Similarly, a probation officer cannot afford to allow pity to have too much influence on his judgement—though frequently, I think, this does happen. That a tragic childhood explained why Denis committed his offence—violent robbery of a room-mate in a Church Army hostel—was beyond doubt. He was then nineteen, but at the age of eight he had been deserted by his mother who seems to have vanished; six months after she left, his father had been killed in a road accident, and Denis was taken into care by the local authority. He was brought up in several institutions, in none of which he was happy: attempts to place him in foster homes during the school holidays always failed after a few days because of his difficult behaviour. He passed his childhood in continual revolt against every form of Authority on which were focused his racking resentment for his personal misfortune. Eventually, after some time in a special boys' hostel, he was allowed to live in lodgings, but after an appearance in court, the landlady would not have him back. To talk with, he was quite amiable but to even an inexperienced eye the taut set of the facial muscles, the restless, jerky eye movements, the scratch in his voice, suggested an uncontrollable hostility. None of the specialist reports—from the children's officer, psychiatrist, schoolmaster—were optimistic: 'devoid of ambition and refuses to work' . . . 'cunning and quite happy to be thought an amiable simpleton which is far from the truth' . . . 'essentially irresponsible and parasitic, vicious' . . . Although, as will be shown later, it is not unknown for a period of probation to prove the gloomiest prognosis by psychiatrists to be mistaken, the decision not to recommend Denis needs no justification.

In the courts I know, reports are normally made in writing, though supplemented by short statements in the witness-box or from the probation officers' table in the well of the court, and occasionally by a few private words in the magistrates' room before the sitting begins. Our justice is rightly proud of its tradition of working in the open and it is laid down that the defendant shall see a copy of the report and have an opportunity to refute it, but great harm can be done if it is insisted, as sometimes happens, that the report is read aloud in open court. This is to turn the principle that justice must be 'seen to be done' into a fetish and on occasions can cause the probation officer, from sympathy with the offender's anxiety at having spicy details of his personal life lapped up by members of the public, to leave out essential information.

A probation officer's report is, legally speaking, evidence, whether or not it is given on oath, and is sometimes, though rarely, subject to cross-examination; he must therefore be prepared to substantiate it, and prudence usually counsels him to omit his more tentative conclusions. I have noticed, for example, that letters by probation officers introducing a client to a psychiatrist will usually be franker and contain more 'hunches' than do reports intended for the court.

'It's surprising, though, how much a good bench can read between the lines,' an elderly probation officer told me, 'once, that is, they've got used to you and they believe they can rely on your opinions. But with a strange judge or chairman it's always best to go carefully. A few of them get very touchy if you give the appearance of upsetting their dignity.'

Inevitably, I suppose, the chances of an offender being put on probation rather than locked up depend to a frightening extent on who happens to be sitting on the bench, on his or her or their ideas about punishment, on their understanding of the evidence, on the state of their livers, their whims, class prejudices, and the gamut of their personal emotional drives and adjustments. If chairman of the bench X. has a 'thing' about homosexuals—owing maybe to a suppressed fear that he has tendencies that way himself—an importuner in a public lavatory has obviously less chance of getting probation than if he has the luck to appear before chairman of the bench Y. who personally happens to believe that our homosexual legislation is badly in need of overhaul. Our magistrates and judges can be counted on to know the law and to apply it without conscious favour, but inevitably the same cannot be said about the severity of their sentences.

In all probation work much depends on there being a good understanding, an easy personal relationship between the bench and the team of probation officers. In most courts this can be said to be generally true, but there are still courts where probation is looked at with suspicion, and where 'common sense' and a 'practical experience of life' are considered altogether more reliable than the 'trickcychological' approach. Though probation in its full sense was incorporated into the legal system over fifty years ago, there are still courts where, while it is accepted, it is treated as a comparative innovation. Its representatives are respected merely for their qualities as individuals, in the same way as were the Police Court Missionaries, those dedicated men and women who in the face of prejudice and cant were probation's pioneers. In the modern, enlightened court, however, the probation officer is recognized as belonging to a profession, as a social worker with specialized skills that can help reveal and influence the factors underlying human behaviour. As well as making a report before the sentence, a probation officer who has the bench's confidence will normally be given an opportunity to say what he thinks about the offender should there be a breach of the order: the court may limit itself to a ticking-off, or it may decide on a fine, an extension of the period on probation, if not imprisonment for the original offence—though of course once the bench has officially recognized the breach the matter is formally out of the probation officer's hands.

Machinery for strengthening the link between the bench and its probation officers is provided by what are known as case committees, set up for each petty sessional division. They consist almost entirely of magistrates, their powers of co-option seldom being used, and are supposed to supervise the work of the local probation officers[1] and to maintain the personal interest of members of the bench in the progress of individual cases. One hears conflicting opinions of how successfully these committees function and it seems that their value varies remarkably in different parts of the country. Particularly where the volume of the work is relatively small, examination of difficult cases can be enlightening to the bench and help them in their approach to sentencing future offenders; at the same time it can be of benefit to the officer and offer an antidote to the inevitable loneliness of his responsibility; yet too often discussion tends to be superficial and the magistrates seem only interested in pursuing cases which, for some unimportant reason or other, they happen to recall from among the dozens that are brought before them.

In many courts the more casual, unofficial contacts with the bench are the most valuable. An experienced bench will get to know the qualities and limitations of each probation officer attached to it and, while the allocation of cases to particular officers is normally determined by where the offenders happen to live, ideally they should be supervised by the officer most likely to

[1] Appointment of officers, payment of salaries, and general administration of the local probation service are the responsibility of separate 'probation committees'.

win their sympathy. Inevitably this degree of 'matching' is not always possible and everyone must expect to take his share of whatever cases the court disposes of, but the nature of the personal impact between an offender and his prospective officer, so far as it can be anticipated, cannot be ignored. A probation officer should have the right to be more choosey than, say, a prison officer.

The detailed functioning of the probation office is outside the scope of this book, but what little has been said will be enough to make obvious the desirability not only of a large measure of co-operation with the bench, but also with every official in the court: the clerk to the justices who can be a useful consultant on questions of law or about breaches of the order, or when an officer finds himself perhaps becoming trickily involved in his client's affairs; the gaoler who, if not on friendly terms, can inflict many minor annoyances when it comes to visiting the cells at awkward times; the various ranks of the police and C.I.D., both in court and at the police stations.

II

In considering what sentence is justified, magistrates and judges must, of course, look further than the probation officer's report, and have other things to take into account besides what may be best for the offender in question. There is the gravity of the offence and the effect of their decision on others. In a district in which juvenile crime is on the increase a probation order, however justified in respect of the individual, is likely to be considered as a sign of weakness and may well encourage further offences; similarly, following the race riots in Notting Hill unusually severe sentences were felt to be necessary which had an immediate and salutary effect. The prime function of the justices is to protect the community whose representatives they are and whose attitudes they tend to reflect. One cannot therefore get far in examining probation without asking questions about the theory and purpose of punishment.

Like most people, I imagine, I am by instinct on the side of the man or woman in the dock. Whatever the offence, whatever the number of previous convictions, I catch myself hoping that they will get off and I am apt to think of the bench, the clerk of the court, the police and gaolers as complacent despots. I was made extra conscious of the dangers of this irrational approach when, in connection with this book, I spent a day sitting next to a Recorder while he presided over the quarter sessions of a County Borough. I owe much to his very kind invitation and to his learned opinions on the uses of probation—indeed this chapter would have been very different without them—but the effects of the experience were both unnerving and unforeseen. There was I, sitting—literally—at the right hand of Justice, subjected from across the intervening well of the court to the direct stare of the accused—cowed, defiant, terrified, resentful, nonchalant, pitiful; as the sentences were declared and new faces kept appearing, I understood as never before the terrible and awesome responsibility of the bench. Some of our judges and magistrates are fortified maybe by thick skins and the power that corrupts the soul; but there are many more who are sensitive and kind and naturally forgiving and it is intended as praise when I say that, however full of experience and wisdom, they must frequently pass restless nights.

It is commonly believed that the first object of punishment is to deter others and the offender from committing a further offence; even this simple assertion has to be protected by some pretty big qualifications. The professional criminal has, almost by definition, to be excluded : the threat of imprisonment may make him more careful but it is no more than an occupational risk—in the same way as a professional boxer risks a cauliflower ear or becoming punch-drunk. In addition many categories of casual offenders would seem to be impervious to most deterrents: there are those who are genuinely unable to explain why they committed their offences—and they include thieves as well as exhibitionists and pæderasts—and there are the hosts of punishment seekers, those who subconsciously seek rejection, also those who find, without perhaps knowing it, the harsh security offered by a prison to be easier than the world outside it. I knew of one probationer who, realizing he was without money or shelter, went up to a commissionaire outside an hotel and asked if he had ever seen an unidentified flying missile; the commissionaire shook his head, whereupon the probationer flung a stone through a plate-glass window and settled down on the pavement to wait for the police to pick him up.

Few cases, though, are quite so obvious, and rational investigation into the motivation of criminals is still so little advanced that over a wide variety of crimes and individuals one can only guess at the true effects of deterrence. It is open, as well, to impressive moral objections: there are many who believe there can be no true virtue in making people do the right thing for wrong reasons; or in making men honest not by changing their hearts but merely by threats and fear; or in punishing an individual beyond his own deserts merely in order to deter others.

'In any event whatever fulfils the purpose of punishment should be sufficient,' the Recorder suggested as we lunched on an excellent steak-and-mushroom pie in his private room. 'If you can shame rather than scare the offender into better ways; if you can divert others from offending, by demonstrating the advantages of doing right rather than the drawbacks of doing wrong; if you can inspire a respect for the law despite its mercy, rather than because of its relentlessness—then you have achieved all that is expected of punishment. The second chance offered by probation can likewise be justified—but remember that lurking in the principle of probation is the full armoury of conventional punishment. A second offence can mean punishment for the first one as well. Probation does not abrogate the criminal law. It asserts and upholds it.'

That very afternoon a young man whom the Recorder had placed on probation three months earlier pleaded guilty to a further offence of housebreaking. This time the offender had used up his ration of mercy and was given eighteen months—six for the second offence and twelve for the original one. As the sentence was being pronounced I noticed in the spectators' enclosure at the back of the court two youths who had been put on probation that morning: it must have been a direful object lesson.

The other dominant element in punishment is society's vindictiveness, the need for retribution, the desire for a scapegoat. This can be difficult to tame. The wish to reform by kinder methods is dubbed as 'emotional'. Insistence on harsh treatment for its own sake is, to say the least, also an emotional response to crime, but this is an awkward argument to advance to the victims of a crime or his relations and neighbours who not unreasonably expect the law to take some revenge on their behalf.

The Recorder put it this way: 'We have to remind ourselves that what looks like excessive leniency can bring the law into contempt. The outraged mother of the little child who has been indecently assaulted will cry out bitterly against a probation order imposed on the unbalanced culprit. "Next time," she exclaims, "Dad will deal with him himself. What's the good of calling in the police when the court is so sorry for him that it sends him home and hopes he will be feeling better soon?" The same applies to the slate club treasurer who borrows the funds to pay his overwhelming debts—sometimes he is safer in prison! If the public lose confidence in the courts, there is a direct incitement to take the law into their own hands.'

It is not unknown for the victims to take it out on the probation officer. I was once talking with Miss Lane when we were interrupted by a telephone call from the Hon. Mrs ——, a furious employer of a housemaid who the week before had been placed on probation for stealing a dozen silver spoons, all of which had been returned, and for maliciously burning some blankets. Why, the Hon. lady demanded, hadn't the girl been sent to Borstal? She was a menace and ought not to be at large. They had not been informed of the date of the hearing, otherwise her husband would have been present and protested to the magistrates. He was taking the whole thing up with his M.P. and a friend of his brother who was a High Court judge. . . . One can appreciate, though in this case only with an effort, how the lady felt, but what kind of menace was the culprit? A mousy, wispy child of seventeen, she was the illegitimate daughter of a Dublin chambermaid who had died of cancer before her baby was weaned. Most of the girl's life had been spent in a convent; she appeared very slow-witted and barely knew how to read. The stealing and blanket burning were, I think, merely her inadequate, feeble efforts to assert her own rights and to protest against being overworked. Miss Lane's tolerant gentleness could when necessary give way to the brand of high-principled obstinacy that often goes with a sound, middle-class, Nonconformist conscience, and I was glad to hear her deal with the employer as if she were talking to one of the more hysterical probationers; but she also took the precaution of reporting the protest to the clerk of the court. Nothing more, though, was heard, and the girl was found a job as ward-maid in the local hospital and the last I knew of her was that she had been promoted to the private wing.

The task of enlightened justice is how to decide between and balance many conflicting claims: the need for deterrence, the protection of society, the demands for vengeance and retribution on the one hand; the welfare and reform of the malefactor on the other. The courageous claim of probation is that it is able very often to reconcile the contradictions, that it can achieve the most worthwhile purpose of punishment, the recovery of the individual, without inflicting upon him the probable damage and taint inherent in imprisonment: instead he is encouraged and helped to readjust himself while living as a normal citizen, to learn how to face normal problems. If there is a risk, it proclaims, even if the proportion of failures is high, is it not a risk well worth taking? How much better to have a man re-established in life, earning his living and making his contribution to society, than another ex-convict re-entering a hostile world! It is tempting merely to accept probation's claim with gratitude, but my purpose is to find out if and to what extent it can be substantiated, at least in terms of the individual case.

From the Recorder I obtained several illustrations of just how delicate the balancing of conflicting factors can sometimes be. Two young men, both aged twenty-six and married with family responsibilities, were once brought before him on a joint charge of housebreaking and stealing property worth £5. They were found guilty. One of them had been put on probation five years earlier; though he was difficult to handle, the two-year period had been completed without further trouble, but later he had broken down again and so had been fined and given a short sentence. Despite these punishments, here he was again, apparently without remorse.

'A further period of probation seemed wholly inappropriate. I would not have so much as considered it, had it been possible to regard his case in isolation from the man who was convicted with him. The other's record was not clean—some juvenile transgression, a conviction of poaching, one petty theft—but he seemed very likely material for probation—had it not been for getting himself mixed up with such a doubtful colleague.

'In a case like this it is perfectly possible to discriminate between the two, but my difficulty was increased when the detective sergeant who gave evidence as to their characters was very adamant in his view that there was nothing to choose between the pair of them; one was as bad as the other, particularly when it came to the offence in question. What should I do? However justified I was in thinking that a prison sentence for one and probation for the other was the fairest—and also the most effective—decision, it would create a bad impression. Why, people would ask, was I dealing unequally with two men for a joint offence of which they were equally culpable? Wasn't the one sent to prison being punished over again for past offences for which he'd already paid the penalty? The choice was clearly between prison for both and probation for both? Which was worse? To burden the probation officer with a very unsuitable subject, merely to avoid being harder than absolutely necessary on the other? To deprive the latter of a chance of probation for the sake of adequately punishing the first one?

'In the end I decided on the more merciful course—and I'm glad to say that both men have completed their probation satisfactorily.'

The Recorder spoke of another joint offence to show how unpredictable were the results of mercy. One of the offenders was a married man of forty-eight with a large family, a heavy drinker, and with two previous convictions: the other was a bachelor of twenty-eight with a clean record. Both were placed on probation for housebreaking. Within nine months the younger man had been convicted of burglary, whereas the older man with the criminal record cut out the drink, worked steadily and settled down with his family, and ended his probation without getting into more trouble.

III

A high proportion of those put on probation are first offenders, but a clean record is by no means an essential qualification: neither do the nature and seriousness of the offence necessarily, of themselves, determine the court's decision. With the majority of the more serious crimes probation is seldom considered but, with the exceptions of treason, piracy, arson of H.M. ships, and murder, every kind of offence or degree of seriousness is eligible, and in recent years it has been used at all levels of court[1] in what may at first appear to be very unexpected instances. So much depends on the total, three-dimensional assessment that emerges from the probation officer's report, when it is allied with the actual circumstances in which the offence occurred and the general requirements of justice. I was surprised, for example, to come across a case of perjury among one probation officer's clients. The culprit's name was Norman and he was in arrears with the payments of the maintenance allowance due to his wife under a separation order; in the witness-box he had failed to disclose certain amounts he had received from the National Assistance Board—not that they amounted to much, his total earnings being around £6 weekly out of which he had also to support the woman he was now living with, who had just presented him with a child. Desperation, hopelessness, and panic, rather than a conscious deceitfulness, had prompted the lies, and all that was asked of the probation officer was to help him sort out his affairs and perhaps find a better paid job.

Obscene libel may seem an unlikely offence to merit probation but it was thought suitable for Grace, a quiet, respectable lady in her late thirties who was jilted by her fiancé after an eight-year engagement. Without notice and without even telling her beforehand, her betrothed had gone and married a widow with a comfortable income. For reasons I could not fully understand Grace was advised by her solicitor not to sue for breach of promise, but the injustice done to her was so painful that she relieved her distress by sending the new bride threatening letters through the post. They contained some surprisingly filthy abuse and on being summoned she was at first bound over, but when the letters started again the probation officer took her in hand. Grace's worst trouble was loneliness; being able to share her unhappiness and grievance with a sympathetic listener was the only treatment necessary.

Although murder is virtually the one exception, cases of

[1] In 1959, 32,816 were placed on probation in magistrates' courts and 6,536 in courts of assize and quarter sessions (total 39,352). *Criminal Statistics, England and Wales, 1959.* Cmd 1100 (pp. 80–81).

attempted murder or of inflicting grievous bodily harm or malicious wounding sometimes end up with probation, though the circumstances usually have to be pretty favourable to the defendant. If anyone ever had justification for assaulting his wife, it was Michael. You would not normally expect to see him in trouble: approaching forty; a successful engineer earning some £1,500 a year; a captain during the war; grey eyes, embedded in smile lines; carefully brushed, rather soft and thinning fair hair—his manner one of tolerance blended with restrained assurance. His only mistake in life, it seemed, had been to marry Frances. It was a quick, wartime affair, their courting being largely confined to week-end leaves, but she was a zestful, razor-witted person who took him to lots of parties and amused him with her quick, diamond-edged comments on the failings of their many friends; tall, tense as a guitar string, with skeletal restless hands, she could perhaps be best described as a very compelling *jolie-laide* rather than beautiful—but in any case Michael admitted that he was soon infatuated. They both used to drink and Frances a good deal more than he did; but she had hollow legs and its only effect was to make her conversation even more glittering and destructive.

Soon after the marriage he was posted overseas, was captured and made a prisoner-of-war. It was three years before he got home, the separation, if anything, fertilizing his infatuation and creating an idealized, gentle and sympathetic Frances, the mother of the son he had never seen. The reality was very different: the son was parked with his mother, Frances was drinking more than before, her gossip was coarser, though still amusing. He put it all down to the war, to anxiety, and they talked enthusiastically about a new start. Being lucky in finding a flat, they settled down together with the little boy. For a while Frances enjoyed being a housewife, painting the flat, collecting small pieces of Regency furniture, and going in for Mediterranean cookery. Her tastes were of the type described as 'faultless'. But then she grew bored, was continuously irritable with the child and wanted to spend every evening in a near-by, very middle-class pub. If Michael did not feel like going she went by herself.

Their married life took on the hackneyed pattern of quarrels, tedious sulks and reconciliations—for some reason, he usually found himself taking the blame. There would be quite long patches when she would be sweet, but then she would suddenly find herself impatient with him, contemptuous and accusing. He was still very much in her thrall—it was the word he used himself: they got on well in bed and this, too, made it easier to recover from the quarrels.

The years went by, the boy was sent to a prep. school, Michael got a better job; he adapted himself, learned to live with her unpleasantness, and the crisis, as so often, was unexpected. One night he returned early from a business dinner and found her in bed with a man they sometimes met in the pub—a bumbling, sozzled, fighter-shocked, ex-R.A.F. type.

'If it had been someone else it might not have happened,' Michael told the probation officer. 'Somehow, taking a man like that made it seem a bigger insult.' It was significant that Michael's attack was against his half-naked wife rather than her lover. Grabbing a poker, he hammered at her face and breasts. With the man's help she managed to free herself, and Michael collapsed weeping on the bed. When the police arrived he was pathetically calm and was himself ringing up for an ambulance. Luckily Frances's worst injury, apart from gruesome bruises, was a cracked collar-bone.

An original charge of attempted murder was reduced to one of causing grievous bodily harm and, with overt misgivings, the assize judge put Michael on probation for three years, with the very strict requirement that on no account was he to attempt to see or to have any direct dealings with his wife.

There was never much fear that Michael might make a second attack, but for a long time he made his probation officer very anxious. The case had received sensational publicity and it was several months before Michael could find anyone to give him the kind of job of which he was capable. He lived in a sleasy residential hotel, saw hardly any of their old friends, and was often overcome with loneliness and a corroding remorse. Though he gave her a very generous allowance, Frances made the most of her advantage by demanding even further sums of money; she even used the son as a lever, threatening to stop Michael's monthly visit to the prep. school to take him out for the afternoon. Tactfully and with hesitant suggestions, the probation officer helped Michael to form for himself a more accurate image of his wife. He still talked of being in love with her, but he slowly gained the strength to accept that the marriage was now finished and, more important, to live with his realization.

I am doubtful if he could ever have reconciled himself if he had not been proffered so much understanding. Once he very nearly attempted suicide and after this the probation officer implored him to ring up immediately he felt depression getting out of hand. Four times the call came and the probation officer would then arrange an immediate meeting, take him out for a meal and a long talk—even though it once meant a trip to Birmingham where Michael had been sent for a week by his firm.

After he had been seen through these crises, which were spread over eighteen months, Michael seemed to make a sudden change—it was like the turning-point in a disease. He rented a small, pleasant flat in a modern block, made new friends, bought an Elizabethan recorder and learned how to play it, showed no signs of being disturbed by the divorce proceedings. . . . The last year of the probation period was uneventful, except that he seemed politely resentful at having still to come for interviews. A few months after it was completed a printed card arrived from Scotland announcing his marriage to a girl called Nina—but I never learned what happened to Frances.

It is not difficult to argue that, whatever the provocation, if it had not been for some basic flaw or inner weakness in Michael's personality he would have been able to control his fateful impulse and would never have grabbed the poker, and yet it is understandable why he gained the judge's sympathy. I know of cases where much greater risks were taken, though they may not have seemed so in the light of what was known of the potential murderer at the trial, and of at least one in which a second violent assault occurred during the course of the probation order—the victim's chest was punctured by a blow from a chisel and the probationer was awarded three years' corrective training. The anxieties these cases can cause were made very clear in an account given me of a man who had tried to murder his wife by the traditional dose of weed-killer added to her morning tea. His probation officer, an Aberdonian, was not given to exaggeration:

'I was doubtful about Paul from the start. Reasonable enough and apparently frank, disarmingly so, when you first met him but underneath he was very immature: the type who panics when things get difficult and does something stupidly dramatic. Ethel, the wife, was the stronger character of the two, though to look at she was an anaemic little thing. But she wanted him back, weed-killer or not. It was thanks to her, and to a report by the psychiatrist and the prison doctor, that probation was tried—subject to his having no contact with Ethel and to treatment for a year as an in-patient in a mental hospital.

'It was only after the trial that I learned from Ethel that there had been a previous attempt on her life—he had tried to push her off a bridge when they were on holiday in Wales. He had a vicious temper and there was no doubt she had succeeded in covering up plenty. Knowing all this made me all the more worried when the year was up and he left the hospital. On my first home visit he was very surly. I snatched the chance, when he went out of the living-room, to warn Ethel of the risk she might be running and begged her to ring me up if she had any reason to feel alarmed. My only comfort was that there were plenty of people living all round, though poisoning is different from knifing—you don't yell for help!

'For a long time I made a point of visiting them once a week, largely to try and satisfy myself that she was in no danger. As I feared, the situation soon deteriorated: Paul was in work but he did not give her enough money, was out most evenings—not that Ethel volunteered much of this. I had to drag it out. I reasoned with Paul, warned him that his whole attitude was irresponsible, that he had a lot to make up for, but he didn't seem in the least grateful for her forgiveness—in fact it probably increased his feeling of guilt for most of his conversation was directed against her, full of complaints about her bad cooking, the dirt in the flat, the way she spoiled the child. All this, mind you, in front of Ethel who merely looked downcast, or shook her head (so that he shouldn't notice) to tell me to pay no attention.

'One night on my way home, I had a sudden fear that she was in trouble. I don't usually pay attention to this kind of hunch—if you don't look out, you're apt to get too many!—but I went straight over. Paul opened the door himself and I thought he jumped: all he said was "You!" and with a look of disgust pushed past me down the steps. I rushed inside but there was Ethel ironing quite calmly, listening to the radio.

'Another time, though, I found her very ill in bed. She had been vomiting all day—Paul, fed up, had just gone out to the pictures. She recovered but after this attack she was seldom really well. Her skin was yellow and each time I called she seemed a little thinner. Everything was all right, she assured me. She even made a sad little joke about weed-killers, but when she'd lost several pounds I insisted she saw her doctor. He sent her straight to the hospital for a thorough investigation. The specialist could find nothing definitely wrong with her, nothing to explain the continuing loss of weight. I felt compelled to tell him about my fears and of course he was very disturbed, carried out further tests and so on, but could find nothing out of the ordinary.

'The rest, however, evidently did her good. They put her on some kind of diet and, after a spell in a convalescent home, she was discharged as fit. Even so, I still couldn't help wondering.... I still do—though my immediate concern has been removed, because, while she was away, Paul got into further trouble. He was arrested for his share in a bank hold-up and was sent to prison for three years. He's still there.'

As he spoke these words, the probation officer's grin was resigned, almost mocking. He looked very tired. It's a job in which each one has to work out his own special way of becoming used to failure.

3

Friendship as a Profession

*

IMMEDIATELY after being released from the dock it is usual for a new client to be formally served with the probation order. He has already answered the judge or chairman that he is willing to be put on probation and the first job of the officer who has agreed to supervise him—provided he is over fourteen—is to hand him a copy of the order and invite him to sign it. As we have seen, the offender gives his consent under the threat of imprisonment, and the ritual of signing the order smacks of bumbledom and hypocrisy. Yet the principle of consent, of a voluntary contract entered into by the probationer to be of good behaviour and turn over a new leaf is central to the whole conception of probation. This first interview after the conviction is considered to be a very important one, particularly where it has not been possible to carry out proper preliminary inquiries. Some probation officers prefer to postpone it for twenty-four hours, particularly if the client shows signs of still being dazed and overwrought, or has been held in custody and is probably hungry and exhausted following an early breakfast of prison porridge, a morning spent in the Black Maria and a cell.

The new probationer will be given further explanations of the meaning of any special requirements included in the order. The Criminal Justice Act of 1948, which embodies the current law and procedures governing probation, leaves much to the discretion of the courts and allows them to specify requirements to suit each case—thus Terry was required to live in a hostel and Michael to keep away from his wife. The 1948 Act also introduced certain safeguards. Probation orders are valid for not more than three years and not less than one. Conditions of residence in institutions are limited to a maximum of twelve months and made subject to review after six months. Strict conditions govern the ordering of psychiatric treatment for any probationers who, while not certifiably insane or subnormal, are considered to be mentally or emotionally unbalanced—but these will be dealt with in a later chapter. The offender is encouraged, whenever feasible, to make good the monetary loss caused by a theft or other crime, and the law enables the court to issue an order for the payment of compensation, usually by instalments (with an upper limit of £100 in magistrates' courts). This cannot be made an actual requirement of the probation order, as it would mean that the threat of imprisonment (for breach of the probation order) could be used as a lever to enforce payment of the damages; but where the probationer is earning reasonable money, there is a good chance that the victim of the crime will eventually be paid back, and this in itself can often help in the battle to rekindle the probationer's self-respect.

With some clients, as may be imagined, it is not easy to ensure that the idea, let alone the details, of the probation order has sunk in; they have to be tactfully reiterated at subsequent interviews. These take place at frequent, though not necessarily regular, intervals—often once a week to begin with. In most cases 'reporting' visits to the probation office are mixed with visits to the client's home or a meeting at a teashop or some other mutually agreeable place. Some probation officers believe in making unannounced visits at times when they are least expected: others frown on this method, saying that behaving as a spy, appearing as if one is trying to catch people doing something wrong, must be harmful to the main objective of winning the client's trust.

When anyone has very strong objections to visits being made to his home, few probation officers will insist on coming, unless they are suspicious that something important to their client's welfare is being hidden; the obvious advantages of seeing the client in his home setting, getting to know his relatives, and so on, are liable sometimes to be more than offset if this means adding to his shame, embarrassment, and insecurity. Young Peter, for example, who had interfered with the little girl, showed distressing anxiety at the idea of Mr Young visiting his new lodgings. He had settled down quite happily with an elderly couple without children—in fact he described it as the nearest he had ever come to having a home—but they knew nothing of his offence and he was certain they would chuck him out if they learned he was on probation. It was undoubtedly best to waive the visits, though I have known other cases where a compromise was reached and the probation officer was introduced as an old friend. For similar reasons, when it is necessary to write to probationers, it is customary to use a plain, unofficial looking envelope.

Some people feel more at ease surrounded by their own belongings, however poor and inadequate, when sitting at their own table, being able to offer a cup of tea: others, though, may use the presence of relations, interruptions from children or neighbours, the duties of a host and the demands of politeness as a welcome obstacle to entering upon a solid discussion of their problems. Making a round of calls can be the most discouraging, lugubrious part of the job, especially on a damp November night when most of the clients seem to have gone to the pictures but, accompanying Mr Young and others, I have often noticed how resentment at the intrusion, alarm and shame at the revelation of unmade beds and unemptied jerries can give way to relief at finding themselves 'accepted' despite it all. The less articulate are sometimes pleased to have the probation officer see for himself the extent of a burden that is difficult to put into words: a bedridden, querulous grandmother; an insanitary, shared lavatory; fungoid-infested walls . . .

Reporting to the probation office can also have its disadvantages. A crowded waiting-room can be as dangerous an incubator for the cross-fertilization of delinquent intentions as is a crowded doctor's waiting-room for germs. So much depends on what the office is like. In the busiest, most urban court in my area, six probation officers—each with a case-load approaching a hundred—depend on a dank, tenebrous little waiting-room, furnished with a few superannuated kitchen chairs; an attempt is made to cheer the cracked, lavatory-tiled walls with posters advocating the pleasures of a winter on the Riviera and I was told that on occasions the mantelpiece had been beautified with flowers—but each time, before the day was out, they had been swiped, vase as well as flowers. The interviewing rooms at this court are equally certain to foster despondency.

Another office I know well, near the centre of a large dormitory area, is incomparably different. Here probation is considered important enough by the authorities to be given an entire house to itself, in a quiet leafy road at a satisfactory but not inconvenient distance from the court. The waiting-rooms—there are two, one for each sex—are carpeted, have neat tubular furniture, and are decorated with Ganymed prints. The interviewing rooms might be likened to housemasters' studies and each expresses the occupant's personality: one has an illuminated tank of tropical fish, another a table covered with model aeroplanes—both useful media for breaking ice! At this court the individual officer's case-load averages only forty.

The extreme differences in the size of case-loads, even more than physical surroundings, add to the many variations of method and outlook. An officer faced with a hundred as opposed to forty cases will not necessarily reduce the average time of each interview, but is more likely to cut down on home visits, keep shorter records, and see less of the clients who he feels are more reliable and nearer rehabilitation—on the other hand they may be expertly elusive. Inevitably, though, the overloaded officer's work suffers, especially as he usually seems to have to spend a relatively higher proportion of his time in court (or hanging about in case he is wanted); with many of his probationers he has to be satisfied with making a far more superficial contact than he would desire.

This can be serious, as the essence, as the core of all probation work is the forming of an intimate, person-to-person relationship. This needs time and a sense of relaxation, hard to attain when you know the waiting-room is crowded; that unhappy young Clive, who has just arrived there after failing to report for six weeks, may not withstand the strain of waiting his turn and will disappear again; that it is particularly unfortunate that Frank is having a talk with David, an innate homo if there ever was one . . . Erle Stanley Gardiner, the American writer, has said that 'giving a probation officer too great a case-load is as fatal as overloading an airplane and then condemning it because it can't fly'.

II

The function of the probation officer was originally described, in the Probation of Offenders Act, 1907, by the picturesque phrase: 'advise, assist, and befriend'; nowadays this is still the aim except that 'befriending' should really be first. If the friendship is heartfelt and genuine then the advice and assistance are more likely to be acceptable and effective. It has to be a special, a systematized, a professional type of friendship, but it is friendship none the less. The jargon word for it is 'casework', and the modern, progressive probation officer sees himself as a caseworker alongside the psychiatric social worker, the hospital almoner, the child welfare officer, and others concerned with individual welfare.

What casework means in terms of probation is too nebulous for concise explanation; its character will, I hope, emerge from the cases described in the ensuing chapters, but before going further an attempt must be made to define its rudiments. The relationship between probation officer and client acts as a bridge so that the latter's capacity for reform and growth can be nourished and made stronger. Perhaps the commonest, fundamental, pervading characteristic noticed among offenders of all types is their failure to make satisfactory personal relationships—*vide* Terry with his stepfather; the controlled, conscious relationship with the neutral caseworker remedies this disability, sets an example of how it can be done. The aim is not to effect a radical change in personality but rather by 'mobilizing the healthy parts of the personality to try to set in motion the natural healing forces present in everyone'.[1] Casework is sometimes ancillary to, yet distinct from, the deeper probing of psychotherapy or psycho-analysis, but as it deals actively with the client's circumstances as well as with his thoughts and feelings, treats him as a case of 'social breakdown', its field is more extensive. It is re-educational rather than clinical. As each client is seen as being unique, the treatment has to be adaptable: one client can be encouraged to solve his practical problems, such as finding a job or a new flat, by himself, whereas another will need plenty of realistic advice. But alongside practical help and advice is the continual bolstering of the client's positive qualities, the quiet support for his efforts to loosen the tentacles of insecurity and anxiety, the relieving of emotional tension, the subtle promotion of insight, the unburdening of guilt and concealed fears. . . .

Put down like this as an abstract, theoretical statement, the casework technique is liable to sound well-meaning but unconvincing—as a meretricious version of the cliché 'kindness works wonders'; it brings to mind the chestnut about the patient at a Freudian clinic who, on being asked what help he needed, replied: 'Well, what I really want is the rent, but I'm quite prepared to talk sex for half an hour.' I can almost hear, too, the derision and scoffs of more than one experienced probation officer, as they read the previous paragraph, and there is no doubt at all that, when considered in relation to some of the morose, refractory, peevish, aggressive specimens to be seen in most probation officers'

[1] A. B. Lloyd Davies: *The Boundaries of Casework*, published by the Association of Psychiatric Social Workers, 1957 (p. 37).

waiting-rooms, talk of social casework can appear remote, ridiculously impracticable and pretentious.

Consider, for a moment, its precepts in relation to someone like George to whom the probation officer is indistinguishable from the police:

'What's the difference?' he asks warily at his second interview, ' 'cept the other lot wear a uniform and your lot don't. What you people ever done that a bloke can trust you?'

There is certainly nothing overtly neurotic about George—you might call him remarkably uninhibited and self-assured. He works as a goods-yard unloader, among men who are used to saying what they think.

'You're not kidding me that your job isn't to keep the tabs on us,' he says later, softening a little. 'You may mean well, but in that case you must be a mug. You should learn something from the coppers. They're like everyone else. They know how to bring off a fiddle. There's scarce a man on the beat that hasn't got his price. Where does being honest get you anyway?'

Diagnosis in George's case is not particularly difficult. On top of a basic, paradoxically frank, amorality is superimposed an exaggerated dislike and distrust of Authority. His relationship with his parents seems to be quite a good one, in fact it was so good that he absorbed quite contentedly their own amoral standards and the result is his violent resistance to society's guardians of good behaviour, including the probation officer. It is hard to know just where to start building the 'prophylactic bridge' prescribed by the manuals of casework or how to stimulate the 'natural healing forces present in everyone'.

In a large majority of cases the client, as one might expect, accepts probation very grudgingly, looks upon the probation officer as a spectre of disapproval. His recent experiences, the arrest and trial, will probably have left him hostile and humiliated. He has failed and been publicly and shamingly told so. He can now react by being cowed and uncommunicative, or resentful and contemptuous, or surly, rude, sullen, and with every weapon in the armoury of unpleasantness. He lies, fails to keep appointments, and it is not difficult for him to discover numerous ways of 'playing-up'. In some cases it takes months for the shock and 'concussion' to evaporate and for this reason alone the offender is at first incapable of facing his problems. Whatever the reaction, the probation officer is likely to be associated with the unpleasant experience, and—is presumably intended?—to be a living reminder of it. The weekly or fortnightly reporting visit brings it all back again, particularly if the office is situated in the court building. The probation officer, despite his welcoming, helpful, understanding mask is, above all, the symbol of hated Authority, of the Establishment, of Them.

Enough has been said to show that as a caseworker the probation officer starts with a burdensome handicap. Probation is not exactly the most favourable situation in which to encourage even a 'professional type of friendship'. The probation officer has to admit to himself that in effect he has a dual role—symbol of Authority and also sympathetic friend; court official and neutral caseworker. No wonder it is a job that demands rather special qualities! Although the willing participation of the offender is normally necessary for success, the probation officer cannot, of course, wait for him to ask for help: otherwise he will be like the apocryphal social caseworker who saw a swimmer in difficulties in a fast-flowing river and merely watched and wrung his hands. The swimmer sank, surfaced, and sank again. As he surfaced for the third time the drowning man managed to gasp 'Help!' 'Thank God!' said the caseworker as he dived in to the rescue. One of the most perplexing skills in probation work is to know how to begin.

As well as assuming many forms, nonco-operation can stem from different and several causes. They have to be analysed and understood before they can be overcome. At least two contradictory phases of nonco-operation could be recognized in a young woman like Lilian, found guilty of stealing a petticoat from the counter of a large store. In the dock, in a torn mackintosh and laddered, twisted stockings, she appeared defeated, hopeless, indifferent; immediately on reaching the probation office she broke down completely. She had been held in custody for over a fortnight and the experience had stunned her, smothered her very small supply of self-assurance. Though there was time for adequate inquiries, these could, I felt—and it was true of so many cases—have been equally well carried out while the offender was on bail and without subjecting her to the indignity and humiliation of what was in effect, if not for the record, a short prison sentence. Remand prisoners are kept separate from convicts, but this does not remove the danger of 'contamination'; the remanded include not only first offenders: if they are adult, they may find themselves lumped with professional crooks, drunks, pathological maniacs, sex perverts, and others. True, there are officers who argue that a taste of imprisonment makes a good start to a period of probation, but this would seem to deny one of its main purposes, and it certainly was not true of Lilian. Between her sobs she declared she was no good, no good at all. She had nothing left to hope for. She was disgraced, proved to be a liar, a cheat. She ought to have been sent back to prison. Her probation officer, a matronly lady who dated back to the Police Court Missionaries, tried to make her see that fundamentally she had not changed; that mistakes could always be turned to good account, even if they could not be undone. Lilian merely shook her head and gave herself up to more weeping.

It was some weeks before Lilian began to unravel her depression, but then she erected quite a different kind of barrier. She seemed to want to provoke disapproval. One afternoon, for example, she teetered into the probation office on three-inch heels and in a bottom-clinging skirt that might have been designed to delight a masochist, and asked for permission to spend the night out. She was living in a church hostel and the warden had no objection provided she had somewhere definite to go. This was reasonable enough, but Lilian refused to reveal her plans, and was studiedly vague, merely murmuring that she had been invited out by two young men and another girl and they intended to explore Soho night life. As she had admitted earlier to a little mild 'hostessing', even though she expressed horror at the mere idea of reverting to this kind of life, the request was delicately charged.

'Do you trust me?' she demanded.

'Of course I do, Lilian.'

'Well then?' She gazed innocently across the desk. 'Why not trust me tonight?'

'It's just that it's a little unusual, isn't it?' the probation officer hedged cautiously. 'I can't very well approve of something when you don't give me enough details.'

'Why should I have to give you chapter and verse for everything I do! You told me that you wanted me to build a life of my own, to make my own decisions, and here you are treating me like a child.'

After more of this kind of fencing, the probation officer gave way. It was a transparent example of 'testing', and far more important than protecting Lilian from the temptations of Soho was to show her that she really was trusted. This was something she appeared to need in her efforts to win back self-respect.

Her telephone call the next morning seemed to confirm this. Sounding unusually relaxed and cheerful, she announced that her throat had not been cut and she's had a gorgeous time. 'You know,' Lilian added warmly before ringing off, 'you're not such an old dragon as you look.'

Testing can, of course, be much more flagrant and provocative than in this case and it sometimes forces the officer to apply for a warrant for his client's arrest for a breach of the probation order. In some ways, though, it is easier to cope with than sulkiness, insolent refusals to answer questions, or the many techniques of polite stone-walling. Experts at the latter are quite different from the genuinely inarticulate. They answer, often brightly and apparently helpfully, even volunteer information, and yet the probation officer knows—without quite knowing how—that it is all a complex disguise and that the true personality is kept just out of sight—and sometimes, though not always, from the client himself. It amounts to a sophisticated kind of *satyagraha*.

Allied with this group of nonco-operators are those who refuse to admit that their offence was bad enough even for probation. To good-looking young Roland the whole thing still appears as a 'mistake'. He intended, he swears, to remit the £30 collected on behalf of his firm to the head office the next morning. He would never have dreamed of borrowing it if it hadn't been for the ridiculous threats from the people who had sold him his secondhand Jaguar—everyone knew what sharks there were in the motor trade . . . It was the kind of slip anyone in business might make. It was just his bad luck. Roland sits among the more normal juvenile delinquents, uncomfortably twiddling his bowler and reading the Births and Deaths in *The Times*. He feels—and in some ways he is—very, very different from them, and at the start of most interviews he makes out that he finds them 'amusing' and tries to identify himself with the probation officer. He does not appear to like the suggestion that human failure is common to all, that some express it in one way, some in another. He is clearly a more unsettled person than he appears; the Jaguar, for example, is probably a reflection of a need to win acceptance in circles which are much wealthier than he is, a need that sometimes comes close to desperation. Tactfully, over the weeks, he is helped to understand himself better, to gain the courage to be more humble.

Righteous humbugs certainly put the 'person-to-person' relationship under some very difficult strains, but fortunately their type of self-myopia often approaches tragi-comedy. There was Florence, a loquacious, angry-looking woman I had often seen in the waiting-room wearing a home-knitted dress like an enormous bedsock, amber beads, and puffing smoke pettishly through an ivory cigarette-holder. I learned she was on probation for the unlikely offence of bigamy. Again it was 'all a mistake'. She had been misinformed that marriages automatically dissolved themselves after five years' separation. The bigamous husband declared he knew nothing of her past—though I could not help suspecting that he was thankful for the excuse to be rid of her. Florence herself showed not a scintilla of remorse for having misled him: she had only 'married' him through a desire to help, to give companionship and proper care to someone incapable of looking after himself—and how had he repaid her? By ingratitude, brutality, and finally desertion! Throughout her life her one wish had been to help others, to satisfy her 'sense of service', but unhappily she only seemed to attract the wicked and ungrateful. A month's remand in prison came as a shock, not because it had happened to her, but because of the other inmates—she had never known that such wicked people existed. She was seriously thinking of devoting the rest of her life to serving them.

The officer supervising Florence—Mrs Grieves, herself a youngish married woman with a sociological, L.S.E. background—told me that at the early interviews it was impossible to get a normal human response from her, to pierce the high-minded mask, to soften for a moment the carborundum hardness in Florence's eye. Her misfortunes, and they were many, had always been the fault of others. It was like ham-acting, except that Florence believed in the part. It was surprising how easily she took people in, though it was seldom for long, and this meant that she could never keep a job for more than a few weeks—people she worked with could not stand the corroding criticism. Untrained for any trade and unused to being on her own, it was not long before her savings were exhausted and, after a spell out of work, she felt for the first time in her life the cold fingers of poverty. Mrs Grieves gave her a pound from the court poor-box, and told me that she could not help feeling rather sorry for her, particularly as adversity seemed to prompt Florence to express feelings that might be genuine.

In time, encouraged by some very skilful coaxing, she became increasingly human. She was told to try and accept weakness in herself and also in others; not to set standards too high for anyone to live up to; that doing things for other people was not as important as merely being kind and understanding.

'I felt I was being an even bigger prig than Florence herself,' Mrs Grieves laughed. 'The poor thing's trouble, I suspect, was her Mum. One of those wonderful, terribly good creatures, but very strict and intolerant with little Flo. Perhaps if she hadn't been brought up so respectable she would have lived in sin and been a lot happier?'

III

What a client *feels* about his offence, about his general circumstances and relationships with others has an important effect on his behaviour—and the feelings may not coincide with objective reality. In all of us, of course, particularly when we are under stress, feelings influence more actions than we normally realize; in the delinquent and neurotic they are apt to be even more decisive. The probation officer has to make great efforts, therefore, to understand his client's feelings, particularly those that may be confusing him. These cannot be reached, let alone eased or changed, by rational discussion alone: the warm and 'comfortable' relationship with the client is as essential as are the microscope to the biologist and the scalpel to the surgeon. True feelings and urges may be too violent or painful to be uncovered—even when not locked in the unconscious. The support of the probation officer can, however, make the process less terrible, show up some of the fears to be paper dragons.

The handling of a homosexual case often provides an example of both the wish to avoid discussion of a painful subject and of how the resistance can be broken down by recognizing it and analysing it. Tony, a promising commercial artist who has just started his first job after finishing at art school, pleaded guilty to importuning. At his first interview he is quite friendly, almost casual, but veers away from discussing his deviation. Later he becomes increasingly hostile and offhand, forgets to keep appointments, until one day the probation officer suggests the reason frankly: that coming to report makes him anxious because it reactivates his memories of the offence and may mean he has to bring to the surface feelings that alarm him. No attempt is made to censure him, to make him feel like a criminal: instead it is explained that probation can help him to readjust himself—that is if he wishes—or at any rate to avoid getting into further trouble with the police; that probation has positive, helpful aims.

'You may be right,' Tony replies curtly. 'I don't want to talk about it—and why should I? I don't feel there is anything wrong with me. There are lots of homos who never get pounced on, people up at the top. Till I came to London I never realized just how many. So why pick on me?'

By way of answer the probation officer starts talking about the Wolfenden Report and the proposal that homosexual relations should be permitted between consenting adults. Tony does not take this up, though he is obviously very interested—even perturbed by the possibility. Very casually he remarks that perhaps he is not a proper homosexual after all.

'Sometimes I don't know what I am—male or female.' Concealed behind Tony's equanimity, and also partly from himself, is a dangerous amount of anxiety: about the degree of his homosexuality; about the extent to which he should give in to it; the social disgrace and maladjustment. In later interviews this all comes out, and a lot more besides, and the probation officer is able to make his life easier, to reduce much of his tension, to give him some insight into his difficulties; eventually he is persuaded to seek the help of a psychiatrist. But none of this would have been possible if Tony had not, in the early stages, been met with friendliness and sympathy, if his feelings had not been understood.

Failure to admit the need for help, blindness to shortcomings, normally have to be broken down before treatment—this is the word always used, for good reasons—can be effective. One old Scottish labourer, a pretty obvious rogue with a long list of petty offences, many of them for drunkenness, complained that he should never have been put on probation for 'loitering with intent'. He absolutely denied the charge, declared he had merely been going for a stroll and was window-shopping; that to get pinched for something he had not done made him feel it was not worth while to try to go straight. He may well have had a sound grudge in this instance, but he was using it as an excuse not to co-operate with the probation officer over his other problems—including the need to find a job, to see that his six children were better fed and clothed, to stop abusing and beating his wife after too much beer. A tough, difficult life can itself become the excuse for refusing help. As one client put it: 'When you have been bashed about as much as I have, you don't trust people even when they really are trying to help you.'

With nearly every kind of offender, except those of very low intelligence, lack of co-operation in all its forms and, in particular, resistance to the court setting, to the whole idea of having to report and be kept under supervision, are defeated only by frankness. The purpose and implications of probation, even the difficulties of the probation officer himself, have to be explained openly and in detail. Reasons as well as advice are given at every step. Above all, the clients are made to feel that the probation office is not a place where they stand to attention and are cross-examined. I have heard it said that with a difficult client it is useful to get him sitting down and for the officer to stand over him, as this makes it easier to appear dominating. This sort of thing may be the practice in some courts—yes, I know it is—and it was fairly widespread some years ago when more thought it desirable to make probation as unpleasant as possible, to force clients to report at inconvenient hours, to take their hands out of their pockets, but it is not probation as I understand it and have seen it in action.

To impute these methods to the probation officers I have known would be to turn truth on its head. They have often to be stern, to show that certain actions and attitudes cannot be tolerated, but they are not bullies. Heavy-handed sergeant-major methods can only make resistance more stubborn. To try and 'knock sense' into probationers is futile. One does not have to read many background histories to realize that the majority have suffered too often in this way already. Discipline, too much of it (mingled, maybe, with over-indulgence), is the frequent midwife of their rebellion. To meet it yet again, to be humiliated, only confirms their previous dislike of those in authority.

This may sound dogmatic, but if one is to consider probation as being something more than a negative restraint, one has to take sides unflinchingly on this principle, for it contains the remedy for most of the forms of nonco-operation I have mentioned—and of many others. A probationer's first attitude towards the—in his eyes—censorious busybody who has been forced into his life is coloured by his existing feelings about people, by what is already in his mind. He often tends—involuntarily—to identify the probation officer with some significant authoritative figure in his early childhood. If it is true that upbringing has any connection with the creation of delinquents, then it is understandable how this happens, how all his old defences, resentments, refusals to obey, desires to hurt—and the emotional power they generate—are transferred to the most likely target of all, the probation officer.

I was told of a young man called Ralph who was seen actually to shudder with nervousness as he admitted that he had been given the sack. When reassured and told not to take it too hard, he replied: 'I thought you were going to shout at me like Father always did.' It was then explained that getting people mixed with important figures from childhood, or rather with one's feelings towards them, was quite usual, particularly when one was under stress. This seemed to help him and later he was shown how an awareness of this tendency could reduce his nervousness and make his relationships generally more relaxed.

The need for exploring the family background becomes therefore even more apparent. The preliminary assessment not only helps in deciding if the offender is suitable for probation but it also provides the first map of his feelings and therefore it may suggest the route to winning his confidence. In fact an increasing number of probation officers now consider the first interview, even if it takes place several days or weeks before the sentence, as the start of treatment. The first impressions made on the client when he is under the stress of uncertainty as to his fate are bound to affect the future relationship. There need be no conflict between objectivity and sympathetic recognition of the offender's fears and hostility: even if a prison sentence is awarded, the probation officer can prepare him and his family to face it bravely and possibly start him on the road to eventual recovery and re-establishment in society—perhaps that sounds sanctimonious but I have been told of such cases. On the other hand, if too much sympathy is shown and the offender is convinced that it is only the probation officer's report that has saved him from prison, he may develop an exaggerated sense of gratitude; this only too easily turns into resentment once there has been a start to the process of getting the client to face reality. Adverse criticism in the report is, of course, an even more likely stimulant of resentment.

At every phase and twist in the relationship the dual role—caseworker and court official—has to be reckoned with. The probation officer has to differentiate between condoning the offence and 'accepting' the offender—if the defences erected by the offender against the expected personal condemnation are ignored, they are more likely to wither quickly. Modern therapeutic technique is in line with the Christian concepts of 'loving thine enemy' and forgiveness of sinners. To an adolescent delinquent, for example, one who has been brought up with few moral standards, or who has become cynical through seeing the standards taught him at school or in church flouted by the people around him, by the popular heroes of films, TV, and the comics, by top people—financiers, politicians, and even bishops—(or so it seems to him) the probation officer, because he is human, may well make these standards again sound rational and worth while.

This was certainly true in the case of Charles for whose parents crime was literally a family business. They were all arrested together, while carrying out a complicated robbery of a cinema : the father got four years, the mother eighteen months, an elder brother and sister one year each; Charles, being only seventeen, was put on probation. Though he clearly felt a strong loyalty to the others, it was surprising how readily he was prepared to recognize the wrongness and futility of their outlook. He was grateful, without fawning, for the probation officer's help in fixing him up with lodgings and an apprenticeship to a plumber; even more surprising was his determination to pay the rent of his parents' council flat so that it would be kept available for them. There was a difficult patch when his mother was released and he was under tearful pressure to return home, but after talking it over with the probation officer, he decided not to. Shortly after this his brother received another sentence, but Charles never wavered—the second chance had been justified, against apparently very long odds.

Charles was probably such a relatively easy case because he *wanted* to discover someone new for whom he could feel respect. As a child he seemed—like George, who appeared earlier in this chapter—to have had a happy relationship with his father but once his reason began to suggest that it was a mistake to be a criminal, he needed a substitute which was supplied in the person of the probation officer. This mechanism, though it may sound very theoretical, can be widely recognized and is the opposite to the 'negative transference', discussed a few pages earlier, in which the probation officer becomes the target for previous resentments.

The value of the positive variety can also be seen very easily in the case of Caroline. She was twenty-two and was living with a man called Monks who was not far off fifty. Her childhood had been unhappy: the father drank, the mother was usually ailing, and much of Caroline's time had been spent with a prudish, very religious aunt. Monks was the first person to show her deep affection or even ungrudging kindness: they had been together for eighteen months and she was devoted to him—he must have been a cross between a lover and a father. Then suddenly Monks, the only stable figure in her life, was arrested and given a three-year sentence for robbery: she was involved as an accessory and got two years' probation.

To begin with she is very unco-operative. Tearfully she declares that she would have preferred to have been sent to prison. She lives by herself in a luxury flat full of expensive furniture and with wardrobes stuffed with clothes—there is no proof, but, as Monks was not known to have had a job, it seems likely that this affluence is the fruit of his earlier crimes. She always declares that she is determined to wait for him. She seems to have little awareness of right and wrong.

As the months go by Caroline changes. There is not much left in the bank and several pieces of furniture and the radiogram are sold. Egged on partly by boredom, she finds herself a job with a dress shop, only to lose it after two months as the result of confiding unwisely in the manageress. This crisis helps her to draw closer to the probation officer: instead of trying to get through the interviews as quickly as possible, she is now difficult to get rid of—she asks plenty of questions but more than anything she seems to need long feminine chats. The probation officer takes her to a dress parade and encourages her to enrol for evening classes in shorthand. Monks is seldom discussed—and then only if Caroline mentions him first—and care is taken to offer only the most hesitant advice.

Eventually Caroline determines on her own accord to break with him; a meeting with an ex-convict, who brings a message from Monks in prison and who talks of plans for them all three to work together in the future, decides her. She leaves the flat, but is scared of what Monks might do to her when he is released. By then her probation will have finished but she is told to keep in touch and ask for help whenever she feels she needs it.

IV

There come times for every probation officer when he or she has to make the difficult decision whether or not to pass on to the police possibly incriminating information received from or about probationers, and in particular whether or not to report to the court a breach of the probation order. If the officer acts as a court official, he destroys the confidence he has carefully constructed as a caseworker; if he decides not to act officially, he is liable to fail in his duty to the community.

'It all depends on the particular case,' Mr Young would explain with the familiar balancing of opposing considerations that is so apt to appear as unhelpful ambiguity. 'You have to take into account the total situation, the gravity of the breach or information, the progress, if any so far, made by the probationer and so on. Of course we continually have to close our eyes and forget what we've heard, but don't give people the idea that we're a kind of crooks' protection agency; if we hear anything really serious and there is no other way, we have to inform the authorities. There is no point either in wasting too much time on a man who for months makes no effort to co-operate. Every now and again you have to write off your losses. I suppose that for some, prison—or what they call the "short, sharp shock" of the detention centre—may be more effective, though for us it's another defeat.'

Technically what amounts to a breach is seldom difficult to define: persistent refusal to work, laxity in reporting or informing the officer of one's whereabouts, or the breaking of one of the special conditions to the order, are all breaches and entitle the officer to bring the client back before the court. But even when the probation order is allowed to remain in force—and in particular when, as can happen, it is extended—the friendly relationship is unlikely to escape at least temporary damage. The probation officer now appears in the role of prosecutor. He becomes starkly identified with Authority. He seems to have turned out to be like everyone else and to have rejected the client. A degree of risk is, as we have seen, inseparable from most probation orders: many clients will inevitably express their hostility in this way, are almost certain to commit a breach, especially in the early stages; others need to 'test' the strength of their new relationship, and so on. Yet it must be added that sometimes failure to report a breach may cause the client to feel bewildered and insecure; as the official probation textbook puts it,[1] '. . . he will be hindered rather than helped if his probation officer, who represents Authority, himself rejects Authority in his effort to get on close terms with his client. If he does this, the probation officer in effect identifies himself with his client's rejection of Authority and only confirms his belief that Authority is outside his scheme of things.'

There are some who tell you that it was easier to win an offender's trust in the days when the probation officer was unofficial and merely a member of the Police Court Mission. The dual role was then less of a problem. He would be more likely to see his cases in a private house or a church hall, away from the court building, and was thus not so closely identified with the Establishment. There is probably some truth in this, though the counter-argument is that the official status of a probation officer is precisely what enables the offender to come to terms with Authority, even to reconcile his ambivalent feelings of love and hate.

The battle by a probation officer to prevent a client from reverting to crime has often to be more strenuously engaged than

[1] *The Probation Service*, edited by Joan King, Butterworth, 1958 (p. 174).

in the cases of Charles or Caroline. It is tempting—and really it would scarcely be an exaggeration—to liken the role of these quiet unobtrusive officials to that of determined, often desperate, guardian angels supplied by the Welfare State. This simile is surely just in the account given me by Mr Young of a television dealer called Robert.

'It was only a small place with a window on the High Street and a workshop behind, but the business seemed thriving—repairs mostly and replacing tubes, but he reckoned on selling three or four new sets each week. That was how he got into trouble. A man called Adams stole a lorryful of new sets straight from the factory; they fitted the registration plates from old worn-out sets and Robert flogged them on the never-never. Adams, an old hand, was lucky to get away with two years; Robert was given probation, as he was not involved in the actual robbery and it was his first offence—or, more likely, the first time he'd been caught.

'The more I saw of Robert, the more I doubted him—though I could never be sure. Not that he was unfriendly—if anything he was a shade too co-operative. The look into one's eyes was too square. You could not distinguish between the real man and the salesman. His assurances that he wasn't getting into more trouble sounded as if they'd been rehearsed. He would invite me to examine his stock, to look carefully at the registration plates—but of course he knew they would mean nothing to me. With a good deal of obsequious, but keep-it-dark hinting he would offer to supply me with a set on trade terms. Then, just as I was beginning to think my suspicions were unnecessary, he took on an assistant called Dickens—a lugubrious little man with a paunch and spade-shaped sideboards. I knew the face, but I could not place it. He might have been an old probation case belonging to someone else, or more likely I had seen him in court? Just to make sure, because it might give me a line on Robert, I made some inquiries. Dickens also turned out to be quite an old hand: seven previous and just finished three years in the Ville, the same prison as Adams—Robert's collaborator.

'Even so, I had nothing against either of them. But I felt I must tell Robert what I knew, as he was my first concern. He made no effort to feign surprise and argued, with sincerity but it could easily have been hypocrisy, that having been in trouble himself he liked to be able to help someone like Dickens, make it easier for him to get back on his feet and go straight. It was only after I had warned him at length of the danger he was running, that he admitted that Dickens had brought with him a message from Adams. I was not prepared to press for its contents, particularly as Robert swore he'd torn it up without reading it and it would have meant showing I didn't trust him.

'I used to drop into the shop nearly every week, though normally I don't like to give the idea I'm snooping. There was never anything definite, only the vaguest indications to make me suspicious—such as the man with the bandaged hand and a bruised eye drinking tea with Dickens in the workshop: the day before there'd been a big hold-up in the West End in which a gang had got away in a stolen car, found crashed upside-down a couple of miles from Robert's shop. Later, about the time when Adams was released from gaol, I noticed Robert was using a flashy, cream-coloured Cadillac, but of course he assured me he'd bought it cheap off a friend. The interviews were still very pally; he seemed even to enjoy my visits or coming for long chats at the office, and yet I still had the feeling I was being buttered up, as if I was one of his customers. I suspected all the time that Robert was on the fringe of some pretty big operators—if he wasn't in thick with them.

'All I could do was to remind him of the dangers, and all he did was to look pained—that is until Dickens was arrested for a dockyard robbery. I could see then that Robert was very frightened: Scotland Yard had already questioned him and he begged me to tell them he knew nothing, that he had only employed Dickens out of kindness. I replied that of course I couldn't help unless he told me the complete truth but he swore there was nothing to add.

'The next morning he was waiting for me outside the office. Adams had visited his place and accused him of shopping Dickens. He hadn't, but what was he to do? He was scared that they would dump some stolen goods in his workshop. My advice was to go directly to the police if this happened, or if he ever received a definite threat, and to change the locks on all his doors. I was by then certain that he wasn't merely using me to gain an alibi. He really did want to escape being dragged back into Adams's circle.

'Adams in the end disappeared—went abroad, I think—but the fact that I was always there, that Robert and I had seen each other every week for some eighteen months, had been enough to steady him, to make him come to us at the crisis of his fight against his past.'

Reform—though it is better to think of it as 'recovery'—in these last three cases would have been unlikely without the establishment of an easy, confident relationship. In cases where the antagonism is greater, where the transference is entirely negative, this is more difficult, but even more essential. The probation officer's function is not to impose reform from without, but to arouse a desire to change, to supply incentives, to rebuild and bolster moral stamina; to plant the seeds of self-recovery and then allow friendship, acceptance, sympathy, to germinate and fertilize them. But if a graph could be drawn to express a client's reform, in few instances would the curve be even. Each case has its own dynamic. Most have their periods of crisis, especially during the early months, their *allegro* passages, their unexpected *bravuras*—particularly those that are most justly described as successes.

4
Reasons for Criminals

*

Alan, aged 18, taking and driving a Ford Consul; stopped by police for erratic control of the vehicle—*two years' probation.*
Francis, aged 15½, taking and driving a Hillman Minx without licence—*two years' probation.*
Peter, aged 17¼, taking and driving a Daimler sports saloon without licence—*two years' probation.*
Desmond, aged 19, taking and driving without licence a taxi to the public danger—*two years' probation.*

'TAKING and driving' has become the classical offence of the juvenile delinquent. What else offers such an exciting, danger-spiced opportunity for expressing aggression, for experiencing a sense of angry power, for cocking a snook at Authority? Also it is easy and, for oneself, comparatively free from risk. The unattended car waiting by the kerb presents a nagging challenge; the desire to accept it becomes compulsive and breeds its own variety of recidivism. In 1959 no less than 40,856 cases of taking and driving were known to the police; this is apart from 12,990 motor vehicles stolen, of which 10,346 were recovered during the year. Many of the culprits find themselves on probation. The four listed at the head of this chapter are taken at random from my notebooks. Their offences were very similar: none of them were insured or had passed their driving tests; they received almost identical dressing-downs and warnings from four different benches. In any court they would be routine cases, but the briefest summaries of the four young men's characters and backgrounds suggest several cardinal questions.

Alan lived with his parents in a well-to-do block of flats and was training to be a quantity surveyor. He was intelligent, easy to converse with, did well at school, had no previous convictions, but he was obviously over-tense and it was not difficult to imagine him being awkward. The trouble was very simple: his father kept a mistress. She lived in a similar, but slightly less luxurious flat in the next suburb and the father divided his time between the two establishments. He was as much torn by guilt as was Alan's mother by self-pity. The mistress—actually an inconspicuous, jolly, rather toothy lady with a part-time job in the city—must have been an invisible, poisoning influence throughout the years of Alan's adolescence. Neither parent appeared to have much insight into the boy's very natural resentment.

Then there was Francis, still at school. He was only the passenger, he explained; it was the other two, older boys who did the driving. Though he admitted he had enjoyed the thrill, it was feasible to believe he had been dared into joining them. Francis's background also concealed tragedy. His mother died when he was ten and his father, after several unaided years of keeping the home going for Francis and his younger sister, had remarried. Judging by the stepmother's acidulous, ungenerous manner, let alone her unpowdered, grey-lipped, flat-chested appearance of chronic spinsterhood, desperation with her too had been the match-maker. Almost her first words to the probation officer were to make sure he realized that neither Francis nor his sister were hers; she insinuated that they both inherited 'their trouble' from their mother. Her husband, she complained despisingly, failed to face up to his responsibilities to the children—one minute he would be spoiling them and the next punishing them unfairly; whenever they were difficult at the week-ends he would escape to his bed with a sick headache and she would be left with the burden. Francis had no illusions about her—with a twinkle of pleasure he informed the probation officer that after the first two months his 'Dad and her never had it together'—but the boy seldom seemed sure of what he felt about his father: there was a strong emotional tie but in many ways he found it difficult to respect him. Francis would often say how very sorry he was about his offence and yet one felt that he did not really wish, so to speak, to be reformed: at his first interviews he seemed to enjoy the idea of someone trying to understand him, prepared to take so much trouble over him. He was probably not really interested in stealing: going off in a car was a dramatic way of getting away from things, 'that sort of lark gives you a lift', made him 'kind of feel strong inside'. A bad end-of-term report at school probably triggered-off the offence but it was unlikely to have happened without a weakness in character structure, related to his mother's death, aggravated by his father's difficulties as a parent and the coldness of a stepmother—a coldness that freezes deeper than any other.

On the other hand Peter—who chose a Daimler for his free ride—possessed a home background that was in no way unusual and in fact appeared to be very satisfactory. His father drove a steamroller for the local council and the mother was a cheerful, if simple, woman whose rosy face would still have looked in place in the milking-shed of her father's Donegal farm. Her other two children seemed well-adjusted, but Peter, who was the oldest, gave the impression of being over-anxious to be liked, of disguising a severe sense of uncertainty; he was just the type to show-off in bad company—and to himself—with some daredevilry like joy-riding in someone else's car. The Daimler gave a possible clue. It tied up with several strands of his earliest experiences. His mother described how shortly after his birth the blitz had become suddenly worse and she was evacuated to a country village in the Midlands. There she had worked as a daily help to one of the big houses in the neighbourhood and, owing to the shortage of domestics, had been eventually offered the chauffeur's flat over the stables. She had been very happy there because her husband was stationed not far away and was able to join them most week-ends; it was an admirable place for Peter to grow up in. His first experiences of the outside world as a toddler took place in the big house's gardens. The middle-aged lady who owned the house—her husband was a Brigadier—had no children of her own and she grew fond of him. When the war ended it was agreed that Peter should remain at the big house while his parents returned to London to find somewhere to live. In fact he stayed eleven months—until after the birth of a second child—and for the next few years, until he was ten, he was invited to go back for long summer holidays. He was treated almost like a son, taught to ride a pony in the paddock, fitted out with clothes from Daniel Neals; the Brigadier, now retired, even bought him a small split-cane trout-rod and showed him how to tie on a fly. Then one day the kindly couple were both killed in a motor crash: from then on Peter had to be content with a week at Clacton along with his brother and sister. The jaunt in the Daimler and his lack of confidence as an adolescent therefore had three possible causes. The emotional shock of the accident; the confusion implanted as a result of being nurtured according to very different sets of values and standards; and, paradoxically, a sense of emotional deprivation as a result of the eleven months spent, when still very young, apart from his mother. A fussiness about his clothes—he saved up to buy a faintly Tattersallish suit from Austin Reeds—his decision to obtain a post as a footman, the care with which he tried to modulate his vowel-sounds, were probably also part of his pathetic, largely unconscious attempt to act out his childhood experiences as a young gentleman, to gravitate to the world of the rich.

Lastly there was Desmond. He came from West Africa and at the time of the offence had only been here two months. He was illiterate and he tended to say politely whatever he thought the probation officer wanted him to, though his accent made him hard to understand. It was very difficult to keep him to the point, particularly as he frequently laughed out loud to himself, and had a habit of jabbing at his collar or indulging in bouts of convulsive shoulder jerks. It turned out that the taxi he borrowed belonged to a man with whom he was lodging, though this was not made clear in court. When Desmond first arrived in London with only five shillings in his pocket he had got into conversation with the taxi-driver at an all-night coffee-stall, and naïvely accepted the surprising offer of bed and food and even money until he found a job. It must have been bewildering to learn that these full *pension* terms were to be settled by sharing the taxi-driver's bed. Apparently he felt he had no alternative, but after a few weeks he could not master his disgust any more and there was a very unlovely quarrel which ended with Desmond, stupefied by anger, driving off in the taxi as a furious act of defiance. He left it stranded somewhere in the East End where a constable, attracted by the uncertain driving and the sight of such a dark taxi-driver, started to ask questions.

As often happens, a single, relatively simple offence led in each of these four cases to the unravelling of a complex of difficult, surprising circumstances and background. The charges were the same and the result was a uniform two-year period on probation, but what lay behind each was wholly and at nearly all points different. Every new client means a separate searching after causes. The police have the task of discovering *who* committed the offence: the probation officer hopes to discover *why*. The search for a possible motivation, or more likely for several, stemming from a collection of factors as subtly various and multiform as the human face, starts with the preliminary inquiries and normally continues throughout the early months of the probation period. Without this diagnosis—it is the term used—the probation officer would merely be coping with symptoms: to try and quieten a client's anger, or censure his rudeness, or comfort his unhappiness, or criticize his weakness, without looking for the root causes, can be as hopeless as smothering a syphilitic ulcer with talcum powder.

II

This approach to crime is of relatively, astonishingly recent origin. It is not very many years since crime, like poverty, was generally considered to be almost solely the evil fruit of selfishness, extravagance, drink, or indolence. These qualities of course are still very relevant, but mere wickedness is not a sufficient explanation: what causes the wickedness is of much greater concern to a more enlightened system of justice. The boundary between crime on the one hand and on the other unhappiness, inadequacy, mental defect or mental ill health has become increasingly smudged. To steal is to 'deviate': delinquency is a form of social illness to which all of us are prone. The Victorians did begin to realize that weak-minded convicts should be segregated in special prisons, but on the whole the care of the convicts' mental health was the concern of clergymen, and the only recognized therapy was a dose of moral instruction. Lady Wootton in her polemical analysis *Social Science and Social Pathology*[1] has examined the revolutionary changes in attitude towards crime with scholarly documentation and asks some important and difficult questions about the effect of the changes on moral judgements, a subject which will be returned to later. She writes: 'In the eighteenth century no clear distinction was drawn between the mentally afflicted and the criminal. Lunatics were treated more or less as criminals. . . . Today, for quite different reasons, the distinction between the two classes has once more become confused: but, instead of treating lunatics as criminals, we now regard many criminals as lunatics, or at any rate as mentally disordered.'

The shift in outlook—of which the probation service is an expression—owes much, of course, to modern psychiatry and to the widely accepted body of psychological description rooted in the work of Freud, Adler, Jung, and others. Though opinions on

[1] George Allen & Unwin Ltd., 1959 (p. 203).

the value of psychotherapy in probation work promote heated, and no doubt unconsciously motivated, differences among the profession, every trainee comes to his first cases fortified by an understanding of the major types of personality disturbance, neurosis, and psychosis; he is familiar with the interplay of the id, the ego, the super-ego, with retardation and regression, anxiety, obsessions, hysteria, aggression. . . . This is not a textbook of criminal psychology but, later, we shall see how these concepts influence the work of the probation service and how, and to what extent, they affect the treatment given to certain cases.

As, so to speak, detectives of their clients' psyches, probation officers have also to be seen in relation to the rambling and, again, young science of criminology. The methods used in reforming or curing wrongdoers are inevitably dependent on the accumulated understanding of the causes of crime. Many branches of criminology are influenced by or related closely to psychology, but it spreads very much further and overlaps into sociology, economics, medicine, statistics, and other disciplines. The most celebrated of the new science's pioneers was the Italian professor, Cesare Lombroso (1836–1909), who in his atavistic theory pursued the idea that the criminal was a throw-back to primitive man and even to inferior animals. This was later modified to fit the belief that the criminal was a clearly recognizable type of degenerate. Lombroso compiled an immense catalogue of physical traits which he believed characterized a criminal tendency—a receding forehead, or a thin upper lip, projecting ears, prominent eyebrows, Mongolian physiognomy, excessive wrinkles, a furrow across the cheek, and many other features. In answer to criticism he also catalogued external factors such as the consumption of alcohol, tobacco, and snuff, extremes of temperature, density of population, race, the price of bread, illiteracy, and other social and economic factors which could increase the crime rate. Most of Lombroso's theories have long been exploded, but he was among the earliest to try to treat crime rationally, as a social disease rather than merely wickedness. Mixed with his pseudo-science was an accurate insight into the minds of the individual criminals he was able to observe; he was also in favour of prison reform.

Since Lombroso's day the problem has been approached from numerous starting-points, in many countries, on the basis of an astonishing collection of hypotheses, and in attempts to seek every imaginable kind of correlation. Some of the best known inquiries into crime and, in particular, juvenile delinquency have examined the influence of such factors as:

slum or neighbourhood cultures;
acute poverty or unemployment;
regularity and type of employment;
number of persons to a bedroom;
rehousing on a new estate;
size of family;
seniority in family;
other criminals in the family;
physical handicaps;
physical health of the parents;
mothers who go out to work;
marital friction or broken home;
maternal deprivation;
illegitimacy;
step-parents;
age-group and sex of the offender;
intelligence quotient and scholastic ability;
cinema and television;
religious beliefs;
membership of a youth club;
hereditary factors;
alcohol or drugs;
truancy at school;
over-indulgence in upbringing or over-strictness. . . .

The list could easily be lengthened, but the findings tend to be either inconclusive or platitudinous. A laboriously compiled sample of, say, hundreds of delinquents compared with a similar number of 'non-deviants', with its bewildering comparative percentages, often tells us little more than that severe overcrowding is likely to increase the incidence of offences or that to be unloved in childhood raises one's chances of becoming a thief. Much of the research carried out so far can perhaps be considered as an essential clearing of the ground, but it would be quite wrong to underestimate the degree to which criminology has clarified and systematized our understanding. In this country the Institute for the Study and Treatment of Delinquency, individuals like Hermann Mannheim, John Bowlby, Sir W. Norwood East, L. Radzinowicz, Max Grünhut, to mention but a few, have done and are doing distinguished work; criminology is likely to grow in scope and importance, it is part of the new humanist, liberal approach to offenders, and it is good to know that Cambridge University has converted its Department of Criminal Science into an enlarged Institute of Criminology, a step that may help to bring the subject nearer to the level of importance attached to it in some other countries. Even so Lord Pakenham, writing in the *Causes of Crime*,[1] his concise and efficient investigation of the chief contemporary trends of research, is forced to conclude: '. . . every reply to our questions suffers, from our point of view, from one of two defects: either it contains no quantitative estimates, however rough, of the importance of the various factors; or, if it does so, its estimate has at present "no proved foundation" . . . Broadly speaking, there was little readiness on the part of any expert to commit himself to a quantitative evaluation of any one factor or set of factors . . . it is tempting to emit a weary sigh and shrug the whole thing off with the reflection "the causes of crime are neither known nor knowable".'

By its nature criminology must be an inexact science. Its propositions are often incapable of strict scientific proof, though improved techniques are being evolved so as to know and refine the factor investigated—the Gluecks, for example, in America are

[1] Weidenfeld and Nicolson, 1958 (p. 106).

currently studying no less than three hundred individual traits. A fruitful line of 'operational' research has been opened up by what are termed prediction methods. These ignore causes as such, but readily classifiable information about a group of offenders is weighted and combined statistically: the results have been found to predict future behaviour with degrees of accuracy that have the advantage of being ascertainable. The practical uses of prediction methods have been demonstrated in a survey of boys sentenced to Borstal training: for example, it was shown that ' "open" Borstals had a better success rate than "closed", even after all possible allowances had been made for the fact that the youths sent to "open" Borstals were "better risks".'[1]

Much of the criminologist's data is 'soft', incapable of precise measurement: how, for example, does one arrive at the degree of over-indulgence in a family or the severity of marital friction? Even experienced caseworkers will interpret them differently. There is a tendency to attach too much weight to the factors that are easier to 'measure' and too little to others that may be more important. It is even impossible to take a sample of the entire criminal population, because the investigator has to leave out the sizeable section who never get caught: the successful criminals, whose characteristics may reasonably be thought to differ from the unsuccessful who supply most of the data, are lost among the non-criminal population and may well form part of the 'control group'. It is frequently difficult to distinguish between a causal and a chance connection. Even the official criminal statistics are said to be very unreliable, owing to variation in their compilation in different parts of the country, in the efficiency of the police, and the arbitrary method of classification—different officers and courts have different opinions on the dividing-line between robbery and larceny, between unlawful wounding and assault, and so on. Lady Wootton devotes the larger part of her latest

[1] *Prediction Methods in Relation to Borstal Training.* Hermann Mannheim and Leslie T. Wilkins, H.M.S.O. 1955 (p. 135).

book[1] to elaborating the difficulties and the weaknesses up till now in research and to subjecting some of the most widely accepted theories to a caustic battering: '. . . few generalizations,' she writes, 'can be made with confidence about those whose behaviour is socially unacceptable, and [it is clear] that not many are applicable even to any one group of these. For the popular theories about the delinquency of latchkey children, about social failure repeating itself generation after generation, about the beneficial effects of boys' clubs or the disastrous consequences of illegitimacy—for these and similar generalizations we have, as yet at any rate, little solid factual evidence. Perhaps we can go so far as to say that the lack of secure affection in infancy is likely to create difficulties in after-life, and that one possible manifestation of these difficulties is a reluctance to conform to what society expects. But that those who are not loved are likely themselves to hate rather than to love is hardly a discovery for which modern science can take the credit. Man has known this truth in theory for as long as he has disregarded it in practice.'

Opinion among the experts differs acutely on the emphasis to be placed on a particular factor, and divides into two fundamental schools: the ancient argument about original sin now takes the form of environmental influences versus defects and disturbance in character. A report prepared for the World Health Organization by Lucien Bovet[2] quotes from a table (given by the Swedish S. Ahnsjö in his book on delinquent girls) that compares the relative importance attached by various experts to external and internal factors. The discrepancies are striking: some attribute 91 per cent, others 12 per cent of cases to hereditary factors; similarly, some experts assert that they have never seen a single case where external factors are alone responsible, compared with a figure of over 50 per cent given by others.

Whatever relative weights one may give to each kind of factor, the inescapable conclusion is that there is never one single cause.

[1] *ibid* (p. 301).

[2] *Psychiatric Aspects of Juvenile Delinquency*, 1951 (p. 12).

A crime is the result of a complex of factors, a train of earlier events, a balance both of social and individual influences that differ in each case: Sir Cyril Burt speaks of 'multiple causation'; Dr Max Grünhut of 'composite syndromes' and 'a coincidence of personal and social factors, none of which does not appear among non-delinquents as well'.

III

How does all this affect the probation officer—face to face with an individual wrongdoer, rather than a population sample or age group? Even if he relies solely on common sense and his technique is entirely pragmatic, he too is likely to assume that there must be some composite explanation for the offence. Though his insight into his client will probably be more penetrating if he possesses a knowledge of criminology and psychology, he will nevertheless be rash if he attempts to impose a ready-made hypothesis—even a composite one: on the contrary this, if at all, can only grow out of the information he assembles. His assessment can seldom be called complete; frequently it has to remain very indistinct and tentative; normally it changes as the relationship with the client becomes closer and more confident, and it is possible to observe him reacting to new events. The kind of information very briefly touched upon in the four cases at the head of this chapter, when looked into deeply and sensibly balanced, can however begin to reveal the 'total situation' and suggest means of avoiding trouble in future. It must be stressed again that the re-educational process, the giving of advice and emotional support usually starts from the earliest possible moment: it does not wait upon the reaching of even a provisional assessment. Treatment and diagnosis run parallel to each other and intertwine: as will be seen, the very process of getting information from the client, of striving towards a diagnosis, can often be helpful, make it easier for the client to release tension, to sort himself out.

The offence itself is a natural starting-point for the investigation, but its circumstances or the events that immediately led up to it may only have 'triggered it off', and the real cause will possibly be harder to discover. Similarly, worries that are uppermost in the client's mind, and which he may be readier to talk about, often mask deeper and more important ones. The probation officer has to be a very sensitive, a 'creative', watchful listener. The tautening of an eye, the quiver of a lip, a sudden alteration in the pattern of breathing may indicate a revealing emotion or attitude. The chance, seemingly unimportant, remark; the context in which something is said; the precise way it is said, the emphasis and overtones to certain words or names—things like this may give a glimpse of feeling or attitude, add a brushstroke to the growing picture of the client; occasionally they may reveal something more important, the key that releases a sudden, clarifying comprehension, though of course it is only too easy to arrive at neat, but dangerously false deductions. Since Freud's *Psychopathology of Everyday Life* the idea that much can be learned from unwitting slips in conversation, from the exact choice of words and phraseology, has become everyday knowledge—in particular they offer clues to ideas and feelings that a person wishes to disguise from himself and others.

Writing for American probation officers, a professor of casework at Ohio State University[1] has said : 'Generally we hear only bits and pieces of what other people say, and these bits and pieces are often filtered through our prejudices, biases, and preconceptions before they qualify for the final action of hearing. . . .

'Choice of words as well as form of expression tells its own quiet story. We observe quickly the violent and obscene in language, all but the inconspicuous conjunction of certain words or the use of certain metaphoric expressions is easily overlooked.

[1] Leontine R. Young, in *Federal Probation* (U.S.A.), December 1957 (pp. 26–27).

The person who makes over-frequent use of the innocuous word "Just", "it just happened", or "I just happened to be there", is usually indicating that he is telling us something less than the whole truth and that coincidence must bear the major brunt of responsibility. The person who clarifies every response with "Yes, but" is probably telling us that he has great resistance to us or that he has a real problem in making decisions. . . .'

Elizabeth Glover, one of the few British probation officers who has written on the technique of her job is equally clear on the importance to diagnosis of listening and watching:[1] 'One observes, for instance, something of the family relationships by the way people speak to or about each other, or refrain from doing so; something of their moral standards by the way they talk about the offence . . . One should note, too, where the client begins his tale, where he leaves off, and what, if anything, he leaves out. These things reveal the way his mind works. Some people begin, "Well, it was my fault, really . . ."; others with a long, involved rigmarole of times and dates and places. This may indicate (or it may not) that the first has already faced the issue, the second is still evading it. Some leave off where other people begin to be involved, others where they themselves are . . . One should mark where people begin to colour up, to shift uneasily or to cry, for these suggest that one is near a sore spot, and therefore a vital one. It may be best to make a mental note of this, rather than to pursue it at the time. . . .

'Left to themselves, if they are sufficiently at ease, people will tell their story their own way. They may begin with their sensations now, or with what happened last Wednesday night; they may proceed backwards, or forwards, or first one way, then another. An interviewer with a logical mind is again and again tempted to interrupt to get what seems to him a rational sequence. If he interrupts, damage is done. The client is telling what is uppermost in his mind, and it is illuminating to the probation

[1] *Probation and Re-education*, Routledge & Kegan Paul, 1949 (pp. 48–49).

officer to know what he thinks is important. . . . By interruption the client is put off his stride, and may be fussed or piqued, while the interviewer has lost a valuable glimpse into his way of going about things.

'One is also sometimes tempted to interrupt with criticism or advice. Both are equally fatal to further revelations. Once suggest "Oh, I would not have done that" or "I think you made a mistake there", and the client's whole attention will be turned, not on giving his own account of things as they seem to him, which is what the interviewer is trying to get, but on trying to defend what he did, or to put it in another light, on covering up other aspects to which he thinks exception might be taken. The interviewer must be absolutely unshockable if he wants his client to speak freely.'

The probation officer has to become very used to lies and has his own methods of detecting them. How he reacts to them depends on the state of the client. It may be a mistake—and also unpleasant—to appear gullible, but sometimes it is wisest to pass the lie over for the time being and return to the subject later, when it can be presented in such a way that it is difficult to repeat the lie—or rather it is easier to tell the truth. To confront a client directly with a lie is apt to increase his resistance, to weaken his self-respect, to encourage him to lie more copiously. To the experienced, lies are valuable evidence in the search for motive and personality structure. What prompts the lie—fear, muddle, spite, vanity, loyalty? Generally, though, deeper worries are not likely to be revealed until the client feels able to confide in the officer; the nature of his worries has to be elicited rather than probed for by direct questions. The probation officer's neutrality allows the client to take stock of his life without having to defend himself against the kind of criticisms he may well have received or feared from relations and close friends.

'It's much better to get the client to see the way things are for himself,' was a favourite remark of Mr Young's. 'Don't present him with a blueprint of his difficulties and a recipe for solving them. It's best just to prompt, to guide gently. In this way he's more likely to consolidate his reform.'

IV

It was Mr Young who told me about Alec and Helen, a young newly-married couple who, one would have thought, had less reason than most to find themselves in trouble. Alec had a good job, Helen was very pretty; his parents had helped them buy the lease of a modern four-roomed flat; perhaps Alec was a little oversatisfied with himself and underrated the effort needed even for minor achievements—I recognized in him my own adolescent illusion that one was born on a different level from the rest, that one was natural material for a success story—but it was not very easy to imagine him as a cheat. His crime was the unrealistic, but surprisingly common one of hire-purchasing something—in this case a vacuum cleaner—and then immediately selling it second-hand: his story was that he had suddenly found himself in debt and, having already borrowed £40 from his parents, this appeared to be the only way of keeping the landlord at bay.

The exploration of his case was like the unravelling of Peer Gynt's onion: several possible causes for the flaw in Alec's character, of the type pursued by criminologists, were revealed one by one, but though they probably each had an effect, there was always the feeling that the fundamental cause was still concealed. He was an only son. His father was frequently away on business. He had been spoiled by his mawkish mother. Almost certainly he was too immature for the responsibilities of marriage, even though his wife still earned as a hairdresser—but this is really to beg the question, a common pitfall because what is another symptom can so easily be mistaken for the cause. Apart from his magniloquent ideas about his career, he had few interests and his reading appeared to be limited to American-style comics.

All this—the outer layers of the onion—was relatively easy to discern, but it was three months before Mr Young realized there was major trouble between Alec and his wife. His mother had once or twice dropped hints but this could so easily have been maternal jealousy that they were ignored; Alec suddenly burst out with it one evening when Mr Young was paying a home visit. He was like a child unable to withstand the loneliness of hiding some private shame. Inquiring casually where Helen was, Mr Young received the reply: 'You may well ask! Out with one of her pick-ups, of course.' After this Alec broke down and eventually admitted that only a few weeks after the marriage Helen had started going out with other men—'a new one every fortnight'. She sounded a proper head-collector. At first she had pretended to be going to the pictures with a girl-friend or on a visit to her mother, but lately she had been quite frank about 'wanting a good time'.

This revelation could well have had a bearing on the offence: Alec would not have been the first young husband to be thrown off-balance by a highly-sexed wife, but the ultimate, essential trouble had even yet to be unveiled. It took several meetings with Helen herself to find out that Alec was impotent.

This humiliating realization, coupled with Helen's lack of sympathy and what amounted to her hysterical reaction, and their ignorance of the probability that his condition was temporary and could be cured, was a convincing reason for his having become disturbed emotionally and thus having given way to panic about his debts and involved himself in a rather ridiculous piece of dishonesty. Even so, it did not have to be considered in isolation, as the more obvious factors—the spoiling, over-possessive mother, his immaturity and self-deception about his abilities, the lack of other interests and the influence of the comics—had previously weakened or distorted Alec's character and left it incapable of withstanding the major disgrace and shock.

Such an analysis always tends to sound too facile, but in this case it was viable. Its complexities put it beyond the reach of statistical criminology—even if someone has worked out a correlation between crime and impotency. The study of many individual offenders, in greater detail than provided by the average case history and by considering them as three-dimensional figures that exist in time, are constantly reacting to events, and are never static, is a fruitful method of adding to our understanding of criminal motivation. When this is followed by a search for common factors, some of them perhaps as yet unobserved, it can be an important adjunct to normal criminological techniques.

The risk of mistaken, and particularly over-facile, assessments is ever-present in probation work. Even when the hypothesis is suggested by the facts—and is not imposed on them—it can happen that the essential facts are missing or not even known to exist. The case of Simon described to me by Mr Compton, the Aberdonian who also told me about Paul (who added the weed-killer to his wife's tea), shows how alarmingly easy it is to be wrong.

'There were no pre-sentence inquiries, no psychologist's report, but as soon as I saw him, I guessed he was in a very nervous state. I wasn't surprised when he told me that a year previously he'd suffered a nervous breakdown. After the trial he sat listlessly in my office sipping a cup of tea. His hands shook so violently that most of it went into the saucer and he could scarcely write his signature on the probation order. He was, however, very prepared to talk and I was surprised how well he understood himself. His present attack of nerves, as he called it, dated back to an accident at work. He was a shunter at the goods-yard and one morning he'd misjudged the distance between his engine and a pair of points and crushed a plate-layer's foot. It was one of those accidents where it could have been several people's fault: the plate-layer's for not getting out of the way, another man with a flag whose warning was said to have been ambiguous, or Simon's. Luckily, they were able to save the man's foot though he was off sick for several months. The court of inquiry seems to have been unable to blame anyone and Simon was given what you might call a half-hearted exoneration. But he told me how the scene that morning preyed on his mind—the man's scream; the tug on the brake-lever; trying unsuccessfully to remove the crumpled boot while they waited for the first-aid team; then once they had carried the victim away on a stretcher, the private retching by the lineside . . . one can imagine it!

'Simon did his best to forget, but he began to suffer again from insomnia, to dislike his meals, and he suspected he was in for another breakdown. His doctor gave him some pills, but they did not help much. What he needed, he told me ruefully, was a wife—but he had never met the right girl. At his age—he was getting on for forty—it was best, he believed, to give up looking, and so he went on living with his mother and a brother, who was also a bachelor.

'It was the accident, too, he more or less confessed, that had triggered-off his offence—the theft of cigarettes from a slot-machine. He went so far as actually to tell me that he felt so guilty about the accident that he deserved some sort of punishment. On each occasion—he asked for three similar offences to be taken into account—the stealing had acted like a drug and it had been followed by several good nights. He put it like this: "I did not think it was enough. I had to do it once more, just to make sure." The police reported that he had broken the glass of the cigarette-machine in the most obvious way—it was around seven o'clock and plenty of people were passing. He'd made no effort to escape or resist arrest.

'After only a few weeks on probation I felt he was rapidly improving. He told me that he felt as if he was coming out of a hideous valley. He found himself a different job in charge of a lathe at an engineering works. It seemed as if the thefts, the arrest, the week in prison, the appearance in court, really had relieved his tension; that he had expiated his guilt. He kept saying that they should not have let him off so lightly, but that things would now be all right.

'As the summer went by he seemed so much calmer and self-confident that I cut down his visits from once a week to once a fortnight. He was always punctual and would ring if anything prevented him from coming. Then one evening he never turned up. There was no message. Two days later the police called to say that he'd been summoned by his brother for assault, but before the charge could be laid he was arrested while breaking into a pawnbroker's shop.'

There is no purpose in recording the rest of Simon's story. Mr Compton believes that his original diagnosis was wildly wrong and was owing to a self-deceptive rationalization by Simon of other, deeper conflicts which he did not dare face. A more complete investigation suggested that they centred round his mother and brother of whom he had always been jealous. According to them, his behaviour had for long been peculiar and he had been subject to violent rages ever since a small boy: according to Simon, they had always sided against him, treated him like a servant, even given him inferior food to what they eat themselves.

'I never did decide who was most at fault,' Mr Compton said. 'I think what Simon told me about the other two being unkind and siding against him was true—but then perhaps he'd brought that about by his own behaviour? On the other hand the mother struck me as being very neurotic and her comments on Simon can only be described as viperish. As for the brother, he hardly ever spoke—I suspect he was a near-M.D. All I could do when Simon came out of gaol for the further offence was to try and get him to move into digs. But he wouldn't. I found him a good place with a motherly landlady prepared to cook and wash for him, but he wouldn't even go and look at it. It's surprising how some people refuse to let go of their hatreds. I believe they would feel insecure without them.'

The attempt to explore the causes of the offence is often

described as being shared. Ideally, the client comes to understand them as much as does his probation officer; in this way he can recognize what had happened inside himself or what external factor, be it a nagging wife or too much beer, goaded him on to commit the offence. Most people, of course, never gain complete self-awareness—and too much of it can be paralysing—but it can and does help offenders to avoid letting themselves be wrongly influenced a second time. Similarly, the probation officer will notice in the history of many cases a tendency for the same pattern of behaviour to repeat itself, perhaps to culminate in some outburst if not an actual offence—despite the unpleasant lessons taught by the previous occasions. He watches for signs of the onset of this stereotyped behaviour, does what he can to head it off, and knows that at these periods he is most needed.

Whatever the causes, there is seldom a dramatic, specific cure, but to understand them a little makes it easier for the probation officer and his client together to work out a plan for the future. The first, positive steps may not always seem very significant—a change of job or lodgings, enrolment at evening classes, perhaps it's merely a new suit or dress—but such an event can mean the start of rebuilding a damaged life, the first quakings of rebirth, provided it is accompanied by friendship and acceptance which—even if it does sound sanctimonious—is jargon for love.

5

In Trouble With Circumstances

*

THE delicate complex of causes behind each case makes any attempt to formulate even a loose system of classification very difficult. For the reasons given in the previous chapter, it is purposeless to classify them according to offences, and other methods are, in their own ways, equally misleading. Certain cases, it is true, group themselves readily together under such headings as 'Juvenile,' 'Adolescent', 'Prostitution', 'Homosexuality', 'Marriage Reconciliation', but for the majority—the larcenies, breaking-and-enterings, bodily harms, embezzlements, that make up the morning list at most courts—each case seems to need a pigeon-hole to itself. For my purpose at any rate, it is safer to think in terms of the 'factors associated with a case' than of causes, and I have felt justified in saying that for each individual case one kind of factor was probably dominant.

This guarded approach has also enabled me to arrive at the headings for this and the next two chapters: 'In Trouble with Circumstances'; 'In Trouble with Others'; 'In Trouble with Oneself'. Admittedly, quite a few cases would look equally at home in all three, but empirically I have found this division to be practicable—or at any rate less misleading than any other—provided one remembers the need for frequent cross-referencing from one category to another. For example, in the case of Michael who tried to murder his wife (Chapter 2) the dominant factor might be said to be jealousy and he could safely be placed under the heading 'In Trouble with Others', but one has also to remember that a serious flaw in personality might have been responsible for his failure to control the angry impulse for revenge and therefore a cross-reference is necessary to the third category: 'In Trouble with Oneself'. A 'classical' juvenile delinquent like Terry (Chapter 1), whose difficulties originated from his mother's re-marriage and an unsympathetic stepfather, also fits into 'In Trouble with Others', but because his unhappy relationships have helped to disturb his personality, he too might also be eligible for 'In Trouble with Oneself'; if he were so seriously disturbed that he needed treatment at a mental hospital, then this would be the dominant factor and he would fit best into 'In Trouble with One-self' and a cross-reference only would have to be made to 'In Trouble with Others'. Such reservations and semantic safeguards make tedious reading and I have tried to avoid them as far as possible, though they are essential to any form of classification—which in itself is part of the process of understanding.

I must add that my choice of cases has been for the most part eclectic: I have tried to present a wide range of clients but for this very reason the proportion of unusual cases is exaggerated. Attention given to female cases in the book is perhaps greater than is justified by the number who are put on probation or who appear in court—something like six adult (over 21) males to one female are found guilty of offences (with variations this is true of all age-groups and countries), though females account for about one in three adult (over 21) probation cases; for juveniles and adolescents the figure is more closely parallel to the percentage of offences and is one in eight. Similarly, I have probably given adults more than their fair share of space compared with adolescents—the actual numbers placed on probation in 1959 were 10,641 adults and 28,711 juveniles[1]. (Juvenile court cases have been omitted from this book as they deserve a volume to themselves.)

In this chapter at any rate the bias in favour of adults is in place, because adolescents, even delinquent ones, tend to be less vulnerable to the lunges and enfilades by the circumstances of

[1] *Criminal Statistics, England and Wales, 1959.* Cmd 1100 (pp 80–81).

debt, the sack, overwork, and other perils of the industrialized rat-race. Of course common to the vast majority of crimes is the desire for money, but that is quite different from saying that they can be easily correlated with poverty or some form of economic distress. 'I wanted the nickers—what else would I be doing it for?' was how Terry put it. The feeling that one should have more money is experienced by members of all income groups and its strength is relative to individual ambition, envy, and other qualities of character, to the wealth of the people one mixes with, to contemporary standards. In a society dominated by cash, in which wealth tends to be the most important index of merit, when God-fearing business men remark daily and truthfully that 'this is a business, not a charity—the two don't mix, old boy', of course money is the incentive for crooks as it is for all of us. Working-class youths sitting in their Wimpy bars have far more in their pockets than their fathers did at the same age, but the rub is that it does not seem all that much when you dream about buying a Jaguar or flying to the Bahamas. Women become tarts nowadays, not because the sale of their honour is the only way to avoid starvation, but because they prefer a night with a lonely sergeant from Wyoming and a handful of fivers to an eight-hour shift in a biscuit factory—though there are plenty of other factors!

It is very doubtful if those who are subject to severe poverty are exceptionally dishonest, though they may qualify more easily for sainthood. Even so I discovered, in very many more cases than it was comfortable to admit, that after more than a decade of the Welfare State, in a nation 'in which everyone nowadays is a Socialist', in which the extremes of rich and poor are said to have been abolished even if 'some are more equal than others'—in so many of them it was impossible not to conclude that the pervading and dominant factor was poverty. Not underprivilege nor membership of a low income bracket, but poverty. By this I mean the poverty of extreme inequality, the poverty of the 'thirties, of George Orwell's Britain; of the bread-and-marge diet and peeling, damp walls; of urine-soaked little children sharing a bed; of the carefully divided household budget that always seems to work out wrong by Wednesday. . . . Older probation officers have told me that things are very much better than they were in, say, the 1930 slump, that nowadays very few can be classed as destitute, that youngsters have little idea of what their fathers and mothers suffered. I accept all this. The really poor may be a minority—and yet my experience of the courts makes me suspect that they are still a disturbingly large minority: for far too many families circumstances are still lamentable and shameful, and for very many more the improvement is still only marginal, particularly among the old, the unemployed, the sick, the widows with young children. The national wealth may be expanding each year, but to what extent do these groups get a share of the increase?

Poverty nowadays has to some extent been concealed by a curious confidence-trick—for which all three of the main political parties can be blamed: comparisons of income, for example, do not necessarily tell us much about real standards of living and leave out such things as expense accounts and capital gains or insanitary housing. In the waiting-room of most probation offices the gloss appears at its thinnest, particularly if among the clients is someone as old as Lucy. She was a first offender at the age of sixty-four. True, some inner weakness or flaw in personality may have prompted the impulse to pinch the two packets of tea from the self-service store right under the eyes of its chicly disguised young lady detective, but with slightly better circumstances the weakness or flaw would have remained snug and dormant as it does in most of us. A few random extracts from Lucy's bulky case-record will be sufficient to explain the dominant factor in her criminal motivation: 'Her husband is nearing seventy, suffers from chronic bronchitis, and is more or less bed-ridden. Illness and boredom make him very irritable and he refuses to take any medicine. He wheezes like a very dodgy old engine.' 'Their joint old-age pensions come to 80s. a week. With National Assistance amounting to 39s. [this included 25s. for rent; 4s. fuel allowance in winter only; and 5s. extra nourishment for the husband] they talk about "just managing".' 'Lucy insisted on taking out her new dentures to show me where they scratched her gum. Her indigestion, according to the doctor, is probably due to her inability to masticate properly.' 'Lucy reports that she has been taken on as an office cleaner—6–9 a.m. She has to do the top two floors and climbing the stairs winds her. But she is pleased about the job and says the work itself is fairly light.' 'Arrives at my office looking very white and tired. Thinks there may be something wrong with her kidneys as her ankles are swollen. Intends to visit the doctor this evening.' 'Has given up the cleaning job because of the stairs, though her ankles have gone down a little.' 'Asked if she would like me to arrange a holiday for her, but she cannot leave her husband and he is not fit enough for the journey. Gave her 10s. from the court poor-box and her fare, as I discovered she had walked all the way to see me.' 'Their two rooms are very clean though the air smells damp and what furniture there is seems decrepit. Their supper tonight is tea and a bread pudding as their neighbour gave them a spare loaf brought back from his work.' 'Organized some coal tickets and gave her a food parcel. Tried again to contact the housing officer about their leaking window-frame.' 'Lucy returned the 3s. 6d. I lent her last week. She is always anxious to show her gratitude and says she dislikes being dependant on charity.' 'Her ankles are "lovely" and her teeth fit a little better, though she only wears them "with company" and when out shopping. It is impossible to eat with them.' 'Tells me that she started scrubbing this morning at a big store's canteen. It was all right except that she found it very difficult to stand up after a long patch of kneeling. The supervisor noticed this, told her she wasn't strong enough for the work, gave her a day's money and said she was not to come again.' 'Took round a secondhand woolly for Lucy and a winter vest for the husband. They were very grateful, but they could not understand why the N.A.B. had reduced their money by 4s. Promised to look into it and let them know. . . .'

The poor's worst offence, we have been told, is to be boring. I expect they would agree and I am not going to compile the catalogue of poverty's symptoms that could easily be made from the average probation office's records. In numerous cases bad housing alone might be reckoned as a strong secondary, if not the dominant factor behind the offence, but I shall limit myself to an extract from the case-record of a middle-aged mother of eleven children who was found guilty of obtaining money from the National Assistance Board on false pretences: 'No one seems responsible for repairs. The outside wall of the top room at the front is absolutely wringing wet. All the wallpaper is off on one side of the window. Much of the ceiling plaster has collapsed and when it rains the water has to be caught in buckets and bowls. They have managed rather ingeniously to divert the trickles of water so that it all falls in the receptacles, but when it rains very hard they have to get up during the night to empty them. The ground floor is also damp and a great wet patch forms between the inner wall of the passage and the front door. The ceiling looks very unsafe. The eldest boy has left home because he says he is fed-up with damp sheets, though I must say the place is always very clean and neat. . . .'

In both this and Lucy's case probation—and thus their offences—led to a sizeable easing of their practical problems. The probation officer knew much better than they how to manage the complex console of the welfare bureaucracy and how to enlist the help of housing officers, health visitors, the Old People's Welfare, and others. The betterment in their conditions, plus the knowledge that they no longer had to struggle alone, prevented the likelihood of any further offences—in the second case the debt to the authorities was repaid in full. In both instances the probation officer acted like any efficient welfare or social worker and had little need to worry about his client's morals. Most probation offices have their store of secondhand clothes, shoes, and blankets—often stacked depressingly in a corner of one of the interviewing rooms—and in many areas the court poor-box or some other charitable fund provides small amounts of cash for relieving severe distress or helping with some sudden financial emergency. Where needed, arrangements are made for paid holidays or visits to convalescent homes.

Though straightforward relief work still occupies much of the average officer's time, in the past its share was immeasurably greater. Indeed the Police Court Missionaries of Edwardian England who entered upon the work with a strong vocation to serve, fortified by religious zeal, must have found their concern for their clients' spiritual welfare frequently overwhelmed by the immediate problems of arranging shelter for the night, replacing their verminous rags, and providing bowls of nourishing soup. Then, at a later period, the probation officer tended to think of himself primarily as a social scientist and the emphasis was laid frankly on what is labelled hideously as the 'manipulation of environmental factors'. This approach, I suspect, became (rightly and inevitably) popular because the overworked, underpaid probation officers of the 'twenties and 'thirties so often found themselves having to cope with endless symptoms of economic distress; a client's rachitic children and the workings of the unemployed's means test were, perforce, of more immediate urgency than the state of his libido. In recent years the disappearance of the worst and most obvious features of economic distress among many offenders, coupled with the post-war expansion of the social services, has caused—'enabled' might be a more accurate word—the probation service to concentrate on their clients' inner conflicts. An offender who is unemployed, badly housed, or destitute is given practical help, but alongside the investigation of his employment prospects, or of his need for new underwear, goes a very serious attempt to understand his personality, to find means of satisfying unmet emotional needs, and the other techniques of casework.

To talk of three such stages in the Service's history is to oversimplify half a century of rapid and uneven pioneering and to be sweepingly unjust to several generations of successful probation workers, but an awareness of the changes in attitude is necessary to any explanation of current methods and, in particular, of the acute differences met with among probation officers today. In a recent lecture an officer attached to the London Probation Service illustrated the three periods in terms of what has been done for drunks: 'The missionary would persuade the drunk to sign the pledge and do all else he could to strengthen a weak resolve to reform. The social scientist would find the drunk a job, new clothes, friends, and perhaps a new house and new interests, and then by exhortation and personal endeavour support faltering resolution. Nowadays attempts would be made to understand his need to get drunk before efforts are made to help him to come to terms with the cause. . . .'

Like the criminologists, the theoreticians of social work are said to be split between the relative importance of the environmental factors and of disturbances in the personality, but in practice most probation officers, I am sure, normally deal with both simultaneously. They do not seem aware of any dichotomy: faced, say, with a young delinquent husband living with obviously difficult and nagging in-laws, the officers I have known would all seek for 'internal' personal weaknesses or inner emotional conflicts that might be associated with the offence—though here their approach and methods might differ dramatically; but they would also, without exception, almost as a matter of routine, think in terms of finding the young couple a place of their own—and thus 'manipulate the environment'.

II

The helplessness of many clients over everyday practical matters, and the squalor into which the 'inadequates' can let themselves sink, must often make it uncomfortably difficult to remember the need to strengthen the chords of friendship and acceptance. It is not a profession for the finicky. I remember how over lunch one day in the café opposite the office Miss Lane described a visit she had made to a young woman remanded on bail following a charge of neglecting her eight-month-old baby. The café was steamy and decorated with Coca-Cola girls, but the food was cheap and on most days Miss Lane and three or four of her colleagues would be found there talking shop; I soon got used to hearing them discuss such things as job vacancies for after-care clients, or the value of Stilboestrol for homos, or the character of the new court gaoler, or bed-wetting—between mouthfuls of hamburger and chips—with the unconcern that teachers might discuss time-tables or a group of builders the price of cement. But I admit that Miss Lane's account of Priscilla's baby made me leave my jam-roll and custard mostly uneaten—not that Miss Lane, for whom cleanliness and tidiness, I suspected, were aspects of morality and whose person, as well as her own flat, was faintly perfumed with Dettol and coal-tar soap, departed from her usual tone of quiet but charitable objectivity.

The baby had been crying in its pram outside the house when Miss Lane arrived. She lifted the cover and found it soaking and dirty. Beside it was a feeding-bottle, half full of cold curdled milk and with the teat damp with urine. Priscilla herself apparently looked rather unsavoury in a dressing-gown matted with cooking stains and her hair tied vaguely in a bandeau made from an old stocking. She was eighteen and in a shy way quite friendly but no one had ever taught her the elements of housewifery, let alone how to care for a baby. She might not be very bright, but she knew that she was failing—her husband was away most of the time in the navy but, she told Miss Lane unhappily, he was always grumbling about the way she did things. I don't want anyone to think I am exaggerating, so I shall reproduce the rest of my notes on Priscilla exactly as I made them: 'Several piles of dirty and soiled clothes on the floor . . . Double-bed covered with a dirty-looking blanket . . . Everything foul smelling and the baby's cot mattress also soaking . . . Priscilla said she only had seven napkins left, as the rest had been pinched while drying in the yard: when asked for baby's clothes and something dry to change it into, Priscilla could only produce two little frocks . . . She is genuinely worried about the red patches on the baby's bottom and thighs, but it never struck her to visit the clinic . . . Kitchen is disgusting with a single bed piled with dirty clothes and rubbish. Table littered with unwashed crocks and open tins of food including one of dried milk from which sticks out a filthy spoon. . . .'

Later it turned out that Priscilla had V.D. and there were other unpleasant details, but Miss Lane was able to 'manipulate her environment' with astonishing effect. After a course of treatment in hospital for V.D., arrangements were made for Priscilla and the baby to spend three months in a special home for neglectful mothers. Here she was taught some of the things she should have learned from her own mother, and the baby put on weight. When she returned to the flat, Miss Lane visited her almost every day to begin with and made sure the washing and house-cleaning did not get out of hand. Tactfully she encouraged Priscilla to improve her appearance and one afternoon Miss Lane looked after the baby so that she could have her hair permed. It would be misleading to say that Priscilla became a model student of domestic science, but by the time her probation finished she was coping with things unaided: Miss Lane said that the flat was still curiously bleak but it was clean and the baby had become a robust toddler, smeared only with the kind of dirt that comes off at bed-time.

Probation officers have to be ready to help, either actively or with advice, with a motley of practical problems. Whenever necessary they bring in other social agencies but they are always there as the neutral, supporting figure, as far as possible nurturing their clients' independence and their ability to act more effectively for themselves. Supplying information about jobs, lodgings, hospitals, night classes, or whatever it may be, provided it is given in a friendly, non-patronizing way and the problem is genuinely shared, can help the client not only to live more efficiently and enjoyably, but it can also help him to think about himself more clearly and relieve his anxiety. This is the first step towards resolving any deeper confusion of feelings and attitudes that may have been at the root of the offence. Simple, practical, everyday help can provide the scaffolding for the building of insight.

An inability to foresee consequences is characteristic of mental disorder, but like so many other symptoms, this, in some degree or other, is common to many of us who are considered normal. Incurring too many debts is an obvious example and one that is certainly a frequent factor among first offenders on larceny charges. Wendy's husband, for instance, stole £15 not because he was essentially dishonest but because he was desperate and in his panic it seemed like a solution. Advertisement proneness, effective salesmanship, gullibility, ridiculous naïvety, rather than any innate criminal tendencies, had made them commit the folly of taking on weekly H.P. payments of £7 17s. 10d. a week out of a weekly income of £11 and with a family of four young children. The shock of arrest, the ten days on bail, the disgrace, were enough to prevent the likelihood of another offence and the probation officer's role was more like that of a friendly accountant. Some of the goods were returned after correspondence with the companies who had sold them; the weekly payments were reduced to under £5; Wendy herself took a part-time job in a factory, her mother coming over each morning to look after the two youngest children; and by the time the year's probation was over the family's affairs were in order again.

The official probation textbook[1] frowns on giving advice as opposed to information, saying, a little optimistically perhaps, that 'advice in telling a client what he should do has little place in modern casework'; the probation officer should only 'put the alternatives . . . and indicate the consequences of certain actions'. It warns against the perils of giving too much legal advice: most probation officers pick up an extensive working knowledge of the law but, apart from explaining court procedure and the client's

[1] *The Probation Service* (pp. 74–75).

legal rights, they would soon find themselves in difficulties if they started to play at lawyers.

They must be prepared for much of their advice on any subject to be rejected. As the textbook says: '. . . some clients want advice only in order to prove its uselessness. A mother may ask whether or not she should chastise her child. She presses for this advice until the officer may feel that he is failing in her eyes until an answer is given. Having been told what course to adopt, the woman may return triumphant at a later date with evidence that the advice she was given has proved futile.'

By definition probation officers, I suppose, are thought to be straitlaced and upholders of conventional virtue, but I found their advice was frequently and refreshingly unorthodox. Mrs Oldfield, for instance, who had gained her first experience as a Police Court Missionary and who had little time for 'all this psychology', told me of a row she had just had with the father of one of her young clients. White-haired and immensely corseted, in a dark-green coat and skirt cut, it would appear, by a military tailor, Mrs Oldfield could be very intimidating.

'He even threatened to complain to the Clerk of the Court. Let him! The man behaves as if Mr Gladstone were still Prime Minister; expects Alice, his daughter, to be in by nine o'clock and to be satisfied with the "nice" kind of friends they provide for her. She may be all he says. She's certainly a miserable slip of a girl, but she's nineteen and entitled to a little independence. No wonder she's let herself get caught up with all these Nuclear Disarmament types, and what's worse, let one of them put her in the family way.'

Mrs Oldfield took an angry gulp from her cup of office tea. As often happened, she was treating me as a neutral but eager receptacle for the relief of her own tension. It was a trait I encouraged perhaps a little too shamelessly.

'Alice "missed" four months before she told anybody, and now her father is insisting that the young man should marry her, make an honest woman of her if you please! The young man is a poor fish but says he's quite willing. It's Alice herself who isn't. She told me that she doesn't really love him, that he hasn't any money, and that anyway she's keen on someone else. And she's right! I told her father that I agreed with her, and now he thinks I'm disgusting.

'Well, let him! There's nothing sillier than getting married just because you've started a baby. Unless there's a lot more besides that, it's likely as not to end disastrously, and no one suffers more than the child, the innocent cause of the mess. It's better to get it adopted or for the girl to bring it up single-handed.'

Ignorance of the Facts of Life, unnecessary worries about sex, crop up in many cases and the probation officer has to help remedy parents' and the schools' continuing funk, despite some enlightenment, at explaining things to adolescents sensibly and frankly. Several probation officers keep a shelf of books about sex, growing up, and so on, as their experience has taught that a perfectly ordinary theft or a case of taking and driving can often be traced to anxiety and tension arising from sex frustration. Strictly he does not belong in this chapter, but Stewart is a more obvious example of the results of ignorance. Aged twenty-two, he was placed on probation for voyeurism, squinting through the cracks between curtains of ground-floor bedrooms of the nurses' home attached to the local hospital. The strange thing was that for the past eight months Stewart had been married. At his first interview he was too embarrassed to say much but, finding his probation officer was not shocked and that, instead, he offered an unfussy sympathy, he managed to mutter that he was mostly interested in the girls' breasts. He was unable to explain this. In fact, he did not even connect it with anything physical in himself, but later he recalled a much earlier relationship, when he was sixteen, with a girl who let him fondle her but always drew the line when his hand reached her brassière. Stewart was later able to talk about his marriage and the probation officer also visited his wife. She was attractive—and also bosomy—but as ignorant about sex as her husband. They had practised what they thought was intercourse but in fact the marriage had not been consummated. A little information and the loan of a sensible book was all that was necessary. There were no more offences. A charge of indecent behaviour had led to the fulfilment and probable saving of Stewart's marriage.

In the more usual run of cases help in coping with a client's circumstances, be it the finding of a job, the answering of a letter from the tax collector, a loan of 15s., or the gift, maybe, of a secondhand jumper, or arranging for a client's head to be deloused, do not merely further his rehabilitation : they make it a little easier to convince him that Authority is not always the enemy, that it can be helpful. This may sound like offering bribes, yet you could say the same of probation as a whole—freedom, if you like, is the bribe to keep the client out of trouble. As we have seen, very many offenders have intense feelings of hostility towards society which are focused on the probation officer. It is important, therefore, that in every way possible the client is able to feel that here is a figure of Authority who, unlike others he has known in the past, is really prepared to be helpful, to accept him as a human being with a right to have problems. The hope is that, unless the offender is too severely damaged emotionally, he will slowly begin to think to himself that here is someone who disapproves very much of what I have done but yet seems to like me, to see some of my problems as I see them, and really does want to help me. If an offender can stop resenting his probation officer there is a chance that he will also stop resenting Authority in general—or perhaps direct his resentment into more positive channels than stealing or getting drunk.

That is why it was an important moment when Lilian (Chapter 3) after her night out in Soho rang up to say : 'You're not such an old dragon as you look'; or when at the end of a long trying probation a client could write : 'The next time I report will be the last. Can't I almost hear your sigh of relief? This may sound funny but in a way I am going to miss coming to the office. In fact I quite like you. At least you try to understand me and I do need someone to pour my troubles out to. Still, who knows, you may again have the honour of my company in the near future. Isn't that a warning thought?'

Every probation officer understandably treasures such tributes, even if the language is sometimes rather treacly: 'Do you remember,' wrote another client, 'the time you used to say I'd never pass these two years without copping another lot? I think now I only done it to prove you wrong, but perhaps you only said it to what you might call goad me on like. But anyway we made it. I mean "we" because I'd not an earthly, had I, without you helping and going on at me. Well, that's all for now, except that I wish you every success with some of them other ripe bastards I've met in the waiting-room. I hope they won't be as trying as I've been.' The writer of this farewell note was Terry.

III

As well as having his environment manipulated, the client is helped to put up with disadvantages that are difficult to remedy, to adjust himself to what is inevitable. As many who get into trouble do so because of an unreal sense of their surroundings—similar to an inability to foresee consequences—insight has to be diverted outwards, though this may sound like a paradox. The client's own solutions are, of course, encouraged, but they may be unsound or impracticable. It is difficult sometimes for the officer to avoid becoming entangled in the client's own distorted view of reality. Guiltiness can be too easily relieved by scapegoats. Someone who blames all his difficulties on to his in-laws or the people next door may be wise to find somewhere else to live, but help in smoothing his general relationships with others may be more important, though not so obvious. Poverty, bad luck, illness create their own attitudes, some of them justified, some distorted, most of them hampering to their possessors, except as defences against despair. Factors such as these are relevant to the attempt at sorting out or rebuilding a person's life.

The surest way of stimulating anxiety and thus perhaps a second offence is to push the client too fast. He must be allowed to tackle his problems at his own pace. By the time many offenders find themselves in the probation office their affairs really are in a dispiriting tangle, and I was impressed by the knack some officers have of deciding which is the most important problem to tackle first of all. Its solution may perhaps be the key to several others; as it is sometimes put, solutions, like problems, breed their own solutions. All too frequently, though, one solution seems to fertilize new problems and with the 'inadequates' it is often a question merely of keeping them afloat and out of trouble.

'Reform and sorting-out a person's life are really the same thing,' Mrs Grieves used to tell me, 'but that doesn't mean imposing your plan on to the unfortunate client. Nowadays that's quite *démodé*. With some, of course, we have to be firmer and more definite than with others, but it never pays to bully them into doing something. That's what Mrs Oldfield's apt to do, poor dear! My room used to be next to hers and sometimes you could hear her through the adjoining door ordering her people about as if she was top brass in the A.T.S.—not that she wouldn't exhaust herself on their behalf.'

For some officers 'class' remains an inescapable handicap. Assuming—with no statistical justification—that the class breakdown of offenders more or less matches that of society, the majority will come from the working-class and the many shades of the lower middle-class. Whatever their own social origins, probation officers find it difficult not to convey the superiority, if not the accent, of those 'at the top'—quite apart from the authority that comes from their position as officials of the court. Compared with other social workers, they have less need to justify their right to interfere in their clients' lives, but a certain hesitation and humility before doing so is perhaps salutary. In addition to the more old-fashioned, patrician attitudes that have always to some extent attended charity, superiority can take another, subtle form which is of more recent origin. 'The psychiatric approach to social work,' writes Lady Wootton,[1] 'in short makes it possible simultaneously to disown and to retain the attitude of superior wisdom and insight traditionally adopted by the rich towards the poor: to retain, to quote Virginia Woolf again, the "easy mastery of the will over the poor", and to preserve class attitudes, while denouncing class consciousness. . . . So we pass out of the frying-pan of charitable condescension into the no less condescending fire—or rather the cool detachment—of superior psychological insight.' The technique and language of modern casework certainly do create their own mystique: there is a risk that to believe that someone is 'inadequate' promotes a similar attitude towards them as to say they are 'undeserving'. Whatever truth there may be in Lady Wootton's castigation of other social workers, those responsible for training new entrants to the probation service seem very alive to this danger. In a lecture given to a conference of probation officers it was put this way: '. . . the students will learn that the laws governing human behaviour . . . apply to themselves and that if they are to be able to help people constructively they will need to develop self-awareness, otherwise the unconscious bias, prejudice and self-indulgent wishes to please others or to be liked will stand in their way.'

More will be said later about the officer's self-awareness, but it needs to be mentioned here as it provides the best safeguard against the damage that can be caused when practical help or advice is flavoured with patronage. After the ordeal of the trial, self-respect needs plenty of bolstering; patronage is its natural enemy. The benefit from material help can very easily be more than offset by psychological harm caused by the manner of the giving. Elizabeth Glover mentions three common reactions by clients to well-intentioned but unacceptable management of their affairs by

[1] *Social Science and Social Pathology* (p. 292–3).

others: passive resistance, an assertion of independence, or complete surrender. She quotes[1] an exasperated social worker as complaining: ' "After I'd made all the arrangements for convalescence she never even went to the station!" This is passive resistance. . . . If she had been more perceptive of the personality she was trying to help she would have seen long since that the client in question neither wanted nor intended to do what was suggested.' However careful, with some offenders this kind of thing happens time after time. Elaborate arrangements are made for their benefit, but they fail to post the necessary letter, to keep the appointment at the foot clinic, to turn up at the factory where a job awaits them. Sometimes it is no more than mental dimness, but quite often it seems to be a wish not to be helped—an irrational motivation maybe, similar to that which drove them to court, but one that has to be reckoned with.

Rejection of help is sometimes asserted dramatically—Miss Glover mentions the sale of 'all the new furniture or clothes'—but this is, I think, probably a healthier reaction than its opposite, than complete surrender, becoming over-dependent. Whether or not material help is given in the wrong way, many clients are only too thankful to be able to lean on their probation officers. The first task of breaking-down resentment and initial resistance can be succeeded by the need to prevent the client's dependence from becoming too strong—to prevent the negative transference from becoming too positive. Those who commit crimes because the rat-race of life is too bewildering and exhausting—crime in some people has been likened to migraine, asthma, indigestion, and other ailments due to stress—can soon get into the habit of leaving it to the probation officer to make all the difficult decisions. An unreasonably demanding view of what the officer can do for them—and tolerate from them—may lead to disappointment and thus a relapse into annoyance and nonco-operation. Women, in particular immature adolescents, sometimes find themselves pulled by an attraction for the once forbidding probation officer—not

[1] *Probation and Re-education* (p. 100).

unlike the schoolgirl crush on the hockey mistress—and this may be further complicated by bouts of provocative 'testing' to make sure that the attachment is reciprocated.

Unless the client is very immature and inadequate, over-dependence and cloying devotion are tactfully discouraged. The eventual aim of probation is that the offender must be able to cope with the world on his own, but with certain people weaning is quite as difficult as winning confidence is with others. I have been moved at the pathetic willingness with which some turn to their probation officers. At last, it seems, they have discovered the friend the aching hollow inside them craves for; others have found a substitute parent.

Olive had never known her father and has only very faint recollections of her mother who ran off with a 'foreign man' when Olive was four, leaving her in the care of a grandmother. Two years later the grandmother died and Olive spent the rest of her childhood in an institution. To even the inexperienced eye she carries the stigmata of deprivation. Sadness, one feels, is in the way she holds herself, in the tone of her muscles. Her voice is as dull and precise as her fawn woollen dress and the regimented waves of her lentil-coloured hair. Her pretty, though rather ewe-like, face is curiously overpowdered as if she is wearing a mask. At twenty-three she has done well to become an under-manager's secretary, but making friends was something the orphanage could not teach her and she lives and cooks for herself in a bed-sitting-room in the suburbs.

Her explanation of the offence is significant. Though she earns more than she needs, she stole a crochetted scarf from a dress shop.

'You see it was my birthday', she told Mrs Oldfield, almost as if this was a sufficient reason. 'I wanted to receive a present. Nobody had sent one.'

Presents were obviously very important to her because at Christmas she arrived at the probation office with a gay parcel plastered with coloured labels showing Father Christmases, holly and robins, addressed to Mrs Oldfield. Inside was an expensive handbag, costing at least four or five pounds.

'You don't mind, do you,' she asks anxiously as Mrs Oldfield unwraps it. 'I've no one else to give one to—a present I mean.'

Unlike some severely deprived people, Olive was easy to help. Her feelings of affection were not deeply buried and indeed when Mrs Oldfield found her a better lodging with a family with whom she could share meals and sit in the evenings knitting and watching the telly, they flowered as readily as a hyacinth placed gratefully in damp comforting fibre. She was still uncertain with people she did not know well and tended to laugh too much, as if this was something expected of her, but towards the end of her probation she announced that she was engaged—to a man met at the dancing classes she had started to attend on Monday evenings. Mrs Oldfield arranged with the bench for the probation order to be ended three months before its expiry. She was invited to the wedding and even gave the bride away!

Loneliness, especially the bed-sitter, gas-ring-cooking loneliness of middle-aged spinsters, lies behind a surprising and alarming number of offences—they are not difficult to interpret as protests of anguish and anger at life. The moment Sybil slipped a packet of unpaid-for hairpins into her handbag forty-eight years of loneliness were bewilderingly broken into. The magistrates believed her when, sobbing, she told them that she could not understand why she did it or why a few days earlier she had taken a tin of cocoa from another shop. The first home visit, though, supplied several explanations. She not only lived by herself: she worked by herself. The tall upstairs room in a Victorian Gothic house smelt perpetually of leather. For many years she had earned a small living cutting-out and stitching leather purses and wallets. She might have earned more if she had not been so conscientious or careful a craftswoman.

'You see, I prefer working on my own,' she used to insist. 'It means I can carry on at my own pace, not be flustered. I've tried going out to work, at several places—but it never does.

People are very nice, but after a few days they say I'm too slow. They like my work, but they always want me to do it not quite so well, to take less pains—always, always I must do it much faster. No, it never does. I'm better off on my own.'

'Perhaps you say that,' Mrs Grieves would remark gently, 'just because you find it such an effort to make friends with people—because you run away from having feelings about them.'

'Perhaps—and perhaps not. Anyway, I like to keep myself to myself.'

Sybil was stubborn about most things . . . about her belief that her largely bread-and-potato diet had nothing to do with her fifteen stone or the trouble with her feet; about thinking that her patched old clothes were all she needed—she usually wore what was once a 'tea-gown', dyed and 'remodelled' by herself; about her unwillingness to attend whist-drives and other social events to which she was introduced by Mrs Grieves. And yet in some moods she showed unexpected insight into her own difficulties and, I think, really looked forward to her interviews or having Mrs Grieves come for tea and potato scones. She talked continuously about herself:

'Don't think I don't want to meet people. I do. I'm eager to find out about them, to know what they think and feel, about their wives or husbands or children. But it's like as if I'm getting to know everyone through a shop-window. I'm always apart from them. And it never lasts. Once you find out about a person, you lose interest in them. What more can they give you?'

Mrs Grieves made the obvious suggestion that friendship was two-sided, that one had to be ready to give as well as receive, that one shouldn't be frightened of the sort of friendship that made regular demands. To this Sybil replied that she had often, when she was younger, given people presents, done things for them:

'But in the end they always let you down.'

'Perhaps you made them feel they were being paid for their affection?'

'But how else do you show that you like people?'

'Aren't warmth and understanding repayment enough?'

The loneliness of people like Sybil comes from what looks like selfishness but is really because their power both to accept and give love has failed to mature. She once remarked that she was envious of widows with young children, because they had something to work for and—this was curious—because they were not left any choice. She admitted never having known the urge to look after anyone else, not even a child; or if she had the desire, she had never dared, or been able to express it. Perhaps her parents had never fondled her? Perhaps her earliest essays at affection had been rejected? At her age the reasons are perhaps a little academic; she had lived on her own for too long and all that Mrs Grieves could do was try to penetrate the outer fastnesses of her loneliness, to encourage her to go to places where she could meet people, to urge her to make one more attempt to find a job away from her room.

Towards the end of her two years Sybil began to get anxious about what would happen to her. She would miss the visits to the office and having the attractive young Mrs Grieves to tea. In the end it was agreed, as often happens, that the contact could easily be maintained on an unofficial basis: she would always be welcome at the office, even if it was only for a chat.

Loneliness unrelieved for too long can degenerate into pathological eccentricity and illusions of persecution. This was almost certainly true of Arnold who, at sixty-eight, was put on probation for maliciously trying to set fire to the house in which he had lived with his sister. Eight years older and partially bedridden, the sister appeared to have held him with a curious power. In a different income group he might even have been labelled 'M.D.' as a child and passed most of his life in institutions. He was now merely a dim, bothered old man, with watery blue eyes and soap-suddy voice that conveyed a gentle bewilderment rather than pyromania. As far as could be found out, Arnold had retired from his job as a Civil Service clerk at the age of forty. Their father had been an officer in the Indian Army and left them the house and a modest income on which they had existed ever since, though its value was, of course, greatly decreased and it is doubtful if they had had quite enough to eat.

It was difficult to communicate with Arnold: he seemed anxious to please, but most questions were either politely overlooked or lost amid some amiable causerie about the weather or the infrequency of the bus service to the office. After his retirement he had occupied part of his days growing orchids in a conservatory attached to the house but in recent years this had become a wreck of broken glass; until the war he had escorted his sister to church each Sunday, but after she took to her bed he, too, had stopped going. The vicar used to call, but there was a quarrel—something to do with offertory bags she had embroidered—and she had refused to admit him. By then she had developed a complex about men—apart that is from Arnold—and would not on any account have them let into the house even to do repairs.

In all this Arnold had acquiesced. They became increasingly shut off. They did not even possess a radio, their only contact with the world being Arnold's bi-weekly shopping expeditions and subscriptions to the *Church Times* and a postal jig-saw club. Their few friends drifted away or died. Though they seldom saw the neighbours, Arnold described how his sister had latterly been in great fear of them: she told him they owned a machine that could see through walls and on Saturdays she could hear them playing a lascivious kind of forfeits. During the last months the ageing brother and sister appeared to have barricaded themselves inside the kitchen and what had been their father's study, eating, sleeping, and doing their jigsaws surrounded by relics of Peshawar and Quetta; the two rooms were kept vaguely clean by Arnold, acting on his sister's instructions, while the rest of the house silted up with rubbish. . . .

Then their inbred existence suddenly collapsed. The sister had a stroke and was taken to hospital where she died three days later. All his life Arnold's weak mind had been bullied and cowed by her; probably he had scarcely noticed how peculiar she had become—but she had at least meant some human contact. Now that she was no longer there to be looked after, what was left? He was really and finally alone. Perhaps he intended the flames of the burning house to engulf him too? Perhaps they were a symbolic rage at his wasted manhood—a sexual impulse is frequently associated with pyromania. The probation officer never found out—except that it had nothing to do with insurance, because the premiums were twenty-three years overdue.

This was one of those cases where probation is used, not because the offender is in need of reform, or capable of changing, but because he has not merited prison or admission to a mental hospital, and yet something has to be done for him. In this instance the probation officer put Arnold in touch with a solicitor who arranged for the house and furniture to be auctioned, and Arnold himself was established in a private but inexpensive home for elderly gentlefolk. He is still visited once a month and seems to be increasingly contented. Most of his days are spent browsing through Victorian volumes of *Punch* and, when he feels like it, he helps the gardener with the weeding.

IV

Every probation office has its selection of clients who are not offenders in the normal sense but who find themselves in court because they are incapable of managing unaided to cope with the normal circumstances of living. They include the loiterers, the wanderers without fixed abodes, the red-biddy soakers, and others in need of some kind of care and protection. Some of these casualties are driven by an inner disturbance that prevents them from conforming; others are subnormal or inadequate; strictly, many belong in the chapter headed 'In Trouble with Oneself', but much of the help the probation officer can give them takes the form of finding accommodation, a few days' work, second-hand clothing, and helping to disentangle them from their worst confusions or to stop them rubbing up against the police.

Among them too are those whose rejection of society's ways is owing perhaps not so much to individual weakness as to a confused kind of revolt: they prefer to drift from one Rowton House to another, to spend their days sunning themselves on a park bench, to wear rags and live on scraps, and only work when they cannot avoid it—they would rather live like this than conform to a time-clock drudgery or return, maybe, to a nagging spouse. It would be fallacious (even a little out-dated?) to sentimentalize over people like this, but they do exist and it is arguable that their nonconformity is a symptom of society's sickness rather than their own. If a probation officer is able to show them that he understands how they feel about life, without condoning what to him is irresponsibility, he is more likely to help them and prevent their revolt from becoming actively anti-social.

It would be difficult to determine the size of this subworld of nonconformers and inadequates. Among its citizens are a proportion of the ex-convicts and of the quarter to half million unemployed. It is said to be a good deal smaller than before the war but it is still there, alongside the upper-world of gracious living; alongside the hygenic schools, the office blocks with curtain-walling, the glossy queues of owner-drivers, returning to their pre-frozen suppers and spin-dryers; it is there despite the gaiety of the commercials and the optimistic swirl of Muzak. Nonconformers cause their probation officers continuous irritation. The stipulation that they must tell the probation officer of any change of address has little meaning for them and, though to move without permission is a technical breach, there is often nothing to be gained in setting the police on to tracing them. It may be equal to getting them sent down for three months and it is sometimes better to go out and look for them oneself.

I once accompanied Mr Young on one of these humanitarian

man-hunts. We traced our man from his original boarding-house to a Church Army hostel and a Rowton House and finally to what described itself as a hostel for working men. It was part of a late Georgian brick terrace most of which had been converted into shops and workshops, and I was surprised to learn that it slept up to 200 men.

'Hope your nose isn't too sensitive!' Mr Young warned as we entered. 'I'm used to it.' The odour was not unlike that of the cells at some of the older police courts: urine, armpits, tired breath, but mixed with it a sooty sweetness compounded of what must have been shag and cigarette smoke, very, very old dirt, and the reek of boiling mutton bones. The latter came from a cauldron of soup that was being served in tin bowls through a hatch in the 'dining-room'—a few benches and metal-topped, grease-filmed tables. Most of the building consisted of dormitories but at the back of the ground floor was the main living-room which at once reminded me of a stage set for Gorki's *The Lower Depths*, though it also had something of Cruickshank's drawing of Fagin's den in *Oliver Twist*: in the centre of one wall was a giant open kitchen-range around which half a dozen shabby men were toasting hunks of bread or hanging up bits of washing. The opposite wall was lined with numbered lockers at one of which an enormous red-haired fellow, bare to the waist and with a brave show of tattooing, was sharpening a cut-throat razor; at more of the long metal-topped tables groups sat reading newspapers and Westerns, playing Solo, rolling cigarettes; an old man in a cap was chumping toothlessly at pieces of toast soaked in tea. They were of all ages, though more were elderly than young and several were old age pensioners . . . you might describe it, I suppose, as a relaxed, contented scene, reminiscent of the mess-decks of a wartime troopship—if it had not been for the squalor, if it had not been for those begrimed, rancid walls, the bleak unshaded lights, the cement floor, pitted and covered with a mouldering matrix of spent matches, Woodbine packets, discarded remnants of thousands of bowls of soup—if it had not been 1960.

The man we were looking for had left only two days earlier for another doss-house which Mr Young said was well known among ex-convicts and a place where, like this one, nobody asked questions. The subworld has a right to its own establishments, and perhaps it was irrational of me to feel disturbed by the discovery that these places are run by private enterprise, that as well as slum landlords there are slum hoteliers.

With chronic nonconformers probation officers have always to watch for scrounging. For some clients their only interest in officials is how much they can squeeze out of them. The complex lies and confidence-tricks they will stage in order to get a few shillings out of the court poor-box are usually very transparent. Often the client as well as the officer is aware that the deception is not working. Even so, scrounging is not easy to counter, particularly when the client shows, as he usually does, overt symptoms of poverty and there may be a wife and children to be considered. Scrounging can indicate both a lack of self-respect and a contempt for Authority, and as such it can only be met, in the view of many probation officers, with sympathy and acceptance—it is analogous to 'testing'.

'If you dismiss a scrounger's requests brusquely, they are almost certain to increase,' was how one officer explained this difficult refinement of his technique. 'When I feel forced to refuse him, I always try to treat the man himself with respect. This makes it easier for him to cope with his disappointment. There is more of a chance that what is left of his self-respect will not be further damaged and it may later begin to restrain him. I always treat his requests fairly and seriously, never let him feel that an outright rejection is inevitable—even if I finally do refuse him over and over again. Then when he does ask for help which I feel is justified, I show him that I'm prepared to give it despite his previous insincerity.'

Every probation officer resists very strongly any tendency in his clients to be workshy. There is little doubt also that in most cases, and in particular with potential professional criminals, failure to take a job or to look for one seriously is a symptom that indicates a poor prognosis as surely as a continuing high temperature does in illness—though I must quickly add that finding a job, especially if you are unskilled or have a police record, can be difficult enough to make the best adjusted individual despair. Though poverty and the crime rate refuse to be neatly correlated, any probation officer knows that the moral platitude: 'a job = security and money in the pocket = less temptation' is for everyday practical purposes true. Regular and satisfying work is spoken of as 'rehabilitating an offender'. When a client discovers that his record is against him, the probation officer can sometimes help by, where it is valid, reassuring the employer or putting the client in touch with local employers known not to be narrow-minded. In most cases there is everything to be said for frankness: if the client knows that he has been taken on despite his employers being informed in full about his past, he has no need to live in fear of being found out and thus dismissed.

The lengths to which some probation officers will go to keep their clients in work, and the lengths to which some of the clients will go to keep out of it, are extraordinary. I know of one officer who, in order to help—or call the bluff—of a young man whose excuse for losing a series of jobs was incurable oversleeping, personally paid surprise visits to the man's lodgings at eight o'clock in the morning—just in case he had not heard the alarum bell. On the other side there was the man who accused his probation officer of telephoning his prospective employers in order to warn them that he was not to be trusted and that he was also in the habit of committing indecent assaults, with the result that he was not taken on. The probation officer of course was able to deny this, though the company confirmed that some official had indeed rung up 'from the court'. When it happened with a second job, it seemed clear that someone had a down on the man and was taking a very nasty revenge—though the client himself swore he did not know whom to suspect. It was not until two more jobs had been lost in this way, for one of which he was paid off the second morning with a week's money, that the probation officer tumbled that the impersonator was very probably the client himself.

V

There can be few who find it more difficult to obtain and keep a job, who find the world so harsh as does the old lag, and it is therefore encouraging that nowadays he sometimes is given a last chance on probation. Each new stretch in prison makes the circumstances of his life as a free man more hostile. Though he may not realize it, he is apt to crave a return to prison because it offers at least a kind of security. Indeed it is difficult to answer those critics of our prisons who liken them to efficient yet uncomfortable hotels: the inmates are given free shelter and food, clothing and warmth, and are freed from everyday responsibilities. The longer they stay in prison and the more often they are sent there, the less equipped they are to withstand the pressures of normal living; despite the now fashionable use of the word 'treatment' instead of 'punishment', despite the introduction of corrective training and other reforms, for many prisoners a sentence is not a preparation for a better life, but a respite from its difficulties. Unpleasant though it is, the security offered by prison is undoubtedly an important factor in any attempt to understand the motivation of many recidivists; if there is also a wish for self-punishment it is scarcely an exaggeration to say that prison amounts to an incentive rather than a deterrent, a satisfaction rather than a punishment.

To see an old lag back once more in the dock—at any rate if he is not an accomplished professional criminal—is, I found, both a terrifying and a tragic occasion, one that must cause all but the most complacent to have doubts about our penal methods. A lengthy criminal record is by no means an unambiguous record of character: the intelligent and accomplished crook may commit many more—and more profitable—crimes than a continual offender who commits crimes because of his own weakness or poor circumstances and who lacks the ability (or the wish) to avoid being caught. In the latter's case the support of the probation officer, the unexpected charity and trust of the bench, can sometimes effect a dramatic reformation.

It happened this way with Chris. He was found guilty of shop-breaking and had twenty-eight previous convictions, ranging from breaking and entering, drunk and disorderly, common assault, to loitering with intent, and living on the immoral earnings of a prostitute. At fifty, most of his adult life had been spent in prison: the Scrubs, Parkhurst, the Moor, nice screws and nasty screws, smuggled packets of snout, stretches and laggings—they were his 'cultural environment'. He was a pale, rather expressionless man with unusually prominent facial bones and the cheapest looking and worst fitting dentures I have ever seen, which perhaps accounted for the curious sunken lines that ran up both cheeks. As one might expect, he appeared withdrawn and emotionally dried-up, but he possessed a recondite knowledge of the history of Charlton Athletic.

The chairman of quarter sessions remarked that the appropriate sentence was ten years' preventive detention, but as Chris had never been given a chance before, and his landlady was prepared to have him back and had spoken well on his behalf, he was prepared to try probation. The clerk was in fact instructed to make a note to remind him that Chris was eligible for P.D. if he should ever appear in that court again.

Things were, of course, not easy for Chris. He had great difficulty in finding regular work. In one prison he had received some training as a house painter, but at his first job he found that his standards were not up to those expected in commerce, and he was sacked. At another place he was refused a union card and, when taken on as a scullery-hand in a restaurant, he was sacked following an anonymous letter to the management. He became very disheartened, but he was enabled to share every set-back with his probation officer and eventually he settled in work that he enjoyed, as a gardener in the public park. He also kept away from his old associates and by the time his three-year probation ended there had not only been no more offences, but he had saved nearly £100, gained over a stone, and was dropping casual but arch hints about 'joining forces' with a widow whom he had met, surprisingly maybe, on the terraces of the local football club.

A number of ex-prisoners are also helped by probation officers in their role as agents of the Central After-care Association. The technique of after-care is sufficiently similar to normal probation not to need elaboration—even though, by definition, every ex-prisoner must have been considered unsuitable for probation. Many, especially those fresh from a spell of corrective training or preventive detention, remain stubbornly unco-operative and fixed in their resentment of Authority, even in its most well-meaning aspects. Sometimes their hostility is but thinly masked by anxiety for the future. In prison they have already been interviewed almost to death and they tend to be experts at saying only what and as much as is expected of them. Often they feel they have 'paid the price' for their crimes and grumble at what they think of as further interference. Bludgeoned into sullenness by months or years of prison discipline, many of these men will only respond to a more authoritarian treatment than is normal in probation, and insistence that they report regularly and punctually, keep in a job, and stick to the conditions of their prison licence, has to be rigid. Even so, the probation officer must show that he accepts and respects his client, despite his record; that he at any rate does not look upon a prison sentence as an indelible stigma.

What happens during the first days and weeks after release can be vital. It is then that the ex-prisoner is most vulnerable. The probation officer has to concentrate on the obvious and very real practical difficulties. Until these are overcome, any attempt at deeper, more personal, casework is unrealistic. Before his release contact will have been made with the prisoner's parents, wife or husband, or other relatives, to prepare the way for his return. If they refuse to have him, every effort is made to fix him up with a friendly lodging. Second, he must be helped to find a regular job; as with the man on probation, it is best if the past is not nursed as a shameful, threatening secret, though frequently the officer's only course is to condone the concealment and white lies necessary to regain acceptance—by a society, the roots of whose charity might be said to be enfeebled by guilt. Unless the ex-prisoner is quickly reintegrated with the community the complex of factors that originally turned him to crime, or a combination that is very similar, is only too likely to find expression in yet another offence; or loneliness and the drive to regain the dismal but familiar security of prison may become too strong to be resisted.

Without a comprehensive system of after-care many prison reforms are liable to be nugatory. Telling support in favour of the quality of supervision applied by probation to the ex-prisoner has come recently from the belated official recognition of the need for more after-care to be given to new categories of ex-prisoners and from the decision that the probation service should carry it out. After-care is already normal for youngsters released from approved schools or Borstal institutions, but only four small categories[1] of adult prisoners so far receive it compulsorily—approximately 1,335 (of the 30,000 or so released each year) half of whom were under twenty-one on conviction; in addition, there are of course quite a few who accept after-care voluntarily, through the Discharged Prisoners' Aid Societies, Norman House, the New Bridge, and other excellent organizations. But unfortunately those who need after-care most are often the least likely

[1] (a) prisoners under 21 on conviction who are released on licence—in practice only those with a sentence of three months or more are released in this way (approximately 700 released each year); (b) corrective training prisoners (500); (c) preventive detention prisoners (125); (d) prisoners with a life sentence whose licence includes a condition that they receive after-care (10). Normally supervision continues only for the unexpired portion of the sentence.

to seek it and the decision has been taken to extend it compulsorily to further categories,[1] including adults imprisoned for six months or more who have served at least one previous sentence and adults serving a sentence of four years or more. Other categories will be added by stages.

The responsibility for these new categories will belong to the Central After-care Association, but in practice most of the day-to-day supervision will fall on the probation service, which already handles 2,000 or so ex-Borstal cases and, outside London, most of the adults in the present four compulsory categories. There is no other suitable body of trained social workers with the necessary nationwide network. Many of these after-care clients will have been earlier, at some time or other, on probation and the increase in compulsory after-care can therefore be described as facing the probation service with more of its own failures. True enough, yet it is also a measure of the inevitability of probation, of the efficacy of its techniques, of the growing and practical recognition that society owes a responsibility to the criminals it gives birth to, that it stands in debt to those it has punished.

VI

As we have seen, in relieving his clients' practical difficulties, the officer, when necessary, draws on the other social services, both official and voluntary bodies such as the Marriage Guidance Council, the N.S.P.C.C., Moral Welfare Association, and others. With some clients, though, one suspects that probation officers are presented with the other services' rejects and failures. As we shall see later, the offender who is referred to a psychiatrist for a report will be diagnosed with scientific skill and perspicacity but

[1] *The After-Care and Supervision of Discharged Prisoners*; report of the Advisory Council on the Treatment of Offenders, H.M.S.O., 1958 (p. 16).

quite often the psychiatrist declines to take him on as a patient if, in his opinion, the client's intelligence is too low to be likely to benefit from treatment. Probation officers have to shoulder many of the more unrewarding cases in default of anyone else. It can similarly be argued that the client often reaches the court owing to the previous failure of other services to act early enough—the local housing department perhaps; or a headmaster or the school attendance officer; the health visitor, almoner or doctor; the youth employment officer; the local authority's children's department; or others—too late to prevent the complex of factors, for some of which each is responsible, from eventually maturing in a crime.

This is equal to saying that when casework is carried out by the probation service, it comes later than it should; after the crime and the stigma of the appearance in court instead of preventing it. So often it seems to be merely a matter of accident whether the client, particularly if a child or adolescent, is brought to the attention of the authorities as an offender, or as a member of an overcrowded family, a truant from school, a bed-wetter, as being beyond his parents' control, or for some other reason. The probation officer, however, does see himself increasingly as being to some degree in partnership with the local officials of the other social services, and therefore he gets to know them and makes them familiar with his difficulties. If he is wise he takes care not to trespass on their special provinces; instead, his aim is to encourage the client himself to make use of them, though there are times when a particularly complicated situation or defenceless client makes his support and intervention necessary.

Inevitably duplication and overlapping with the other services are likely to happen; this is not only wasteful but may well mean that the individual or family being helped ends up as no one's responsibility. In recent years much thought has been given to this difficulty and solutions have been put forward, such as an integrated family service[1] which would have prophylactic as well

[1] *Families with Problems: a new approach*, Council for Children's Welfare, 1958.

as curative aims. Administrative reforms fall outside the scope of this book, but my survey would be very incomplete without at least mentioning the need for this particular one: I have listened to too many probation officers complaining of cases where anything up to eight different social workers and agencies are involved, and I have come across so many examples where too little has been done, and done too late.

I remember one in particular—that of Ernest and his sister Mabel who are discussed in the next chapter—in which the family had been known as a 'problem' for years and some half a dozen separate social workers had been in contact with them. But when I visited the parents in company with Miss Lane, they were still living in a leaking, insanitary house and sleeping several to a bed. That family very probably would constitute a problem however much was done for them, but if they had at least been found some better accommodation, Ernest and his sister might have been less likely to have found themselves in court—at any rate on a charge of incest.

Of those who get into trouble largely as the result of difficult circumstances, the group which I have come to the conclusion deserves the most generous mercy and sympathy are the women who have to bring up children single-handed—the widows, the deserted, the wives of men in prison or chronically ill in hospital, the unmarried mothers. For them circumstances must often seem implacable and besieging. Three of these cases provide me with a pertinent ending to this chapter.

First, Mrs Hook whom we met earlier on, the mother of six whose husband had been in prison for ten of the fifteen years of their marriage. Miss Lane had long discussions with her over her debts and worked out that she would have to put aside eleven-and-eightpence a week out of her National Assistance money in order to pay them off during the course of a year. Advice was also given about how to handle her eight-year-old girl with spinal disease: because of it she had been very spoilt both in hospital and at home and Mrs Hook was encouraged to be firmer with her over small things, to try and ignore the inevitable screams and sobbing.

'Someone ought to have done the same with my old man!' was Mrs Hook's ironical reply. 'The girl takes after him, I shouldn't wonder! His mother, I reckon, always spoiled him, gave him all he asked, to stop him making a fuss. So did I for that matter—that is at the start; when we first went together—and look where he is now! It mustn't,' she added shaking her head thoughtfully, 'the same thing mustn't happen to any of the children.'

Later the chairman of the bench arranged for Mrs Hook to be given a grant of £15, to pay off some of the debts and help the family have a week's holiday at the seaside. On the whole, though, Mrs Hook was against accepting gifts and once she refused a long-term loan from one of her husband's old friends because, very wisely, she felt he was not a type to whom she would want to be under an obligation. Her life, of course, continued to be very difficult and on top of everything her rent was increased. Mrs Hook was undespairing and determined not to pay. With Miss Lane's support she fought the landlord and insisted on repairs being done to the roof.

Meanwhile the husband wrote from prison asking for his clothes to be got out of pawn and for his wife to place bets on various horses. He seemed to have no idea of how little she had to manage on. On one of her visits to the prison he even accused her of spending too much on her own clothes, but this was going too far and she became very angry and, if it had not been for the plate-glass separating them in the interview cell, they would have started what she called one of their 'special rows'. Though she was beginning to have more insight into his personality, to understand that emotionally he was in some ways still a spoilt little boy, she could not help feeling resentful that, compared with herself, he had little to bother about in prison. Yet she still loved him—perhaps because he was such a child, but also as a man—and the days after the prison visits were always the worst. Mrs Hook had plenty in common with Brecht's Mother Courage.

Mrs Hook's husband might be in gaol, but at least she did have a husband, and her children were born respectable, within the sanction of wedlock. In recent years the unmarried mother has been the subject of earnest study—though this is not equally true of the unmarried father—and society's attitudes towards her have become more tolerant; but while she is made to feel less of an outcast, less of a menace to the institution of the family, she has to face practical difficulties that are beyond the imaginings of most of us, especially if we are men. Even when the father pays an allowance, it must need courage to reject the alternative of adoption. The will to rear a child is a tenacious force and it appears even in the most unstable women. No one was less suited—at one level less inclined—to bring up a daughter than Muriel. I was in court the day her probation order was discharged and over lunch Mrs Grieves told me something of her story, beginning with a cynical little jibe, her defence against letting her feelings become too involved with her cases:

'I expect most of the male readers of your book like to sentimentalize about tarts, especially when they are also plucky little women! Muriel fills the bill all right and, unlike some, she has the right kind of looks. She told me that one of her gentlemen, an actuary I think he was, said she reminded him of Anna Karenina. When I first knew her she was nineteen but she had been on the game for some time; she shared a flat with another prostitute, and they went out soliciting in the streets around the big railway stations. Then Muriel discovered she was pregnant, though she'd no idea who was the father. She managed to keep on the game until she was six months' gone—this is what she told me and she did have the type of figure where it doesn't show much—and by then she had enough to see her through the confinement.

'The baby was born in hospital and she planned to have it adopted. But after seeing it once or twice she told me she wanted time to make up her mind. I tried, very gently of course, to persuade her not to let herself grow too fond of it, but she decided to put it into a nursery, and there it stayed for several months. The baby was christened Carol and once a week at least Muriel would visit her and if it was fine they would let her take her for a walk. She always paid for Carol's keep. For a few weeks she worked in a florists but before long she was supplementing her wage with the odd bit of soliciting. Then one Sunday she took the baby for its walk and failed to return her to the nursery. The next morning she rang up to tell them that she would in future be looking after Carol herself.'

Mrs Grieves, though she could not herself be much more than twenty-eight, used to surprise me with the certainty of her opinions of people: not that she was dogmatic, in fact I think she only reached them after intense observation. 'Muriel was the type,' she went on, 'who needs someone of her own to look after. Her maternal instinct was very strong though she was quite intelligent enough to know that circumstances were against her. She was not one of the well organized, big earning tarts—she was too vague for that. I think she always wanted to get off the game and only went back to it when things became a bit tight. You know,' Mrs Grieves added looking at me almost accusingly, 'it's not easy to run a one-woman brothel on your own with a bawling baby wanting its feed in the kitchen next door.'

Muriel managed to keep going like this for some eight or nine weeks, but then she lost her room and she had no choice but to put Carol back in the nursery. This time she seemed reconciled to giving her up and talked seriously again about adoption, but every Sunday she would still visit the nursery, spend the afternoon playing with her. She told Mrs Grieves that she, as well as the child, always cried when it was time for Carol to be handed back to the matron.

Meanwhile Muriel had found herself a job in a Soho club—something to do with the bar and only a small amount of hostessing—'for pin money' as she put it. She now shared a flat with one of the other girls who worked there, even saved some money, and her life became a little more regularized, but she still fretted for Carol.

'On Carol's first birthday it happened again. Muriel came straight to the office carrying her in her arms, saying she did it on impulse. She could not bear the idea of letting the nursery have her again. It was no use trying to persuade her, so I rang up and explained things to matron, and Muriel took Carol back to the flat. But only for three days as the girl she shared it with had found herself a semi-resident man-friend, a Yorkshire business man who was paying the rent, and perhaps understandably he didn't much take to Carol. Muriel—bless her!—walked out in a rage and turned up here once more with suitcases as well as Carol, and asked "what next?".'

This time it was suggested that, if she really wanted to keep the child, the best thing might be for them both to enter a hostel. Muriel disliked the idea, but she had nothing else to propose and agreed that the possibilities might be investigated, Carol meanwhile being taken again into the nursery. It happened that for various reasons no hostel could be found to receive them. There was talk of a friend lending her a caravan in one of the home counties; of her finding a domestic post where Carol would also be welcome, but all these plans fell through.

Mrs Grieves opened her briefcase and handed me a snapshot of a dark little toddler in a pinafore. She was clutching a wooden cooking-spoon.

'Muriel again started to talk of adoption and even got hold of the documents. I really thought she was weaning herself from the child—if you can use the word that way round! She was working hard—that is, not at a job, but going round with well-to-do business men; I could scarcely be expected to approve, though I confess to sharing Muriel's opinion of them. After all, she was on probation to me for helping in a robbery and I had no jurisdiction over her private morals. I decided she had opted for a good time rather than motherhood—but how wrong I was!

'Her mind was made up by a bruise. A not very large bruise on Carol's arm. She was then eighteen months and a tough little person and matron explained it happened during a tussle with another child. But Muriel did not believe her. She declared they were neglecting and maltreating her daughter, and in a flaming rage carried her off to the station. It was the same kind of impulsive, over-emotional reaction she was apt to exhibit when she was defending herself. Her own difficulties were due to a fairly deep insecurity, a feeling she'd often expressed as being "got at".'

But this time she had a solution. Marriage. Not to one of her business men—they were all married already—but to a bald-headed man who seemed as unstable and emotionally starved as herself. But he had a steady job.

'I suggested point-blank that she was only using him as a means of getting Carol back and she said I could be dead right. On the other hand he did seem to take to Carol, though by all the rules he should have been jealous of her. I was surprised, too, how readily—almost with relief—Muriel settled into the housewife's routine. The affection inside her had perhaps at last found its release. That's why I asked the bench to discharge her early; not that she is quite ready for it. She wants her second child to be born free from any shadows. To her that is very important.'

The proportion of illegitimate children—about one in twenty—still being born every year has always puzzled me. Ignorance and prejudice against birth control may still be widespread and passion can make people forgetful, but are these quite sufficient reasons? Neither taboos nor lack of them seem to make all that difference. In Victorian days householders forbade their female domestics 'followers' and the penalty for indiscretion was to be cast out into a nocturnal snowstorm, whereas today every mother's help has little excuse not to know all about Dutch caps, and experience in bed is becoming almost a necessary part of a young bride's trousseau. But in both periods illegitimate babies have been copious.[1] The will to conceive as well as to mate is even more forceful perhaps than we suppose. Few illegitimate births may be planned consciously, but I find it impossible not to believe that much of the carefree acceptance of the risks of intercourse, a proportion at least of the 'ignorance' and of the passion-induced 'forgetfulness', are expressions of the resolute, innate urge to procreate. I have read that some unmarried mothers are emotionally sick and are compulsively acting out an infantile fantasy, that as children themselves they were either mother-dominated or father-dominated: perhaps most of them were but to me their achievement seems exceedingly natural.

Few of us can approach this subject free of our own personal emotions about sex, about life itself, but whatever we feel, however much social disapproval we believe is justified, being an unmarried mother in a basically monogamous society is unlikely to be very enjoyable. Each year thousands of potential mothers, torn between demands of their biology and practical reality, let alone fear of censure, drink gin, jump down staircases and subject themselves or are subjected to more drastic means of abortion. A percentage of the abortionists[2] and their clients find themselves in court, usually only in connection with some gruesome clinical mishap. A very much smaller percentage, though I imagine the figures[3] are inevitably very imprecise, wait until the baby is born and then commit infanticide.

The law, as I have watched it operate in two of these cases, shows how enlightened and merciful it can be. In one instance the woman was married but had impulsively destroyed her baby a few hours after the birth. She was spoken to by the judge as if he was her personal medical consultant: she was assured in open

[1] Apart from the war years (the peak was 9·1 per cent in 1945) the percentage of illegitimate births has remained fairly constant since 1890, when it was 4·7 per cent the same as in 1958. Has the prevention of illegitimate births by contraception been offset by an increase in promiscuity?

[2] Forty-two were convicted in 1959. *Criminal Statistics, England and Wales, 1959.* Cmd 1100 (p. 34).

[3] Ten were convicted in 1959. ibid(p. 34).

court that she had only done it because she was mentally ill and she must try and forget, not blame herself too much; subject to agreeing to mental treatment, she was placed on probation. The other was eighteen-year-old Gladys. Though she may have felt impelled to destroy her illegitimate baby by more practical fears, the judge treated her in the same way. She was not very bright, but she had had a forbidding Baptist upbringing and her vapid, peaky, ordinary face, with its chapped lips and a frizzed home-perm, concealed a desolate weight of guilt and horror. There was no question of returning to her parents in South Wales and the probation officer arranged for her to live in a hostel. Gladys was able to release very little in words and her misery seemed, week by week, to spread with the inevitability of leukaemia, and the probation officer worried for her reason.

She spent as much time with the girl as possible, and so did the hostel warden. They tried to divert her mind, to plant new interests, or merely to keep her talking about trivial things . . . and slowly the clouds lifted, and one became more conscious of the Welsh sing-song in her voice. After six months the guilt appeared to be tamed, though it could never vanish, and she even enjoyed spending Christmas with her parents. But by the spring Gladys entered another crisis. She had been going out with a dull, very respectable young Londoner whom she met at a chapel social; it never entered his carefully brilliantined head that Gladys was still anything but an unsoiled, prepackaged virgin like himself, and as a result the guilt in her restarted its daily ravaging. She had told him nothing, not even that she was on probation.

Burying her face in her hands, Gladys cried that she must give him up. When she was calmer the probation officer refused to let her believe this and insisted that he must be told the truth—or perhaps she could tell him for her. If he loved her as he said, it would upset him, but it would make no difference.

It took Gladys five more days before she dared. He was more distressed even than she had feared but she told him herself one Sunday afternoon on a park bench. He sat for a long time staring across the grass—there were children, Gladys said, roller-skating up and down the path in front of them. He kept repeating that he was the one she now wanted to damage. She had insulted him even by letting him kiss her. He spoke nonsensically and brutally . . . but by the end of that evening he was mumbling that it must not come between them . . . only that he must have time to get used to it.

The next day he came himself to the office. He wanted to hear it all over again, to make sure he knew every detail. The probation officer described him as looking physically shocked. It demanded her long experience of unhappiness and unapproachable people to decide what were the right things to say to such an affronted, correct, unimaginative young man, yet I can picture how in stages, by just avoiding to say the key words herself, she helped him to see how such a thing could have happened; that perhaps Gladys had already paid the worst part of the price; that she was still the same girl he had learned to love; to convince himself that he ought to go on doing so. After that it was all right.

6

In Trouble With Others

*

TO help an offender sort out his relationships with other people—usually a parent or wife or husband—the probation officer has to make very sure of his own neutrality. The more neurotic type of offender, especially, can be a compelling advocate of his own point-of-view and entrap the unwary in his own fantasy: this can only be offset by understanding the offender in his family setting—not just during the initial assessment but at every stage of the probation order. One of the job's maxims is to see life through the eyes of the client, but if the probation officer identifies himself with him and his problems too closely, the advice and suggestions offered may be harmful and possibly disastrous. This book is about the technique of probation and the motivation and character of offenders rather than about the probation officers themselves: Mr Young, Miss Lane, Mrs Grieves, Mr Compton, and others appear, I know, only as shadowy, not fully rounded figures, but I have limited them on purpose, first because to describe their lives, so full of unusual stresses and satisfactions, would take up too many pages and detract from my main objective; and second because probation officers are quintessentially individuals—whether the job only attracts such, or it makes them so, or both, I do not know. Even if I were to portray a dozen or so very different, contrasting officers, the number would be insufficient and the result inadequate. Nevertheless, before taking my argument much further, I ought to record rather more lucidly something of what I learned of the probation officers' own inner manifestations, of the emotions and reactions stimulated by this very curious profession. Every officer has to understand how these affect him or herself if they are to keep their balance in the swirl of unhappiness and ugliness that passes through their offices.

'They teach us a lot about the need for self-awareness,' I was told by a student officer, undergoing a theoretical course at Rainer House, the residential training centre for the Service. 'We are supposed to be able to understand ourselves as well or better than we do our clients. One can't afford to let one's feelings, whether of sympathy or disgust, fog one's objectivity.'

Many of the clients—for example, interferers with little girls, or sponging, verminous alcoholics, or surly adolescent thugs who bully their younger brothers—are apt to arouse immediate dislike in the kindest individual. To spend hours each week being lied to, scowled at, subjected to every weapon of nonco-operation, to conscious and unconscious stupidity; to pass much of your working life in the company of over-dependent, inadequate people who are frequently letting you down or are the cause of disappointment or for whom each week seems to bring a new, genuine misfortune—the job would put the most charitable saint to an unpleasant strain. Nor is it any good suppressing feelings of revulsion or disguising them behind a gauze of sentimental pity. An inability to recognize his feelings for what they are, to admit his own disgust or anger, is said to increase an officer's anxiety and tension and, worse, to impair his power to think about the client clearly.

'The idea apparently,' the student continued, 'is that if you can understand what the client does to you, then you are more likely to understand the response he evokes in others. This knowledge helps you to give him insight that will perhaps make it easier for him to avoid being quite so irritating in future, or to stop being so mean to his wife, or whatever it happens to be.'

Mr Young explained it rather differently: that a probation officer had to avoid feeling too sympathetic towards his clients; in some ways he had to be like a doctor or hospital nurse—to feel a patient's death or a probationer's relapse into crime too personally is to court a nervous breakdown : tragedy happened too often. Just as relief workers in a famine have, in the interests of the starving, to feed themselves first and eat their full quota of protein and vitamins, so probation officers have to consider their own mental health and balance before that of their clients.

'But don't get the idea,' Mr Young added, as he relit his pipe, 'that we can ever hope to be completely neutral. We wouldn't be much good for this job if we managed to suppress all our feelings. To do so, would use up too much energy. You must be able to offer the client plenty of—what I can only call "emotional vitality", if you know what I mean?'

The reasons why a person wants to become a probation officer, including unconscious ones, are always important and are investigated during the selection procedure for candidates which, as well as normal interviews, includes a skilfully concocted application form, an intelligence test, group discussion, a medical examination and, if thought necessary, a report by a psychiatrist.[1] As few as 17 per cent are accepted for training and only some 12 per cent eventually qualify. Among the candidates will be some who are attracted to the job because they associate themselves very closely with Authority: these may be unhealthily eager, though without realizing it, to dominate and control people or to inflict punishment. There are also likely to be some who do just the opposite, who identify themselves too closely with the accused, with the underdog. The first group will have a tendency to impose on their clients an inflexible, unattainable moral code; the second group may well turn out to be flabbily over-tolerant. There may even be candidates who have suppressed criminal impulses of their own and thus might enjoy a vicarious satisfaction from the offences of their clients. Likewise, those who are keen to work in a juvenile court may wish to compensate

[1] This gives too good a picture, because at the time of writing would-be probation officers can be admitted by means of a less rigorous procedure known as 'direct entry', arranged by local probation committees.

themselves for their own unhappy childhoods and are thus perhaps themselves emotionally immature or liable to be excessively anti-parent.

Mr Young put it squarely: 'Our reasons for wanting to help others, if we really understood them, might give some of us a shock. Of course probation work amounts to a vocation. You can't stick it or be any good at it unless you believe in what you're trying to do . . . and possess a little of the madness of the zealot.'

Too deep an investigation of the motivation of any vocation is likely to be as unrewarding as metaphysical solipsism. From observation of the officers I have known my guess is that most of them at times are subject to the kind of sub-conscious drives just mentioned but, as with the 'normal' individual compared with the neurotic, these drives are controlled rather than suppressed; or, if the Freudians are right, sublimated in constructive directions. At times they certainly do show symptoms of anxiety and irritation, and each has his own method of finding relief—by grumbling to each other; in a superficial, jocular form of cynicism; and so on. If they did not react in these ways, they would not be human. If they were not human, intensely so, they could not hope to do their job.

II

I have often noticed that probation officers easily forget the details of the offence that has brought a client under their care. The type of robbery for example, or the way it was carried out, is only of interest if it can yield a clue to the client's personality or the factors associated with the offence. This chapter is about people in the second of my two very general categories: those for whom the dominant factor can be said to be a conflict or bad relationship with someone else—whether this is expressed either directly in a physical assault or indirectly in a theft, a reversion to homosexuality, a bout of drunkenness, or in some other deviation from the normal.

In quite a few cases someone other than the probationer should be debited with the major part of the responsibility. William, for example, was put on probation for unlawfully wounding a man called Taylor; he admitted it in court but there was no doubt that Taylor's attitude was insulting and provocative. A quarrel arose because William's eighteen-year-old daughter had become engaged to Taylor's nineteen-year-old son. William and his wife approved of the match, though they hoped the couple would wait some months before getting married: Taylor disapproved. On the evening of the offence he had come round to William's house, his breath vaporous with Scotch, and declared that no son of his was going to marry into such a low-bred family, that the girl was nothing but a prostitute, who wanted to be made respectable before it was too late.... Understandably William hit him on the head, though unfortunately with a Number 2 iron, which resulted in a minor concussion and six stitches.

William had never been in any kind of trouble before, but Taylor was known to the police as a boozer who himself had been twice successfully summoned for assault. In fact when he left the hospital he bragged to his friends in the lounge-bar that it was only a matter of time before he gave that little runt William something that would need a bloody sight more than six stitches. One night he got as far as William's front door and shouted insults up at the bedroom windows. The situation was made more dangerous because Taylor's son had by then moved in with William and his wife—it was all very respectable: he occupied the spare room—having no mother of his own and finding it impossible to stand his father's abuse and drinking sessions any longer. William confided all this to his probation officer who had a quiet word with the local police and advised him another time to dial 999.

Even so, for weeks William went in fear of Taylor, seldom

leaving the house after dark and sleeping with a hammer on his bedside table. His wife thought the worry was giving him an ulcer and indeed he often did look ill and very tired. But Taylor never turned up again and eventually he agreed to the wedding. Perhaps he saw there was nothing he could do, or perhaps his bullying and drunkenness concealed, as so often, the kind of insecurity most people call cowardice.

A rather less obvious example of how fear of someone can prompt a crime is provided by young George who was found guilty of housebreaking in company with an older youth called Ken who lived in the same road. Three earlier offences were recorded against Ken and he was sent to Borstal; George, previously of good character, was put on probation. Talk with George's parents suggested that he had been very much under Ken's thumb; though superficially the two were good friends, Ken and the other boys in the street always bullied George who, to win acceptance and perhaps to escape a whack with Ken's studded belt, had sunk to being his sycophantic lieutenant. George's probation officer spoke of him as 'lacking spunk' and having a personality like a 'marshmallow, though without the sweet's resilience'; indeed George's character was as limp as his handshake. The treatment consisted therefore in trying to rebuild his moral stamina by repeated reassurance, encouragement of anything even vaguely positive or successful in his fortnightly account of his recent doings, and by suggesting wider interests, including membership of a youth centre.

It seemed to be having little result and when after fifteen months Ken was released from Borstal, George's parents were worried lest the old friendship might be renewed. At several interviews the probation officer pointed out the dangers; also that Ken might purposely egg him on to more trouble because of a grievance that he had received a severer sentence. George, as usual, readily said he understood this, that of course he would do whatever the probation officer suggested. There were few enough reasons to believe him, yet, inside, George had after all been changing. The soft gristle was becoming bone. This time he did not waver. Even when Ken jeered at him in front of several other youths leaning on their handlebars at the end of the road and called him a 'nark' and a 'softie', it had no effect. George had added a decimal, if a wobbly one, to the percentage of successes.

Among Mr Compton's cases I discovered a remarkable contemporary throwback to the feud in *Romeo and Juliet,* a cockney *West Side Story.* In place of the Capulets and Montagues, the Jets and the Sharks, were the Foxes and the Hopkinsons. Both families lived in neighbouring tenement blocks that backed on to the main line railway that divided my district roughly into two. No one quite remembered how the feud started, but it dated back to the war years, and for long young Foxes and Hopkinsons had used their parents' differences to add an ugly authenticity to the raiding parties of screaming roller-skating Cowboys and Indian cavalry that swept endlessly through the cemented tenement courtyards. It was John Fox, at nineteen the one but youngest in the family, who found himself on probation. The evidence in court was difficult to follow. Mr Hopkinson, father of the other family, agreed he had started the fight but swore that it was to revenge an uninvited visit to his flat by the Foxes during which they had slashed his furniture and the American cloth of the kitchen table. The Foxes maintained they were innocent: John and his older brother, they declared, had stopped at a stall near the station to buy some whelks, when Hopkinson senior and one of his sons had seen them from the other side of the road, walked over and knocked the whelk saucers out of their hands; unfortunately for the Foxes, it was Mr Hopkinson whose head was cut open with the broken neck of a sauce bottle and this was still in John Fox's hand when the police arrested them.

According to the police, the Hopkinsons were tougher than the Foxes. The elder Hopkinson boy was at the time half-way through his second prison sentence for burglary. Mr Fox senior told the probation officer that the week before his arrest this young man had broken most of the shop-windows in the street near the tenements and, though the shopkeepers knew who was responsible, they were too scared to go to the police. As if to ape the familiar drama, John's sister was engaged to one of the Hopkinson boys, though the lovers could only meet secretly and were trying to find a place to live on the opposite outskirts of London.

John was an agreeable person with ginger hair and was the one least likely, I would have thought, to have been violent, but naturally he had been influenced by his father and older brothers. It was a case where the 'total family setting' was alarmingly relevant. A few days after the trial Mr Fox senior telephoned the office to say that the Hopkinsons had been round on Sunday night shouting abuse through the letter-box; a week or two later he rang again to say that three Hopkinsons had surrounded John on his way back from work, grabbed hold of his overcoat and threatened to use their razors on him. The probation officer doubted if these attacks were as one-sided as the Foxes suggested, and told him that another time they should dial 999 and call the police—but Mr Fox said the coppers were always on the Hopkinsons' side, so what was the use?

John found himself a better job and was talking of cycling to the Lakes for his holiday. For months he never spoke to a Hopkinson. It did seem that things were quietening down—that was until the elder Hopkinson boy was released from prison. One night the Foxes came back from a football match to find the glass of their front-door shattered and slashes in their furniture and their American cloth. The next day a van drew up beside John in a deserted side street, out jumped three Hopkinsons, but he just managed to reach the safety of the crowded High Street. This time he went straight to the police station, explaining who he was and what had happened. The sergeant on duty noted it down but again—according to the Foxes—nothing was done. The effect of this on John was to make him resentful and unco-operative and, to his mind, it confirmed the belief that the police were basically on the side of the Hopkinsons. It was especially unfortunate as since the start of the probation order the Hopkinsons, not the Foxes, had been the more aggressive. This became even clearer when the elder Hopkinson was again arrested for burglary and put away for another two years, because after his trial there was no more violence. Both families contented themselves with jeering at each other across the street.

Though I studied this case with extra care, I still find it hard to believe that the vendetta survives into the age of community centres and quiz programmes, in the land of brewers' English and Christmas broadcasts from Sandringham, in which every sixth former can spell 'moral hygiene'; yet it can be argued that the neighbourhood patterns of the Greater London sprawl are diverse enough to produce almost any offence codified by law or history—plus some new ones as well. Some criminologists have indeed carried out social, 'ecological' surveys to plot the geographical incidence of crime. They speak of juvenile delinquency as being the behaviour of an underprivileged neighbourhood, where the law-abiding are the deviants. Investigations have sought to discover if slum districts, for example, show a higher crime rate or what happens to it among families rehoused on new suburban estates—to what extent does the old slum 'sub-culture' survive or does the uprooting create new tensions? These studies can be very complicated and cordoned in by endless reservations, but I think they are likely to prove an increasingly fruitful field of research.

The probation officer, at any rate, automatically constructs what might be termed a rule-of-thumb ecology for his own area. He knows that a certain neighbourhood, for a complex of reasons, generates delinquent gangs and that another one does not. I have heard probation officers speak of two near-by streets which outwardly look very alike, though in fact one contains several families with members who have criminal records, whereas the other produces—according to the records at least—nothing but honest citizens. I have been struck by the amount of crime that stems from respectable suburban roads; many of the strangest sort of sex offences, for example, occur behind net-curtained bay-windows as opposed to the clubs and honky-tonks of Soho. The difficulty of obtaining an accurate understanding of the ecology of a district can be seen from the two London areas of Notting Hill and Brixton: both have relatively large coloured populations and one might imagine that feelings about colour, allied with housing shortages, worries about employment, differences in diet and custom, and so on, would be apt to produce very similar tensions among the inhabitants of both districts, but it is interesting that so far Notting Hill has seen far more violence than Brixton.

In the areas covered by my courts there were no obvious pockets of racial minorities, though there were quite a few individual West Indians and West Africans, some of whom landed up in the probation office. One at least has a place in this chapter as the dominant motivation behind his offence—taking money from a gas-meter—had a close relation with his colour and his difficulties with white people. Up till then John's record had been clean. He told the magistrates that, apart from being short of money, he had felt disheartened with life in England and 'felt a need to do something desperate'. He was very different from young Desmond (the West African in the taking and driving case discussed in Chapter 4): John, twenty-eight, had come four years earlier from (what was then) the Gold Coast to study law, his whole family contributing to a fund to pay his fare and make him a small living allowance. But things had gone badly: John had failed to pass his exams and still had quite a few dinners to eat at the Temple. He had lived with an English girl who bore him twins and then, when they were eight months, left him—and the twins—for a West Indian. There was no alternative to placing the babies in the care of the local authority, even though another young lady now shared his room. She already had a small child of her own from an earlier liaison and was about to produce one of John's: in an attempt to meet the extra expense he had spent a calamitous evening at the dog-track, as a result of which he had to pawn the watch and chain presented to him on his twenty-first birthday. . . .

Nothing of all this had been written in his letters to the Gold Coast, but the day came when his father, displeased at his failure as a student, had stopped the allowance. . . . It was a mess, yet rather than return home in disgrace, he had tried to find work as a clerk in London and carry on studying in the evenings. Employers, he explained, were usually polite at the interviews but always the vacancy turned out to be filled already. He applied also for several positions of shop assistant, and once as a storekeeper, but the reply never varied: the vacancy was filled.

John was convinced—and rightly—it was because of his skin. After weeks of unemployment he was taken on as a temporary postman over the Christmas rush and since the trial he had worked for short periods as a builder's labourer or an unloader in the goods-yard. For his visits to the probation officer, however, he always appeared in a black, legal looking suit, a bowler, and with a furled umbrella. His sensitivity about his social position was strengthened and complicated by an even greater sensitivity about his colour. 'Before I came to London, I never thought of it, but here . . . here, they never let you forget it.' Of course his touchiness was understandable, but he was apt to detect prejudice in what was probably normal everyday rudeness; simple events such as buying groceries or being part of a bus queue easily led to his being swept up in an indignant fury and finding himself the centre of a quarrel—even a visit to the town hall to inquire about being placed on the housing list ended with his tearing up the application form and throwing it in the official's face.

It was impossible to make John see that, however justified, reacting in this way only made his position more unpleasant. To some extent I think he may have clung to his racial difficulties because they provided an excuse, one fortified by very real experience, not to face his failure in his exams and in other ways. With so many clients their difficulties seem to have become part of them and at one level they do not wish to be without them.

Providing a stage upon which John could release some of his bitterness, sympathizing and sharing his problems were all that the probation officer could offer, but it was not enough—perhaps a coloured probation officer would have been more effective? In the end John accused a tobacconist of giving him short change and punched him across the counter; for this he was awarded a month's imprisonment by another court. As it amounted to a breach of the probation order, he was also brought before the original bench and the order was extended for another year.

John's angry refusal to be treated as an inferior had qualities that were admirable but his life would have been easier if he had been more like one of Mr Young's Jewish probationers who remarked: 'If you've got the conk, there's nothing you can bloody well do about it. It's best to learn to live with it.'

III

As a dominant factor in cases involving conflict with others, mothers-in-law come well up to expectations, though I know of at least one case where roles were reversed and a mother was driven to assault her son-in-law. However, the case of Mildred, who stole the neighbour's necklace and bought a ticket back to her own home town with the proceeds, satisfied the classical form more exactly. It also shows how a human conflict can cause one of the distraught contenders to commit an offence not merely in order to end it—in this instance to escape from it—but also to make what appears very like an act of protest and outrage. Mildred explained her feelings unequivocally:

'I never really wanted to marry him. It was she who made us. Because of the baby. We had nowhere to go, see. Do you really think I'd have agreed to live at her place if she hadn't been the one to suggest it? It wasn't my idea of a home, but that's what comes of marrying a man without a proper living. What's more he's always on her side, does whatever she asks—however much he promises not to. Never can make up his mind—not that she doesn't make it up for him. D'you know, I think he hates her really, but he daren't let go, see—like a kid he is what won't let go of his mum's pinny. Be better really if he never saw her again. Better still if she were dead. Then I might be a sort of mother to him as well. . . .'

The mother-in-law's jealousy of Mildred, the virile young usurper who was taking away her first-born, expressed itself not only in the usual criticism and interference but in meanness. If Mildred switched on the light in their bedroom earlier than was considered necessary, mother-in-law would walk in abruptly and switch it off. Most of their furniture was hers, also the rugs and linen, though she had made a great show of it being a wedding-present. Her generosity was another stiletto. On one occasion Mildred had won a row over whether her husband could take her to the pictures; when they returned shortly before midnight they found the bed stripped of sheets, the floor bare, and most of the furniture piled up on the landing. That happened four days before Mildred decided to become a thief.

'I had to get away, see. For baby's sake as well as mine. A silly way of doing it if you like, but my old lady's on the old age and a widow. Couldn't very well ask her for my fare, could I? I was wrong all right—not that it's any good saying you're sorry. The old cow—the one next door, I mean—she's got the thing back anyway. She's just as bad, always nattering over the fence—the two of them together. The hints she dropped when she noticed I was expecting—about it being lucky the poor little mite was to be given a name. . . .'

As well as listening and helping Mildred to disgorge some of her anger and telling her how nicely she looked after the baby, the probation officer was able to provide practical help. Mildred was temporarily lodged in a Salvation Army hostel and then, after a few weeks, a meeting took place in the office between Mildred and her husband. With the probation officer acting as referee they were able to discuss their difficulties more calmly; the furniture removing incident had upset him quite as much as the trial and he agreed they ought to try and find their own place. But he had no plans. He just sat dejectedly on the office chair, repeating that he could see no hope of their managing it for some months. His uneasy picking at the fluff on his coat sleeve was somehow a reminder of the formidable mother waiting for him on his return, ready to smack down the few feeble props to his resolution.

Only a *deus ex machina* could keep the couple together and the probation officer felt justified in producing it. A new town. After an hour's telephoning she discovered that one of these could offer small two-bedroomed houses to men in the husband's trade. Before they left that afternoon a date was fixed for the probation officer to take them in her own car for a visit, to meet the personnel officer at the factory and see over the house. Mildred was promised that nothing would be said to his mother until they had decided on the move and he had actually signed the papers for the lease.

In addition to reforming a thief, another marriage was saved—though who dare say for how long? Unsatisfactory marriages probably prompt more crimes even than bitchy mothers-in-law. Successful marriage reconciliation—where neither party is necessarily a probationer—forms a distinct and growing activity of the probation service, one that is outside the scope of this book, but for certain offenders it can also be the method of reform. More males than females commit crimes against property, but how often are these the end-result of a wife's recklessness with the housekeeping money or her grumbles that he does not earn as much as their friends? Marriage is said to 'settle a man', but how often does the onerous process of adjustment cause anxiety or emotional disturbance that expresses itself in a crime? For well-balanced, secure people the early years of marriage can be difficult, and for the unstable they are likely to be even more so. One can imagine, too, how those who have been starved emotionally find that a relaxed intimacy is beyond their reach; how women dogged with inferiority fear the stigma of spinsterhood and are likely to accept impulsively the first proposal in case it is the last; how those deprived in their own childhood are apt to feel jealous of the love given by a wife or husband to the children. . . . My attempt at imposing a system on my cases is again tottering and I am anticipating what is planned for the next chapter. The clients themselves are taking charge of the narrative, but my point is that with some unstable or deprived people the responsibilities of marriage can trigger-off an already existing tendency to commit a crime.

Ewan, for example, was a man who should probably never have married. His offence was a very minor one and most of his interviews were taken up with his troubles with his wife. He had already left her four times and he was now wondering if he should make it five. His wife was also invited to come to the office for a talk and there were several home visits. She, one felt, relished the chance to display how much she despised her partner, whereas he seemed merely grateful that someone appreciated his point-of-view. A thin, freckled woman, with greying yellow hair and two girls at primary school, she was the music-hall's idea of the nagger: 'Ewan never tried to get on at work.' 'Ewan was a sight too fond of the beer.' 'Ewan never did a thing in the house.' 'Ewan scarcely spoke to the children. . . .' When later some of these accusations were put to him, he would be meek and half-agree, but he mumbled that he too was fed-up—fed-up with being bossed about worse than the children; and then he would recount some occasion when he had told his wife where she got off and he would at once begin to look happier. His probation officer suspected that it was usually a fantasy, that he was romancing about what he would like to have done.

After some months there seemed no doubt that Ewan felt so uncertain about himself that he would never be able to mend his relationship with a wife who was so dominating; that his four attempts to leave her were instinctively reasonable. On his own or living with people with whom he need not be emotionally involved, he could potter through life and be quite happy—he was not unlike H. G. Wells's Mr Polly. In his case not reconciliation, but a return to bachelorhood could be justified: this could mean the removal of stresses that might lead to a second offence. The probation officer was careful not to suggest it in so many words, but by cautious comments he helped Ewan to perceive segments of his situation that hitherto had eluded him and eventually to accept a conclusion he had really already reached by himself. His affection for the children had for long been the only cord of any strength attaching him to the past; he was able to decide that even for their sakes to leave home would be less harmful than staying.

IV

It can scarcely be reiterated too often that the essence of probation is a relationship between two people, but in a sense it is a one-sided relationship, because it exists for the benefit of the client only. The officer is justified therefore in consciously controlling his part of it, so as to match the altering needs of the client. By turns he emphasizes his sympathy, his warnings, his criticisms. There are right and wrong times to impose demands or moral evaluations. He is rather like the comedian's 'feed' because he enables the client to act out his confusions and unsnarl his twisted feelings. He reflects back what is already there. He prompts and tests his ability to become independently responsible and to conform to society's rules. Problems are shared. Feelings of disturbance are expressed and thus perhaps eased. The client is helped to gain a clearer picture of people who are close to him.

How much insight the probation officer can foster depends very much on the accessibility of the client and his intelligence.

For many the process never gets much further than an attempt to clarify the client's general situation and relationships with others, pointing out inconsistencies in his statements or his actions, and helping him plan his life more realistically—and indeed sometimes even less than this is needed. With others a deeper insight can be given, so that the client does begin to understand some of the conflicting feelings and worries that linger just below the threshold of consciousness and have caused him to distort the world around him, to feel so unhappy, and react so mistakenly—particularly the strong feelings inherited from his past that are apt to become related to the demands of the present: if he understands his feelings, there is hope that they will disperse or be controlled and diverted.

Jealousy is a familiar of every probation office either as the instigator of an assault on the rival or the loved one, or, similar to other disturbances of matrimonial harmony, as the dominant factor in some more humdrum offence. Sometimes the probation officer finds himself buffeted from all corners of the amatory triangle—or maybe quadrilateral—as happened to Mr Young in the case of William Green:

'It was an hysterical kind of offence—a back-door hold-up. With a handkerchief tied over the lower half of his face and pointing a toy revolver, he told the housewife who had opened the door to produce all her money. It was Thursday and she only had twelve and fourpence; while she was handing this over, the milkman turned up, gave the alarm, and within ten minutes William was being charged at the police station. He told the court that he had spent most of the night before the hold-up rowing with his wife, with the result that he didn't feel up to going into work. Fed-up as well as short of cash, he thought he'd have a shot at some easy money. If he'd had any previous convictions and if it hadn't been for my report, prison would have been a safe bet.

'They had four lovely kids—two of each; the youngest, only seven, looked ridiculously like William. The house was all right, though a bit untidy, and he had regular work down at the docks. But I didn't take to the wife at all—large and big-boned, with hard, good looks; plenty of wrinkles but well-preserved. She didn't seem to like me much either, though she was frank with her answers. She was in love, she told me, with a man called Preston—had been for years, even before she married. Started seeing him again regularly eighteen months earlier and she didn't intend to stop.

'Preston had his own business and his own car—he came out of a much higher drawer than unhappy William. But he, too, had a wife and kids, and the day after the trial the wife rang me up at the office and introduced herself. Begged me to stop her husband from seeing any more of William's wife. The next day she came to the office and wept so much that I had to get Miss Lane to give her aspirin and see her home safely. Poor woman, she was unable to understand that we had no power to interfere, even though William, like her, wanted to put an end to the liaison; even though it was in the interests of both lots of children to keep the marriages going. Of course I did my best to remind Mrs Green of her responsibilities but even when asked what she would do if it came to a choice, she declared she would rather keep Preston than the children. "Call me what you like, but I've been waiting for him for more than fifteen years. Just you tell me why we should have to wait any longer?—especially now all this has happened."

'I kept on warning William not to let himself be provoked, for I suspected this was what his wife was angling for. Very sensibly he tried to reach a workable arrangement with her for the sake of the children, but she refused even to speak to him. In the evenings she would leave the house as soon as he came home; sometimes she didn't return until early the next morning. She did no more than the minimum shopping and cooking, and each time I visited the house it was visibly dirtier. This distressed William, particularly as their home had always meant a lot to them both. They lived like that for several weeks, with him sleeping on the sitting-room sofa, cooking the evening meal when he came home from the docks, washing-up and seeing the children into bed. Imagine the effect on them—though I think it was only their affection, their obvious need for him that kept him from further crime or a nervous breakdown.

'It couldn't go on like that. One morning Mrs Green rang me to say that she'd left and had taken the children with her. William didn't yet know. When I asked for the address, she cut us off. Luckily I was able to get round to the house before William returned from work, so as to break the news to him as kindly as possible. He took it well. He'd been expecting it to happen and in one way I think it was even a relief that she'd felt the need to take the children. But, as I've often noticed when people go through a crisis like that, he was not letting himself feel the full misery—as if the body secreted its own tranquillizer. It's a state that can suddenly break down and I soon became very worried about him : alone in the house, with most of the furniture gone, Christmas a few days ahead. One night I found him hanging up balloons and paper decorations in the hope that the two older children might be able to come back for Christmas. By then I'd traced Mrs Green via the furniture removal people. Things weren't going quite as she'd expected. Preston had installed her in a large flat but hadn't himself moved in permanently. He wanted—this is what he'd told her—to give his own wife a little longer to get used to the idea, that there were various matters he must attend to first. . . . I suspected he was shilly-shallying because his wife still used to ring up and, though she knew about the flat, she sounded more hopeful. Her mother was French and perhaps had taught her it sometimes pays a wife to be broad-minded.'

Once Mr Young began to describe a case, he was almost too thorough. His memory had electronic efficiency. Like most officers he made a point of never making notes during an interview—nothing is more certain to hamper a client's confidence—and what he jotted down afterwards was only skeletal. Though the Green case was several years old, he gave me far more details than I have space for here, and I shall limit myself to recording how it ended.

'When Mrs Green realized that, at best, she would never be more than Preston's salaried mistress, she changed—in fact it depresses me how often misfortune makes people nicer. On her own she was again looking after the children properly, but she was puzzled why William had not applied for custody. She was even more so when I told her that it was on my advice that he'd done nothing. I felt that court proceedings would only widen the breach and that, anyway, single-handed he just wasn't able to cope. Besides, by then, I was able to get her to agree that two of the children might visit him every other week-end and this was making him happier, though I feared it would unsettle the children—the younger ones especially would worry as to which side they belonged.

'But there I was wrong. One morning there was a message asking me to ring Mrs Green urgently. Very alarmed, she told me that the youngest, eight-year-old Emma, had disappeared. The police had not yet traced her. Mrs Green had been unable to get in touch with William at work and I promised to visit him that evening. I got there round about six to find he had Emma with him. She'd been waiting on the back-door-step. Walked all the way—must be six miles. She knew the route from having travelled several times by bus.

'After that things were soon all right again. I rang Mrs Green and she came straight over. Freed from the anguish of thinking the child had been kidnapped, she embraced her and then sank weeping into William's arms. I think William wept too, but I didn't stop. Little Emma was a better marriage counsellor than I could ever be.' Mr Young looked at me with much satisfaction. 'Now there,' he concluded, 'is a nice sentimental ending for one of your chapters.'

When I told him that it was more likely to read like very bad fiction, he was, I felt, rather hurt. Few cases contain anything approaching a 'story line'; many, especially the successful ones, peter out in a string of uneventful, more widely spaced visits. In particular, many of the cases involving jealousy have the quality of 'truth that is stranger than fiction'—and nothing is so apt to sound false. The story of Miriam, for example, would as it stands be rightly thrown out by the editor of the hammiest, purplest magazine. I shall give it only in the bleakest form of synopsis:

She comes from Southern Eire, the daughter of a small farmer. She was educated by the nuns and is very devout: both her older sisters have entered the convent. Working near London as a nurse, she falls in love with a man called Nicholas: he is taciturn and unoriginal, except that he has his hair cut like Perry Como and has rather advanced ideas about making love. Miriam is very shocked at his suggestions, for a week refuses to see him, but then relents and he has things as he wants them. They become engaged. For her, life has been transformed into rapture, but mingled with her joy is fear and the flavour of sin which is only partially removed by her visits to the confessional box.

Before the marriage she goes to Ireland for a holiday. Then the day before she is due to return comes a letter. Nicholas has changed his mind. All is over. He thinks it will be easier for her if she learns this while she is still with her parents, though his consideration does not prevent him from adding that he now loves someone else. But he underrates the passion he is capable of awakening; he does not understand what it can do to someone as uncomplicated as Miriam. She says nothing to her parents and the next day leaves as arranged for London. She does not yet quite believe his treachery, but in Dublin she buys an eight-inch knife and hides it in her clothing. Without even dropping her suitcase at the nurses' home, she goes straight to his rooms and, finding him with her rival, stabs him in the chest. . . .

Nicholas does not die, in fact he is out of hospital within a week, yet even to continue to describe in the flattest, simplest terms what happened to Miriam while on probation would be to arouse critical accusations of oversimplification. Each case may be unique, each is full of subtleties, but I am beginning to wonder if the sophistication and elaboration of modern fiction—without which I agree it would not be credible let alone entertaining—has not made us expect the world to be rather too grey, if it has not disguised to some degree the black-and-white qualities of the kind of drama to be found in the courts, especially when the principals are simple but passionate. It will be more convincing perhaps if I complete Miriam's tragedy by means of a few documentary extracts from Miss Lane's case-record:

'Miriam feels that anything that matters in her life has been destroyed and there is nothing to live for. She both loves and hates Nicholas . . .' 'Visited Miriam in Holloway. She is now able to talk about her feelings and this may help her. I felt she was an extremely tragic figure overwhelmed with bitterness. Half-way through our conversation she broke down and showed that a much gentler character underlay the hard defensive mask. I came to the conclusion that there are positive qualities that can be built on eventually . . .' 'In her present state she is quite capable of carrying a passionate wish for revenge through any period of imprisonment and acting on it when she is released. In view of this it might possibly be safer to have her on probation than in prison which would only add to her bitterness. Yet will it be safe to have her released? Anything might happen . . .' 'We had a long talk during which she cried a great deal. I asked if a priest could not bring her comfort; in great distress she answered that she had lost her faith in God. The priest never seemed to understand . . .' 'She could forgive Nicholas but not the girl. Later she said the opposite—how could she ever forgive Nicholas for having betrayed her? She is obviously working through her feelings and trying to get herself sorted out . . .' 'I found her lying with her face to the wall, apparently asleep. On looking closer, I saw she was crying. She said she had been like this for two days. I sat beside her and she held my hand and cried quietly. We only talked of trivialities . . .' 'To my surprise she told me that before her probation ends she wants to meet Nicholas. Will I fix a date and time? No other explanation. I cannot help feeling this is rather sinister and I feel very perturbed. We had met in a tea-shop and it wasn't easy to talk, so we wandered round the streets. I pointed out that Nicholas is now married and asked what she could hope from such a meeting. She couldn't give me any real reason, but went on insisting. I think she feels it would make her easier just to see him. She argued that if I didn't arrange a meeting, she would certainly see him by herself after her probation ended. . . .'

I have quoted enough to show how Miss Lane's calm, commonsensical friendship was equal even to the vengeful grief that inspires a *crime passionnel*—though only just. In the early stages she could do little more than provide Miriam with an outlet for her misery and anger; letting her express herself freely automatically brought relief and lessened the tension. Lurking behind the aggressive act was probably a fundamental lack of self-confidence and, as well as sympathy and acceptance, Miss Lane offered encouragement and reassurance. Only when Miriam's morale had been raised a little, did she try seriously to make her come to terms with the reality of her situation, to turn her mind to fresh interests. Even so the success was only partial; the memory of Nicholas twined round her feelings like an ivy that still lives though its roots are severed. But whereas she yearned to see him again—she probably still nursed the irrational hope that he might be prevailed upon to return to her—it was Miriam herself who wanted Miss Lane to be present. Her passion still flamed, but it was something she herself had learned to fear. She was also learning how to live with it and a second assault was unlikely.

Infatuation can be recognized as the dominant factor in bringing many into the courts who would normally not find themselves there. It is almost certainly safe to state that it explained Mary's offence: a girl of twenty-six who by combining a good complexion, eyes, and accent with shorthand and a history degree, had gained herself a job in public relations at a fair salary plus an expense account, she would never have been charged with selling stolen silverware if she had not fallen in love. He was a Hungarian refugee much older than herself but still lean and distinguished—his family before the Revolution had owned an estate near the Rumanian frontier. In court she refused to say how the silver came into her possession, but later she confessed to her probation officer that it came from her Hungarian: he had given it to her to guard but she had sold it—six weeks after he had dropped her for someone else.

For eight months he had lived on-and-off in her flat. At first she suspected and eventually knew that his absences on 'business' could be either an affair with another girl, or a robbery, or both, but as she put it: 'what did it count against what I felt for him? I knew what he was like all right. Of course he was bad. What my father calls a rotter. But it just didn't matter very much.' When at last she admitted to herself that she had lost him, she began to drink heavily; her work was neglected and, after turning up muzzy-eyed at a Press conference and having forgotten to bring the handouts, she was sacked. Largely because of the Hungarian's aristocratic expenditure, she was already in debt and so naïvely took the silverware to the pawnbroker.

In one sense Mary was an ideal client. Though a far more complex person than Miriam, she was scarcely in need of further insight. She required no one to tell her that her feelings for the Hungarian were wrong, irrational, disastrous but, though she promised to try, she still felt unable, or she refused, to master them. For the first few months of her probation he was serving a sentence for robbery and she did quite well. She cut down her drinking, was taken on by another advertising agency, though at a lower salary, spent week-ends with her parents in the country, and seemed to have returned to a respectable, middle-class pattern of living.

'She appeared to be all right,' her probation officer told me, 'but with her type you can never be really sure. We get so used to hostility, awkwardness, shyness that it is very easy not to take enough trouble with people like Mary. You have to keep reminding yourself that the good manners, the ready conversation, the comfortable middle-class *rapport* is only froth; that, though they may be much more articulate, the froth can hide unhappiness and dangerous drives in the personality.'

It was several months later, by which time Mary's reporting visits had become something of a formality, that the probation officer suspected she had started to drink again—probation officers appear to develop an extra faculty capable of assessing alcoholic intake!

'I accused her point-blank of seeing the Hungarian again. I knew he'd been released four weeks earlier and I took a risk. She admitted it, saying she'd happened to bump into him accidentally at a party. He'd spent several nights at her flat and he'd even suggested they might go to South America together. Of course there was no condition in the order preventing her from seeing him, yet she agreed it could be fatal for her not to break with him immediately—but, poor darling, she was honest enough with me, and with herself, to doubt if she could do it. My only course was to see her as often as possible, to keep reminding her of the danger she was in and that I was there in case of emergency.'

The capacity of love to sustain and indeed to be nourished by maltreatment, hurt, and exploitation is only too familiar, yet few possess Mary's power to observe within herself precisely what was occurring. Even when the veneer of Hungarian cosmopolitan *savoir faire* had been shattered, even when he stole her belongings, insulted her, or jilted her in front of her friends . . . even when in a temper he rang up her employers to inform them that she was on probation—it was worth all of this to have even a small part of him for herself. In such a case, more than in any other, the probation officer's function is similar to that of a doctor at the bedside of a patient with an acute infection—except that there are no antibiotics. She must be prepared merely to offer a continuing support. Human relationships, even in a happy marriage, are seldom static, and with an infatuation like Mary's it was a matter of waiting until, like a virus, it burned itself out. Meanwhile she was encouraged to let other men take her out; by working extra hard, and helping, at the probation officer's suggestion, two nights a week at a youth centre, Mary slowly, if rather obviously, found alternative means of emotional satisfaction. She still saw the Hungarian from time to time, but the day came when he tried to lay the blame on her for one of his thefts; it was then that her revulsion overspilled and like acid cauterized his power to attract her. It still existed, it would linger perhaps for a long while, he could still make her unhappy, but, like a damaged muscle, Mary's spirit had rehabilitated itself.

V

When physical attraction turns in a direction not tolerated by society, it is also liable to end up as a problem in the probation office. Homosexuality—including lesbianism (though not as an offence)—incest, sexual intercourse with minors, even bestiality, the probation officer is expected to take in his stride together with the normal run of larcenies and taking and drivings. One tends perhaps, due to revulsion, to think of such cases in purely physical terms, but sometimes they can flower in a love as intense and pure as that created by any accepted relationship.

Mabel and her brother Ernest came from the problem family mentioned in Chapter 5. Like quite a few of Miss Lane's clients Mabel usually brought her baby with her to the office. She was feeding it herself and apparently it was healthy and normal, though Miss Lane told me of another incestuous child who was born stone-deaf. At the time of the trial I had visited Mabel's home with Mr Young. The conditions were classical: a family of six children—two girls and four boys—lived in three rooms; the parents, particularly mother, struck me as lumpen though quite good-hearted. At four o'clock in the afternoon the beds were unmade, the jerries unemptied; there was an odour of soiled clothing, damp brickwork, fried fish, and something that reminded me of sour tea-leaves; in the kitchen-living-room among hulks of furniture spewing horsehair like hernias stood the only modern item: an enormous television set in a walnut cabinet. Both parents seemed puzzled though not particularly upset by the offence. Mabel, aged seventeen, had by then been removed to a mother and baby home to await the child: Ernest, her elder brother and the child's father, was in custody awaiting trial.

'The boys kip in with me,' the father told us, 'and the girls share the other room with their mother.'

'Mabel and one of her sisters usually come in my bed', the mother assured us. 'Case of one turn left and we all have to, if you see what I mean——'

'Can't think how it happened', the father cut her short. 'No more than an accident, you might say. An accident, that's what it was.'

But the mother thought differently and admitted that she had suspected them of 'meddling' for some time and that she had once or twice told them not to. Interviewed in the remand prison, Ernest also agreed that he had been sleeping with his sister on-and-off for some months. He seemed slower-witted than Mabel and showed no regret at what he had done, though he asked anxiously about her, if she was happy at the hostel, and when the baby was expected.

Ernest was sent to gaol and Mabel was put on probation subject to her residing where directed by the probation officer; she was to stay in the hostel until the baby's future was decided. When Miss Lane visited her in the maternity ward, Mabel was told that, if she wished, arrangements could be made to have the little girl adopted; but she must make up her own mind and do only what she felt was best for the child. On another visit Miss Lane gently touched upon her feelings for her brother, but Mabel denied that she looked upon him as a lover. They had always been close to each other, being the two oldest, and she was fond of him, but that was all.

'Somehow,' Miss Lane told me, 'I didn't feel satisfied. I explained once again the law of the land and that if anything more should happen between them, she too would probably go to prison. But she shook her head and said I'd got it all wrong. There was nothing more to worry about.'

Mabel and the baby in due course were allowed to return home. The baby slept in a converted orange crate and Mabel on a lilo in the room with her mother and three sisters.

'If things weren't already bad enough, Ernest as soon as he was released also came straight home. His mother became very indignant when I protested. I realized then that the offence had never possessed any real meaning for her. She assured me that Ernest now stuck to the men's room; she even implied that I was the only one with nasty ideas! The father was more reasonable and said he'd given his son a good talking-to and made him promise nothing more would happen. But on my very next visit I found the boy nursing the baby and it was obvious he was already becoming fond of it. I asked him point-blank if this wasn't so and he nodded sheepishly. He also agreed that his affection for his sister was still far more than brotherly. I can't remember the words he used but he made me feel that in his own eyes his love was innocent.'

This situation could not be allowed to last, particularly as the baby was not being well looked after. With the help of the children's officer it was boarded out with a foster-mother. Mabel visited it every Sunday, though she was advised to keep quiet about its history. Miss Lane also insisted that unless either Ernest or Mabel went to live elsewhere she would have to report them to the judge. The mother complained that if one went, the other would go too, and then no one would have much control over them, but in the end Ernest agreed to find lodgings. Naïvely he asked what he should do if he met Mabel in the street. Could he speak to her? Wouldn't he even be allowed to take her to the pictures? Miss Lane tried to make him see that a clean break would be best, that in time he would forget Mabel and fall in love with another girl, that Mabel would understand if he ignored her.

For a few weeks the danger seemed to have passed, yet Miss Lane was wrestling with a force that the most regular visiting and persuasion could scarcely hope to limit. She was told by the police that Ernest had several times been seen walking with Mabel and the baby in the park; then the children's officer rang up to say that they'd been seen kissing under the church porch. Disarmingly, Mabel admitted meeting him, though she swore they had done no more than go for walks.

I find it surprising that, a year or so later, for the last entry in Mabel's record Miss Lane was able to write that the case concluded satisfactorily. Eventually, rather than risk a return to prison, Ernest was persuaded to sign on for a job up north. Mabel, too, found herself a job she liked in a factory and after two or three months she was prepared to accept the idea of having the child adopted. Eight months passed without brother and sister meeting and towards the end of her probation she told Miss Lane that Ernest was engaged to a young lady he had come to know in the north. Mabel looked dejected but she agreed it would be for the best. She denied sadly that she would ever be likely to get married herself.

'But Mabel was then not quite twenty. I don't know what's happened to her but you could say she possessed a great capacity for loving. It was only the other day that I visited the foster-mother in connection with another case. She told me how Mabel had often come to see the baby with her boy-friend, someone she called Ernie. She described him as being such a nice young man; what a pity, she added, he refused to marry her.'

The age of 'consent' remains at sixteen, yet it seems that the age at which many girls nowadays essay their first sexual adventures has, in recent years, become steadily lower. 'Most girls admit to initial sexual acts between the ages of thirteen and sixteen', was the opinion of a children's officer, Miss J. O'Hara, in a paper presented to a recent congress of the Royal Society of Health.[1] This accords with the tendency for girls to marry at an earlier age—in recent years a quarter of those who married (for the first time) were under twenty, compared with one-tenth in 1936–40—and with the strange biological phenomenon of the lowering of the average age for the onset of menstruation—estimated to be about two years earlier compared with what it was fifty years ago. Earlier physical maturity is not necessarily matched by earlier emotional maturity, and this can be a further source of conflict in the adolescent personality. Despite these trends, and whatever one may think of the altering pattern of sexual morality, the law must, of course, retain its power to protect young girls from unhappy men like Peter (Chapter 1) and from more dangerous creatures. The seduction of innocent girlhood by experienced, maybe cunning, middle-age arouses in most of us natural and healthy reprehension, but the circumstances of this kind of case always need extra careful probing. It is only too easy to be mistaken, particularly about two such people as Wilfred and Lilian—even though he was thirty-five and she only fifteen, even though he had a son of twelve and two daughters under ten while Lilian was yet at school.

Lilian would have passed anywhere for seventeen at least but at his trial Wilfred did not try to make excuses about not knowing her age. He was conscious that he had done very wrong. He told the judge he could not remember when he first met her, that she lived two streets away and he had known her parents for some years. Some months before the offence Wilfred's own wife had deserted him, and both Lilian and her mother had from time to time dropped in to give a hand with the housework or to help out if one of the children were away from school with a cold. Lilian was stout and rather dumpy in the face, but she was kind and practical and the children soon grew used to seeing more of her, to her cooking meals or bathing the youngest. In the juvenile court Lilian's parents blamed themselves for not suspecting what

[1] Quoted in *The Times*, 26 April, 1960

would happen—it was owing to Wilfred, they explained, being more or less their own age—but she had always been headstrong, a girl who kept her thoughts to herself. In her case a supervision order was made for two years; because of his hitherto clean record and his domestic difficulties Wilfred was put on probation.

The law was merciful and the probation officer was understanding rather than censorious. He managed to find a home-help who would come in every morning and cook the children's midday meal during the school holidays. When Wilfred spoke of his loneliness, of the fondness he could not help feeling for Lilian, he was given sympathy and told to get in touch whenever he wanted, even if it was only so as to have someone to talk to—or if he ever suspected that he could not trust himself. The trouble was that, though Lilian was supposed never to visit his house, she still lived very close and it was impossible to avoid each other entirely. Whereas he was prepared and able, if sadly, to accept the situation, this was certainly not true of Lilian. She would be waiting for him at the station of an evening and insist on walking with him to his front door. She would weep and tell him how unhappy she was, how she could not settle down to her school work, that all she asked was to be allowed to love him and be with him.

Wilfred, very worried, tried to comfort her a little, to make her see that it would be best for them both, and for the children, if she kept away. It could not have been very easy for him, because except at a superficial level he did not believe this. Lilian's parents, who all along were very reasonable, told her own probation officer what was happening and she was brought back before the juvenile court. It was decided that in her own interests she must for the time being be kept in a remand home. Eventually it was arranged for Lilian to remain for a period in a hostel in the country.

She had been there only a fortnight when the warden wrote to Wilfred's probation officer to say that one of the girls at the hostel had reported that Wilfred had been ringing Lilian up at prearranged times at a call-box. Questioned, Wilfred said it was the other way round: she had rung to say that she was so miserable that she would do something desperate unless she could see him. He admitted having met her illicitly, but with the aim of persuading her to stay where she was for the time being so as to give each other time to think things over. He pleaded with her to see that they could do nothing until she was old enough.

Later Lilian absconded but Wilfred once again persuaded her to return to the hostel. By this time her parents were ready to approve of the relationship and Wilfred discussed with them the possibility of his getting a divorce, though he still hesitated to think of a new marriage. Very soon Lilian became restless again. No one could now hope to reason with her. Even arguments in favour of waiting she rejected stolidly and with contempt. Again she absconded and this time the court had no option but to send her to an approved school.

There she had to stay until her eighteenth birthday, after Wilfred's probation order had expired. The day she was released she went straight to him, and as early as possible they were married. Psychology can explain quite convincingly why and how Lilian's emotional development had gone askew, but for me she will always be one more reminder of the perilous ease with which one can be induced to revere the norm, to despise the deviant because of one's own fear. A love like Lilian's that can resist the entire dominion of judiciary, police, probation officers, wardens and parents, of social and moral disapproval, is a measure, maybe, of the power of life itself.

VI

Until very recently Wilfred would have been officially charged with having 'carnal knowledge' of Lilian. Fortunately this gruesome description has been done away with—it is now called 'unlawful sexual intercourse'—but for certain homosexual offences the law still clings to the charge of 'buggery', a word that sums up the obscurantism and irrationality with which this subject is only too often approached. Each time I hear the cultured voice of a bewigged clerk of the High Court formally demanding of some poor devil in the dock if he is guilty of buggery, it is as if Darwin and Freud, Einstein and Jung had not yet been born.

The extent to which homosexuals are prosecuted varies a good deal from county to county and town to town, dependent on the attitude of the local police. Only a tiny minority ever find themselves in court and of these very few cases are concerned with homosexual behaviour between consenting adults in private—which the Wolfenden Committee thought should no longer be a criminal offence, though their recommendation was rejected on a free vote in the House of Commons. Over one three-year period only 1·6 per cent of indictable homosexual offences were in this category; the most frequent charges one hears in court are of importuning and indecency in public. Although the police cannot ignore complaints from members of the public and one's sympathy is very much with the detectives employed on unenviable duty in such places as public urinals, the actual offences are often very far from flagrant. What amounts to an affront to public decency is inevitably debatable; not that anyone, as far as I know—not even those who are prepared to be most tolerant—has suggested that homosexuals should be given free licence. The Wolfenden Committee, for example, did not suggest any changes in the laws governing public decency but they did propose stiffening the penalties for homosexual offences against young people. Though it is true that the proportion of homosexuals prone to make conversions is often exaggerated, and in any event their seductions are unlikely to be successful unless the predisposition is already present, there is always the danger that tendencies that would otherwise remain latent may be awakened. Minors have to be protected.

Whether or not one holds the view that a sentence served in a normal prison is a necessary and suitable method of dealing with homosexuals, there is no doubt that in probation the courts have a more humane alternative—provided it is a case in which there is no risk of other people being endangered. So far as the probation officer is concerned, the homosexual is primarily a client, someone who needs help, and from the start the officer accepts the fact of the other's deviation, offers to share his problems and aid him to re-order his life so that he keeps out of further trouble with the authorities. In fact, with many homosexuals this is about all he can hope to achieve. In a proportion of cases the court will make psychiatric treatment a condition of the probation order and in others the officer will persuade the client to attend a clinic voluntarily, but a complete 'cure' is by no means always possible.

Indeed probation officers are expected to deal with homosexuals despite an admitted lack of certainty as to the nature and causes of their client's condition that to the non-expert is bewildering. Theories of fixation at earlier levels of sexual development, hypotheses based on neuroses or psychopathies are advanced; the many degrees and variants of homosexual behaviour are often described as being either congenital or acquired, 'active' or 'passive'. I imagine that many probation officers believe the widely accepted psycho-analytical theory that in childhood the male homosexual fails to transfer infantile attachments away from his mother to his father, continues to model himself on her, and thus his reactions become too feminine: with adolescence this expresses itself in sexual urges towards his own sex.

On the other hand the late Alfred C. Kinsey and his colleagues at Indiana University scouted all such theories, and spoke[1] merely in terms of the 'basic physiologic capacity of every mammal to respond to any sufficient stimulus', and laid importance on the 'accident which leads an individual into his or her first sexual experience with a person of the same sex' and to the 'conditioning

[1] *Sexual Behaviour in the Human Female*, W. B. Saunders, 1953 (p. 447).

effects of such experience'. Their dramatic, and controversial, large-scale survey suggested that far more people had homosexual tendencies, in some degree or other, than was generally believed. Their findings[1] were that 4 per cent of white American males are exclusively homosexual throughout their lives and that 8 per cent are exclusively homosexual for at least three years between 16 and 55. Their estimates of the number of men who are partially homosexual were even more startling: they record that 37 per cent of the total white male population have at least some overt homosexual experience to the point of orgasm between adolescence and old age; and that only 50 per cent of all males have neither overt nor psychic homosexual experience after the onset of adolescence. The Kinsey figures do not, of course, necessarily apply to the British male and the estimates of other investigators are lower—'the most generally accepted figure is that one in twenty or twenty-five of the male population is or has been a practising homosexual'.[2]

Others point to the deficiency of male hormone, to genetic or constitutional factors. In the U.S., for example, Kallmann investigated eighty-five homosexual men, each of whom had a twin brother. Half of these were binovular twins and half identical twins. Among the former just under half the brothers had homosexual traits (a proportion similar to the general Kinsey figure). Among the identical twins, all the twin brothers were a practising homosexual.

Mr Compton, who had several homosexuals on his case-load, understood very well the limited changes which he normally could expect to bring about: 'I find that getting them to understand their peculiarity, not to feel too guilty about it or ashamed, sometimes makes things easier, helps them to restrain their desires —though Heaven knows it's not easy. They suffer a lot from

[1] *Sexual Behaviour in the Human Male*, W. B. Saunders, 1948 (pp. 650–1).

[2] Kenneth Robinson, 'The Time for Decision', *New Statesman*, 25 June 1960.

loneliness, frustration, fear, not to mention jealousy and heart-break, which seem even more violent than with normal lovers. Many have no wish to change, they see nothing wrong in it, but there are others who wish desperately to give it up. When they are genuinely bi-sexual, there is, of course, a greater chance that they'll reorientate themselves.'

Leonard, who was on probation for importuning, had his first experience of homosexuality in the army and explained that he was the 'active' type rather than 'passive', but half-way through his probation he became engaged to a girl. He was very frank with Mr Compton and admitted being still attracted by men in the street, but he was increasingly confident that he could control these feelings and was finding genuine satisfaction in his relationship with his fiancée.

'Yet I often felt he was pushing himself to be heterosexual with what was almost desperation. He told his girl all about himself and she said it could make no difference, but I was worried lest she didn't fully understand the risk she was running. She was very young. I felt I could but persuade them to delay getting married, not that this had any effect and it seems that, so far at any rate, they are very happy together.'

As with normal offenders, the probation officer 'manipulates the environment', does all he can to see that his client has regular work, a good place to live, and so on, because external stress can weaken restraint and trigger-off a homosexual act—just as it can cause alcoholics to spend the evening in a pub or an emotionally maladjusted housewife to shoplift in Woolworths. I came across one case where the sudden death of a brother was followed a week later by an indecent act on a park bench, though the offender, who was middle-aged and had always known himself to be homosexual, had not been in trouble for some years. Discussion with the probation officer about the nature of homosexuality, its possible causes and social aspects, was enough to alleviate his tension and shame and to lessen the likelihood of a relapse.

(I was interested to notice that a lesbian relationship was admitted to by several clients, but as female homosexuality is not illegal they were never on probation for this and the probation officers always made it clear that they were not empowered to prevent it. On the other hand in one case, that of a mannish young woman who always came to the office in slacks and spent most of her evenings at a lesbian club in South Kensington, the probation officer arranged for her to see a psychiatrist about her peculiarity; permission was also obtained from the chairman of the bench to spend £12 on buying the girl a new outfit of more feminine clothes, whenever she felt able to break away from her lesbian friends, so that she could feel proud of being a woman. . . . The offer was rejected.)

Though probation is by far the most rational and humane method of dealing with male homosexuals whose offence does not make prison unavoidable, its results are not very promising. A survey of over 3,000 offenders, charged with various sexual offences, in fourteen different areas, initiated in 1950 by L. Radzinowicz and the Cambridge Department of Criminal Science[1] showed that 16 per cent of those convicted were placed on probation; grave, as well as minor offences were included, though probation was used much less frequently for offences against males than females, a difference explained by the large number of adult homosexual offenders who were fined or convicted under by-laws. The cases were followed up for four years from the making of the probation order: 70 per cent of all offenders were not reconvicted (this figure compares reasonably well with the percentage for all offences: see Chapter 8) but for homosexual offenders the proportion of those reconvicted for sexual offences (as opposed to non-sexual ones) was almost twice as high as for the other categories (heterosexual and exposure cases); of the homosexuals who were also given medical treatment no less than 52 per cent were reconvicted within the four years.

[1] *Sexual Offences.* A Report of the Cambridge Department of Criminal Science, Macmillan, 1957.

These discouraging figures reflect, I believe, not so much the failure either of probation or medical treatment, but that society's whole approach to the problem is intransigently unsound and misinformed. Treatment can, in individual cases, be successful, at any rate as far as further convictions are avoided, as is shown by the work of the Portman Clinic and individual psychiatrists, but the trouble is that the objectives of the law and of the psychiatrist are often out of step. Dr Denis Parr, writing in the *British Journal of Delinquency*[1] gives a good example of this: homosexuals are known to be more promiscuous than heterosexuals, yet he tells us: '. . . men caught indulging in mutual masturbation in public places are sometimes placed on probation with a condition of medical treatment. The psychiatrist treating such a case may find that his therapeutic efforts lead to the establishment by the patient of a stable friendship with another homosexual with whom he practises, in private and undetected, varieties of sexual acts including buggery. Socially the new behaviour is less undesirable than that which led to the conviction, but legally at present it is deemed more reprehensible, and even carries a maximum penalty of imprisonment for life.'

Similarly, Dr Hermann Mannheim has pointed out that, because homosexual practices are treated as serious crimes, the homosexual himself, who is unable to regard them as abnormal, is only too likely to become profoundly anti-social and adopt the mentality of an outlaw. The fact that homosexuals feel themselves to be persecuted produces a special and peculiarly resilient form of resentment to Authority; to appreciate it, a normal person has to try to imagine what he or she would feel like on being told that heterosexual love was taboo and must be avoided. Homosexuality is said to be often associated with emotional disturbances and disorders of the personality. How far are these the result of their isolation and persecution? How many of those who, despite arrests, continue to importune in the public urinals, do so as a compulsive protest and release from depression and anxiety,

[1] 'Psychiatric Aspects of the Wolfenden Report,' July 1958 (p. 41).

caused by society's attitude to their sexual character? As I hope to show in the next chapter, one has to reckon with the paradox that the very threat of punishment to people distraught with shame and self-disgust is capable of provoking an overt offence.

Shortly before writing this chapter, I read that a young man awaiting trial on a homosexual charge had hanged himself in his cell. The judge remarked: 'In a decent world an adolescent would not be prosecuted on a criminal charge arising out of a sexual offence. He would be handed over to some intelligent, sympathetic person who would help him out of his difficulties.' Despite the harshness of the law, probation officers are able and do offer this kind of help. But their task would be less discouraging if the rest of us treated the subject with less emotion and more knowledge.

VII

By placing homosexuals in this chapter I am perhaps breaking my own rule and classifying cases by offences rather than factors that may have led to their being committed but, though their difficulties arise within themselves, it is their relationship with others which gets them into trouble. The same considerations apply to the prostitutes met with in the probation office. In the district covered by the courts to which I had attached myself there are pockets of semi-amateur prostitution based on the drabber type of private drinking club, but most of the prostitutes on the local probation registers had been transferred by the probation offices at the courts in whose areas they were charged with soliciting, usually in or near the West End. It was to these courts, therefore, that I was compelled temporarily to transfer my researches. Another reason was that few girls are actually put on probation for prostitution, and the probation officers at these inner London courts have evolved their own semi-official and short-term methods of helping them.

One morning, shortly before the Street Offences Act, 1959, became law, I was sitting in one of these courts, watching the farcical 'morning parade' shuffle in and out of the dock. The girls, gum-chewing and off duty, for the most part looked washed-out and messily uncoquettish. Each resignedly nodded her guilt, heard herself described as a 'common prostitute' and her number of 'previous' intoned like an item in an inventory, and went off to pay her maximum £2 fine. The cases took about thirty seconds apiece and, though the girls would occasionally grumble that it was not yet their turn on the rota to be picked up, they looked upon the fine as a form of income tax.

Half-way through the parade the magistrate paused and laid down his pen. The plea was once again guilty but the girl grasping the handrails of the dock was different, as if she had got there by mistake. Perhaps eighteen, she was the dream daughter of every sentimental suburban Dad, with golden wavy hair, pretty eyes and fresh little mouth, crisp print frock. Instead of '17', '38', '24', '63' previous, it was a shock to hear 'none'.

'Put back to see the probation officer.'

I heard afterwards that at the interview she had remained composed and determined. She had only recently left her home in a small manufacturing town in the Midlands, where she had worked as a shorthand-typist, earning £8 10s. 0d. a week. She told her parents that she had been offered a better secretarial job in London but, instead, she had taken a half-share in a flat with a girl she met in a café near Euston. She admitted, not without a hint of pride, that she had already entertained over twenty customers. One of them, an American sergeant and an 'all-nighter', had given her fifteen quid. No, she was not badly treated at home but her parents were perhaps a little stuffy, particularly Dad, who'd always nagged her, and grumbled if she came in after midnight; there was no trouble at work; there was even a nice young qualified accountant who wanted to marry her . . . but she was bored. *Bored!* She wanted excitement, what she kept calling 'glamour' and lovely things to wear—negligées and real furs and maybe even jewels. If becoming a prostitute was the only way of getting them, well, she was not one to worry what people said.

'She had it all weighed up,' the probation officer told me. 'As hard a little miss as I've seen in a long while, but at least she was honest—understood all the risks including V.D. I couldn't do a thing with her, except make her feel she was always welcome to drop into the office whenever she wanted help or maybe just a chat.'

Sometimes that first interview is effective; is enough to make the girl hesitate, really to understand that the money will not always come easily, that she must think now what will happen to her when her looks and figure begin to go, and that she must reckon with a high rate of wear-and-tear. An attempt is made also to explore the girls' feelings—about themselves, their relationship with their families, whether they feel ashamed.

'If they're not Londoners, and many of them aren't, I get them on the train before they change their minds. Send them back to their lodgings for their things and meet them at Euston with the ticket. If life is too difficult at home, I usually arrange for them to be fixed up in a hostel and send them round to the employment exchange. A job with evening shifts has its advantages.'

What are known as long remands, lasting several weeks, are sometimes used by the courts as a kind of temporary probation order, to see the girl resettled in normal life. Young girls just starting prostitution—Edward Glover calls them the 'larval' type —and women who lapse into it now and again when things get difficult, are the only ones the probation officer can hope to reform. The professional, particularly the successful call-girl with her own apartment and regular clientele, are beyond her reach. On the other hand, the initial interview, even when it is a failure, occasionally has delayed results, maybe even years later. There is always a regular trickle of women who want to give the game up and they know the probation officer is there to help them.

'Retiring can mean a considerable financial adjustment,' another officer told me. 'One of my girls, who charged £2 to £3 a time and had as many as fifteen customers a night, decided to become a waitress. She dropped from perhaps £40 a week to £5 plus tips. Her expenses had been heavy—clothes, the share in a maid, eleven guineas a week for rent—in fact she couldn't come off the game until she had settled her commitments. But with encouragement and some practical advice about selling things secondhand she did manage to reorganize her life completely. She had been on the game for some years and the change took some getting used to—no wonder she started to get migraines!'

Another young woman had taken up prostitution immediately after her husband had deserted her. At first she declared that she did not need any help but the probation officer doubted this. Her childhood, as well as her marriage, had been exceptionally unhappy; defiance and bitterness against men made her prostitution seem like a protest. On a long remand she was encouraged to take a job in a haberdashery shop and eventually she agreed to attend a psychiatric rehabilitation unit. While there she threw off her depression and spoke openly of her determination not to lapse again into prostitution. The case ended with the court giving her an absolute discharge.

There was also the bored housewife who, up from the suburbs on the spree, fell in with an attractive man who not only bedded her but soon had her out soliciting on his behalf. She must have been very naïve. However, after her first appearance in court, a discussion of her difficulties with the probation officer led to a reconciliation with her husband who never learned what she had been doing. Then there was the ex-prostitute who had married happily but had to be helped secretly to defeat a blackmailer who threatened to publicize her past. Most touching case of all was the experienced, motherly professional who walked one afternoon into the probation office, propelling a girl of eighteen: she had found her 'working' the car parks and demanded that something be done to 'save' her before it was too late.

The probation service has its successes with prostitutes but I do not want to exaggerate their number. It can only influence a fraction of the women involved. The excellent study of prostitution made by Rosalind Wilkinson, a social worker employed by the British Social Biology Council,[1] describes the occasional talks the girls have with the probation officer as being 'undoubtedly very important' and records that '. . . from early interviews and from regular court attendances, most prostitutes acquire a familiarity with its [the probation service's] workings and know that when they wish and are prepared to co-operate they can invoke its aid. Priscilla was full of praise for the sympathetic help given by the probation officers, "in genuine cases. It doesn't matter whether you've been on the game for ten years, they'll still get you a job if you want to go straight".'

Prostitution, as such, not being illegal, the girls normally are liable only to be charged with 'loitering for the purpose of prostitution'. Under the Street Offences Act, 1959, the penalties have been greatly increased. After a couple of cautions and an invitation to call at a police station, where women police officers will advise her and put her in touch with a welfare organization, a known prostitute is liable to a maximum fine of £10; for a second offence the fine can go up to £25; for a third offence she is liable to £25 or three months or both. The new Act was certainly, in one sense at least, immediately effective. Nearly all the girls vanished from the streets overnight. In Curzon Street, Mayfair, which I walk down regularly, I used to be accosted on an average six times, but now I seldom get so much as a wink. There was a rush for ground-floor rooms but this was not much use as doorways are part of the street for the purposes of the Act. Nor are we likely to see girls displaying themselves in illuminated

[1] *Women of the Streets*, edited by C. H. Rolph. Secker & Warburg, 1955 (p. 34).

shop windows, as they do in Amsterdam, for a London court has interpreted tapping on a window as soliciting. One girl, with an upstairs room, tried dangling a paper ball on an elastic in front of passing men's faces and told the police that it was her way of attracting her cat, but neither did she get away with it.

Customers can in the main only be contacted in clubs or by means of small notices pinned up—presumably for an expensive fee—outside newsagents. Common practice is for customers to be coaxed into the clubs by attractive girl touts who are often not established prostitutes and thus can only be charged with obstructing the footway (max. penalty forty shillings). The prostitute therefore meets her customer indoors, or he is directed to an address round the corner. On the notice-boards most describe themselves as 'models' and give vital statistics and a telephone number, but some offer specialized services: outside a single shop near Edgware Road I noted such fetching extras as 'Continental Boot Treatment' and 'Full Wardrobe of Rubber Underwear'; code words such as 'Bondage', 'Corrective', 'Corporeal', hinted at entertainments to delight the sado-masochist, and one lady called herself unambiguously 'Miss Fetiche'.

One probation officer, with years of experience, assured me that no amount of ingenuity will compensate the girls for the disadvantages of not being able to work the streets.

'It's the older ones who felt the Act most. A prostitute I've known for years was up here the other day on a drunk-and-disorderly. It wasn't like her at all. She's not the type. But she told me she'd got depressed waiting for the phone to ring—or waiting for men to turn up after they'd rung! She found that several of her friends were equally fed-up and so they'd gone out on the booze to cheer themselves up.'

Some of this officer's contacts are known to have taken jobs, as the 'alternative to working for ordinary wages is now too unpleasant', but some gave them up after a few weeks and relied on moving continually to fresh districts where they were not familiar to the police. One middle-aged prostitute, who for years had started her nightly soliciting when the pubs closed, asked indignantly:

'How do they expect me to change at my time of life? I haven't had an ordinary job since I was twenty. I'm only used to night work and that makes it even harder to take up anything else.'

Since the Act, probation officers are convinced, it is more difficult and there is much less encouragement for a young girl to start being a prostitute. It is also not so simple for a man to pick one up—even in the clubs the 'hostess', reasonably expected to be on the end of three rounds of ten-and-sixpenny blackcurrant juices, is apt to disappear—and the total amount of prostitution has very probably declined. Fewer young prostitutes reach the courts or the probation office, but it is possible to do more for those who do than it was previously, if only because the probation officer's advice is reinforced by fear of the heavy fines and imprisonment. On the other hand, the Act can be said to be unfair in that it is directed at the girl, rather than her clients; that for some girls the only way of paying the fines is to borrow from a colleague and hastily seek more clients so that they can pay it back; that imprisonment lessens the chances of finding respectable employment. An even more serious objection is that the Act is driving prostitution underground. There was always a measure of complacent hypocrisy in the campaign to 'clean up the streets'—it was too like sweeping the mess under the carpet. An inevitable consequence is that the prostitute is now in greater need of a male protector. Before the Act, organized vice on a big scale was rare in London. The Messina brothers were an exception, as most girls had no need of the kind of organization they supplied. But now that prostitution is being much more severely harried, if not persecuted, by the authorities, it seems almost inevitable that a more elaborate underground network of ponces and pimps will grow as a reaction, with corresponding corruption, gang rivalries, and exploitation of the girls.

Not that there have not always been ponces; indeed probation officers quite often have to protect girls from their influence and cruelty. But to date it has been more customary for a woman to *keep* a man rather than to be one of a number of women under a male employer. Many girls have great affection for and cherish their ponces. The reasons why a prostitute is so ready to hand over her earnings to a man are not easy to understand but they throw light on the prostitute's psychology and social determination. Their profession makes them outcasts socially, rivals to each other, and to have a man of their own reduces their sense of isolation. The short-term, usually frigid relationships with their customers increase their need for a relationship that is permanent and that means something; in fact their need to have a man to love leads them very often, in addition, to bear his children and keep house for him. It is understandable that the courts and public consider that to live on a woman's 'immoral earnings' is a particularly unsavoury crime and feel it must be punished severely. Many ponces have a police record and their backgrounds usually suggest plenty of reasons why they should have become anti-social: 'The histories of these men and women reveal them as the counterparts of one another; people who have gone through parallel desocializing processes. . . . Our judgement of the men derives from the desire to protect the prostitute from what she wants, and might be less harsh had we a fuller appreciation of her way of living and the reason for it.'[1] With the normal ponce, who is a distorted kind of husband, as opposed to the Messina-type of employer, the girl is certainly less subject to coercion than is popularly imagined, for both partners know she can always report him to the police and get him a long sentence. As is only to be expected, the insecurity of the relationship, and of its two individuals, is very apt to express itself in violence and alternating feelings of love and hatred, loyalty and treachery.

The strength of the ponce's attraction can be seen in the case of Suzie. She was on probation for some minor larceny offence and not as a prostitute, but she had been soliciting for nearly two

[1] *Women of the Streets* (pp. 115, 131).

years, during which she had been living with and presumably keeping a good-looking Irishman, rather older than herself. She was still under age and a condition of the probation order was that she must return to her parents in the outer suburbs. The mother was a plausible but dominating woman and Suzie was continually rowing both with her and the father who declared regularly to the probation officer that he had 'washed his hands of her'. Their own personalities explained Suzie's. The girl was described as bitter and lethargic and as having intense 'feelings of badness' about herself, because she was never wanted by her family and now believed herself, rightly, to be persecuted for her recent behaviour. Her attitude towards people—her parents, the Irishman, the probation officer—was typically ambivalent. Having never had a satisfying love relationship as a child, one could see with what satisfying abandon she must have thrown herself at her Irishman. She had worked for him, cooked for him, borne him a child which had died; but perhaps he had given her some happiness? The probation officer suspected he no longer had any use for her but Suzie was set on eventually returning to him.

'Don't think I'll go back on the game. I've finished with all that. I'm sure once we're together again I can make him see that he must work properly, give up his visits to the dogs. Not that he wanted me to go with other men. It was my fault, not his, but what else could I do? We owed so much.'

This was not very convincing and her mother swore that he used to thrash Suzie if she refused to go out at night. Suzie denied this furiously, yet at other times there would be signs of disillusionment. No one could prevent her from meeting her Irishman occasionally and, whenever she did, he would tell her that he was only waiting until she was twenty-one so that they could get married. But then the promised telephone call would not come, her letters were unanswered. News that he had another woman flung Suzie into a worse despair. It was after hearing this that she confessed that at their last meeting she had given him £5 from her wages. She talked of reporting him to the police. 'Sometimes I think he's only nice to me, to stop me telling of him to the coppers'.

The probation officer realized that Suzie's best chance would be to fall for someone else and until this happened all she could do was sympathize, help her cope with her difficult parents, develop a new circle of friends. She also warned Suzie that she might find herself being inclined to punish other men for what the Irishman had done to her. Miserably Suzie agreed that this had already happened. Too much criticism of the Irishman, though, would only add to Suzie's resolve to stick by him. The only course was to co-operate with her on the assumption that she would one day return to him, but at the same time the officer tried to open her eyes to the reality; to help her begin to understand, through the mist of her emotions, that while he might believe himself to be fond of her, her essential attraction for him was as a source of income; that he required her love to be symbolized in pound notes.

In the end Suzie got her own way. She did go back to her Irishman. Her case has the inevitability of so much tragedy. It was as if she wanted to destroy herself. For a while they were happy and he worked in a factory, but then he started gambling again; lost the job; he wanted her to go back on the game and for a few days she refused, but then he threatened to leave her and she became a hostess at a club run by one of his friends. He appeared not to have noticed she was five months pregnant. . . .

I could write a lot more about Suzie and other girls like her but this is enough to show that the reasons they become prostitutes are very similar to the reasons other girls begin to steal or join a gang—there is, in fact, often an early history of truancy, pilfering, and other forms of delinquency. The factors behind their prostitution are equally complex and manifold. Easy money is certainly one of them, though virtually none nowadays are driven to go on the game by economic necessity; money is the lure, but of course it does not explain why one woman becomes a prostitute whereas most women do not. The answer usually has to be looked for in some social and/or personal maladjustment. Edward Glover[1] describes prostitution in terms of psychopathology—his diagnosis of the 'gold-digger' and 'enthusiastic amateur', and also of the customers, is in similar terms. For example, he argues that the choice of prostitution is determined by the early history of the girl's infantile sexual impulse, that prostitution is a kind of sexual backwardness, that 'so far from indicating strong heterosexual tendencies [prostitution] is, in a sense, a denial and denigration of normal sexuality'.[2] In professional prostitutes, in particular, there is often an unconscious antagonism to the male which she relieves by exploiting men financially. It is well known that some prostitutes are lesbian : a prostitute client of Mrs Oldfield's had a long-standing affair with another prostitute, and when one of them had a baby—presumably a customer was the father—the other solicited on behalf of them both in the same way as she might have done for a ponce.

There is no single factor that makes a girl a prostitute, but commonest of all, though I scarcely need say it, is an unhappy or deprived childhood, a history of parental strife, inadequate affection. This brings me back to the inter-human conflict most frequently met with in the probation office : the conflict between the client and his or her parents.

VIII

Though I have left it till last, the parent-child conflict appears, in some degree or other, with disheartening regularity in background case-histories; this is true whether the client is adult or adolescent,

[1] *The Psychopathology of Prostitution.* Institute for the Scientific Treatment of Delinquency, 1957.

[2] ibid. (p. 12).

though with the latter it is, of course, more likely to be of immediate significance when considering the path to his reform and recovery. Adolescence, too, is apt to re-ignite the deeper conflicts and disturbances of the nursery. The quickening that comes with puberty, the unstable alternation between the states of childhood and man- or womanhood, between innocence and maturity, the final striving for independence, result in friction and emotional turbulence that make 'teenagers susceptible to delinquency—particularly when the revolt, often a healthy one against the values of the parents, is displaced and directed against adult society as a whole; when the frustrated anger against a stuffy, unimaginative father or mother finds release perhaps in smashing railway carriage bulbs or the excitement of stealing. The mechanism of adolescent revolt is so familiar and has been written and spoken about by so many people, by everyone from bishops to beatniks, that I shall avoid adding to those aspects that are by now obvious, even though they are central to any discussion of delinquency. The cases of Terry and several others introduced already entail this conflict, and I shall limit myself for the moment to only one more, that of seventeen-year-old Nicky, a client of Mr Compton's. As occasionally happens, this was what is known as a 'voluntary supervision', there having been no offence. Nicky's parents, respectable, law-abiding, but with more prejudices than ideas, visited the probation office because they were at their wits' end.

There was 'nothing we can do with him', they said; 'he's scarcely addressed a civil word to us, not for months he hasn't . . . the slightest thing sends him off into one of his tempers . . . sometimes, Mr Compton, he really seems to hate us. . . .' Since school Nicky had dropped his old friends and was now mixing with 'a peculiar lot who look as if they need a good scrub and a proper haircut—and as for those girls with their pointed shoes and scarlet stockings!'

It is surprising how frequently clothing and hair styles are used to symbolize the clash with parents. In case after case they complain of pointed shoes or tapered trousers, of crew-cuts or hair that is too long: the adolescent expresses his independence—and 'tests'—by making himself look markedly different from his parents who are quite disproportionately and irrationally upset. Nicky's father admitted having once actually cut up a pair of the boy's Italian-type trousers with the bread-knife.

'Mother, here,' he said, nodding to his wife, 'said I ought never to have done it. Perhaps I oughtn't, but why should he want to wear such things? Proper nancy boy stuff. . . .'

Like so many parents of the younger clients, Nicky's father was sincerely baffled. He could not see that his own dark-blue serge suit and bowler, the British Legion badge in his lapel, or even his wife's moulded maroon felt toque and 'sensible' thick-heeled shoes might be equally provocative to Nicky.

They were doubtful if they could persuade him to visit Mr Compton, but after a few days Nicky turned up at the office unannounced. As was to be expected, he was unhappily self-conscious; unusually tall with a narrow chest and oddly pendulous arms, a cluster of angry pimples on his chin, he was almost a caricature of coltish, lubberly youth; the convict-like crew-cut added to the general impression of tense defiance. Very slowly this was dissolved by Mr Compton's matter-of-fact kindness, though at that first interview Nicky would only mumble a few words at a time and seldom unfixed his eyes from the office lino. But he was quite agreeable to coming regularly and after a few weeks he seemed to be grateful for the chance to release some of his constricted animosity. He admitted to being difficult and having tempers and when asked why, he replied unhesitatingly:

'I suppose it's because I'm so unhappy.'

Though he had so little in common with his father and despised him for his petty-officer brand of discipline, one felt that the greater part of Nicky's resentment was directed against his mother. One guessed she was the harder personality of the two.

'She's always on at me. Follows me round the house till she has her own way . . . somehow, though this sounds daft, she makes me say the opposite to what I mean. It's then that I start to get mad with her.'

Visiting Nicky at home one evening, Mr Compton found him alone in the kitchen, washing a cabbage at the sink. His mother was spending a few days with her sister who had jaundice, and Nicky was preparing supper for himself and his father, who was not yet back from work. While they talked Mr Compton helped by peeling the potatoes.

'I don't like to say this,' Nicky went on, 'but with Mum away it's better somehow. 'Course I miss her—not having her to look after us—but Dad and me, when there's just the two of us—we get on pretty well. . . .'

Beneath Nicky's resentment there was a good deal of fondness for his parents. As Mr Compton put it, 'if he could let himself recognize the ways in which he *dis*likes them, he would also be able to like them better.' Nicky's lack was similar to that of many delinquents: they need an older person outside the family with whom they can build a straightforward relationship, who will be sympathetic and reasonable yet not take them too seriously, who can at any rate make up for a few of the shortcomings of their parents. A probation officer can supply this kind of relationship, can suggest attitudes and standards that the adolescent would find difficult to accept from his parents. What most 'teenagers are seeking basically is some form of stability, an 'identity' they can feel comfortable with, one that does not entail a loss of face.

Nicky's response to this kind of support was little short of dramatic. After three months his parents were saying that he had never been so easy to get on with; he even looked fitter and was putting on weight. This also was in part directly thanks to Mr Compton who had encouraged him to attend physical training classes at an evening institute.

He was very sensitive about his thinness, mumbling that he would be ashamed to be seen in bathing-trunks. Mr Compton repeatedly reassured him, saying that he should feel proud to be so tall and that he could not expect to grow in all directions at once.

He talked to Nicky also about his shyness—sometimes it was so bad that it made him break out in a sweat—and pointed out that many of those who appeared the most self-assured—the apparent 'insiders'—concealed a nervousness as intense as his own.

To be able to discuss these topics was the fruit of a patient, drawn-out process of winning Nicky's grudging confidence; even so there were still some worries that were too intimate for him to speak about with ease, and so Mr Compton had the idea of making use of the tape-recorder normally employed for dictating case-records. Left in a room by himself, Nicky was able to say into the microphone things he could never have communicated in any other way. Not that there was anything very extraordinary or shameful in these confessions—the usual worry and guilt over masturbation and sex fantasies, and the anguish caused by the acne on his chin—but ignorance allied with his aloneness had turned his anxieties into malevolent spectres, and caused his fear to fester and burst out in rudeness and tempers. The mere act of releasing it all on to the tape was in itself therapeutic, and some reassuring advice from Mr Compton and the loan of a simple book on sex did the rest.

Mr Compton was also able to enlighten Nicky's parents, to make them more tolerant than I would have thought possible. At first they tended to look upon Nicky's supervision by Mr Compton as a weapon against the boy, the carrying out of a threat. They reacted unhelpfully to most suggestions that Nicky's trouble could be their fault. But slowly, by giving examples that were akin to parables, Mr Compton straightened some of their own confused feelings, and explained why the uneven development of a child had to be met with elasticity; that it was unfair to expect him to behave like a grown-up and at the same time insist on his always being home by nine or be resentful if he questioned their opinions; that adolescence was a phase of exaggerated self-consciousness and uncertainty in which despair was never far away, that behind the boorishness lay fear.

There are times when the conflict with parents has become so severe that the only course is to advise the client's removal from home, usually either to lodgings or, as in the case of Terry, a hostel. For adolescent offenders whose record does not merit an approved school or Borstal, but whose home circumstances make a further offence only too likely, a stay in one of the special probation hostels can be effective, and (up to one year) is made a condition of the probation order.

I have visited a couple of these hostels, each a converted Victorian mansion catering for about twenty-five 'teenage boys. They included first offenders and those with fairly bad records. Nearly all came from the north, and the majority from homes wrecked by quarrelling, drunkenness, by one of the parents dying, by the father being in prison, or going off with another woman, by physical or mental illness, overcrowding, lumpen poverty . . . In both hostels the resident warden and his wife had managed with very inadequate resources to create something of a 'family' atmosphere, though the small dormitories and the over-polished corridors were reminiscent of the meaner type of prep. school. The boys told me that they went out to work each morning—mostly to labouring jobs—but that apart from Saturday afternoons their leisure was controlled.

'There's plenty to keep them occupied,' one of the wardens explained. 'One night each week I take them to the baths; a few go to night-classes. On Sunday there is compulsory church, perhaps a trip to the museums, and of course we give them plenty of games—you've seen our new billiard table; that's something we're very proud of.'

To me, I must confess, the régime seemed very grim. It was one of benevolent discipline with 'kit inspections' and sensible rules about not smoking in dormitories and books not put away in lockers being confiscated. After sharing a couple of evenings of 'controlled leisure' with billiards, table-tennis, and the 'Army Game', I could not pretend to have pierced the barricades of deferential reserve erected by the boys against even an unofficial visitor such as myself or to have heard their viewpoints, yet I believe the system has much to be said for it. At least it is better than going to Borstal. It is still 'probation in the open', though the supervision is much more intense.

'It's best if the probation order extends to the period after they leave here,' the warden explained. 'Most of them need all the support they can get when they are readjusting themselves to normal life—not that we aim to offer an escape-hole. On the contrary, by relieving lads from the pressures they are up against at home, we hope to make them more self-reliant and less vulnerable. Merely to insist on regular work, regular bedtimes, and regular and substantial meals is often enough to set a pattern of stability—you'd be surprised how many, when they first arrive, don't even seem familiar with using a fork and put their meat between pieces of bread and won't touch green vegetables.'

In the 'semi-protected' environment of a hostel the boys are also freer to concentrate on their personal difficulties. As well as long private talks with the warden, they have interviews with a probation officer who visits the hostel regularly; he keeps in touch with the probation officer in the boy's home area who will probably be 'working' on the parents and trying to improve the home situation pending his return. The community life of the hostel can in itself be a valuable part of the 'treatment'. Getting to know other boys who have been in trouble, and who may have to cope with similar personal and home difficulties, is comforting and has been found to foster a change of attitude, the realization that delinquency is not really a 'solution'—though I was told that a single innately disruptive boy can have the very opposite influence and may be capable of undermining the general acceptance of benevolent authority. For this reason, as well as the small number of hostels in existence, only the most suitable cases are selected. Even so, the percentage of 'failures' can be as high as 40 per cent of whom more than half may have absconded—though, as I shall explain in my final chapter, statistics like these can be misleading.

As the probation officer attached to one of the hostels

remarked ironically: 'There'd be virtually no delinquency at all, if it wasn't for parents.' Throughout the Service, as among psychologists and other social workers, there seems to be little disagreement that the seeds of criminality are most frequently germinated in the family and childhood—though there are differences of opinion as to at what age it is most likely to happen and how it happens; that a bad or incomplete relationship with one's parents (or a step-parent or guardian), or being deprived of any relationship with them at all owing to death or separation, is apt to lead to the obtuseness, emotional insecurity, awkwardness that expresses itself in violence or delinquency. This, if anything, might be called delinquency's true H.C.F. Lord Pakenham describes the psychological and moral influence of the family—especially during the child's first few years—as the 'most fashionable category among those who write and talk about the causes of crime'.[1] The bad parent-child relationship may still exist or it may have done its mischief to the personality in childhood. It lies behind the offences of many adults, even though the damage is more heavily overlaid by other experiences. The conflicts that seem to be the dominant factor behind their offences are, one feels, a continuation of earlier, unresolved conflicts that date back to adolescence and possibly the cradle.

To be on the wrong kind of terms with the first people one meets in life can lead, years later, to being in trouble with oneself: to put it the other way round, to be in trouble with oneself is owing to having been in trouble with others earlier on. My clumsy categories are again overlapping and collapsing, for I am already entangled in the subject of the next chapter.

[1] *Causes of Crime* (p. 121).

7
In Trouble With Oneself

*

'(ACTION, to *Diesel*)
'Dear kindly Judge, yourHonour,
'My parents treat me rough.
'With all their marijuana,
'They won't give me a puff.
'They didn't wanna have me,
'But somehow I was had.
'Leapin' lizards—that's why I'm so bad!

'(DIESEL, *imitating a judge*)
'Right!
'Officer Krupke, you're really a square;
'This boy don't need a judge, he needs a analyst's care!
'It's just his neurosis that oughta be curbed—
'He's psychologically disturbed!...

'(ACTION, *to A-rab*)
'My father is a bastard
'My ma's an S.O.B.
'My grandpa's always plastered,
'My grandma pushes tea.
'My sister wears a moustache,
'My brother wears a dress.
'Goodness gracious, that's why I'm a mess!...'

From (*Gee, Officer Krupke*): song in *West Side Story*[1]

THE concept that much crime is akin to and is a reflection of some mental or emotional disturbance is essential to an understanding of modern probation technique. This does not mean that all offenders can be classified as maladjusted or neurotic—nor that the maladjusted and neurotic are necessarily delinquent; as the previous two chapters should have made clear, the dominant factor associated with an offence is by no means always a psychological one, though of course any offence must involve the mind (or more accurately the psyche) to some

[1] From *West Side Story*, book by Arthur Laurents. Published in Great Britain by William Heinemann Ltd. © Copyright, 1956, 1958, by Arthur Laurents, Leonard Bernstein, Stephen Sondheim, and Jerome Robbins. Lyrics © Copyright, 1957, by Leonard Bernstein and Stephen Sondheim. Reprinted by permission.

degree or other. It is also true that every offence I have discussed so far has a stake in this chapter; the inner weakness or proclivity must always be present, even when it requires friction with external circumstances or with others to trigger it off. In this, the last of my three very imprecise categories, I have grouped offenders who would probably have found themselves in court even though the stresses imposed by their environment were relatively normal; whose offences were owing to some degree of mental deficiency or relatively severe mental disorder; or they seem to have been primarily the expression of unmet emotional needs or of inner despair or of a fundamental instability of personality; whose stealing or aggression concealed a disabling lack of confidence, emotional immaturity, a sense of failure or rejection; and so on. These symptoms can lead, in particular, to generalized feelings of insecurity that can only too easily engender a disastrous vicious circle[1]: insecurity leads to anxiety, the fear without an object → anxiety builds up tension that can only be broken by some act of aggression (which may be a crime) → the aggression in its turn leads to guilt → guilt leads to more anxiety → and so the process grinds round once again. . . . Another way of putting it is to say that many offences can be interpreted as compensatory, protective actions by a damaged personality.

This view of crime, owing, as it does, much to psychology and psychiatry, is—it must be emphasized—by no means accepted throughout the probation service, especially its influence on methods of handling the client. Its opponents are concerned lest too little emphasis be laid on moral standards and feel that there is a danger that psychology may lead to the gradual replacement of a code of morality by a negative determinism. I have been given monitory—and convincing—descriptions of the application of half-baked, misunderstood Freudian principles to clients whose real need is to be made to settle down to a regular job or to lay off the booze. The apologists for the psychiatric approach retort that

[1] Lucian Bovet, *Psychiatric Aspects of Juvenile Delinquency* (p. 42).

inevitably it is a subject which not only disrupts dearly held sentiments and prejudices but also rouses in our unconscious deeply buried feelings of aggression and guilt. Among older officers, among those who came into the Service late in life, or who have not taken a degree course or diploma in social studies, it is natural to find people whose resistance and suspicion is to some extent a rationalization of their unwillingness to make the effort to gain even a superficial knowledge of the labyrinth of conflicting psychological theory. They find the language as bewildering and irritating as that of, say, nuclear physics with its neutrinos and antiparticles. There are many more—Mr Young, for example—who though able to accept the psychologist's description of the basic components of the personality and of the conflicts that can arise between them—and in fact recognize these in their clients—do so without being convinced of classical Freudian theory: they can agree that a delinquent's ego and instinctual drives may be out of harmony but they find it hard to see the relation of this to, say, nipple-biting as an infant or freedom to mess on their mother's laps or alarm at her lack of a male genital organ. I think most would agree that psychological knowledge does help them to understand their clients better and, so to speak, to systematize their individual intuitive methods of handling a case.

The conflict between the two wings in the Service is, to a certain extent, false and one of terminology. Whereas one officer will speak of 'mild psychotherapy' and 'positive transference' and another speaks of 'giving him a chance to let off steam' and 'administering a dose of common sense,' it often comes to very much the same thing. In any event it would be profitless for me to explore this conflict; I have therefore written this chapter from what seems to be the standpoint of the majority of officers whose work I have studied and limited myself to psychological interpretations they would have little difficulty in accepting. As far as possible I have avoided the terminology of the clinical textbook, though this has meant skirting the twin chasms of misinterpretation and oversimplification—for example, I have tended to convey the false idea that the various classifications of psychological abnormality are separate from and unconnected with each other.

Helping people to behave is seen as being the same process as helping them to be happier and more stable. With quite a few clients one cannot achieve much more than merely enable them to keep within the law, but with the majority there is always the hope that one may succeed in fostering independent responsibility; the intention is to cure rather than to lock the client in a strait-jacket of conformity. Explanation of why people commit offences does not mean exculpation. The influence of psychology on probation has, on the whole, been one of science rather than sentimentality. Its rediscovery of the healing power of love has grown from man's first attempt at submitting his own mechanisms of thought and emotion to a systematic inspection.

With certain offenders, of course, the connection between the offence and mental abnormality is only too probable and will be accepted by every probation officer irrespective of his opinion of psychiatrists. This category of offenders includes those who are obviously mentally subnormal, or who show clear signs of one of the severer neuroses (e.g. acute anxiety, obsessions, hysteria) or of being psychotic (e.g. paranoia, schizophrenia, manic-depression). When the court asks for a psychiatrist's report, if these conditions are present, they will normally be diagnosed and the probation order is likely—though not with mental subnormality—to be made subject to the offender agreeing to treatment at a psychiatric clinic or as an in- or out-patient at a mental hospital. The law provides safeguards against the misuse of this power by insisting that the court must first obtain a report from a doctor 'experienced in the diagnosis of mental disorders'; this must state that the offender both needs and may respond to mental treatment. The probationer has the right to accept or refuse the treatment—though admittedly to refuse may be equal to exchanging probation for prison—and later to apply for the discharge or variation of the condition to his order. A refusal to submit to electrical or surgical treatment is in any event not regarded as a breach of the probation order.

In these cases the responsibility for the offender is shared; thus a client in hospital can be visited so that he can feel able to rely on the probation officer's friendly support when the time comes for him to face the world again. Difficulties can arise when, as sometimes happens, the client fails to keep his appointments at the clinic or intends to discharge himself from the mental hospital against the advice of the doctors. The latter have to consider him as an informal patient who is free at any time to leave, whereas the court is in a position to impose sanctions and may feel it has to for the protection of the community. Persuading clients not to miss their appointments at clinics or to complete their stay in hospital and coaxing them to return within its walls has to be included among the job's normal duties.

II

On most occasions psychiatrist and probation officer work well together; even where it is decided that treatment is unnecessary or pointless, the psychiatrist's advice is always available and his report provides a guide to what can be expected of the client.

'Not that I always pay much attention to what they say,' a member of the 'anti-psychology school' told me. 'They are too ready to sum up an offender's personality on the basis of a half-hour interview and a few doubtful tests. Too often a man is labelled 'psychopath'—in other words he is a more or less hopeless case. It would be more honest if they said they didn't know how to cure him.'

Many would agree that the term 'psychopath' is used too readily and too vaguely—and this is true of probation officers as well as psychiatrists. There appears to be no agreed definition.

Edward Glover,[1] who has done much to clarify the description of this condition calls it '. . . the stepchild of psychiatry. This was due in part to the fact that it did not fit comfortably into existing psychiatric classifications, in part to general psychiatric neglect of characterological disorders, and in the case of criminal psychopathy, to the circumstance that it has always been difficult to distinguish on the one hand psychopathic criminal conduct from that of "responsible" criminals and on the other the apparently normal conduct of psychopaths from that of law-abiding persons.' He also explains how psychopathy manifests affinities with the whole range of classical mental disorders, 'all of which are interwoven and held together in a sometimes superficially charming personality-frame which the psychopathic swindler exploits to his frequent undoing. Psychopathy is in short one of the great groups of character disorder vying with schizophrenia for pride of pathological place.'

Some psychiatrists always link the psychopath with delinquency and lack of moral scruple: others deny there has to be such a connection. Three main classes of psychopathic personality are usually defined: those who are predominantly creative; aggressive; or passive and inadequate. Psychopathy is talked of as varying considerably in intensity—'mildly' or 'partially psychopathic' are phrases frequently met with—but so far as the courts are concerned a psychopath is generally taken to mean someone whose mental disease makes him, to some extent or other, constitutionally anti-social and lacking in morality; though there may be no evidence of mental impairment or of neurosis or psychosis, symptoms may include pathological lying, laziness, swindling, alcoholism, and other vices; psychopaths are said to be insensitive to the rights of others, egocentric, and lacking in feeling; normally they are unable to profit from experience. Though in recent years some advances in the treatment of psychopaths have been made, and Glover[2] is able to write on the basis of great experience that

[1] *The Roots of Crime*, Imago, 1960 (p. 117).
[2] ibid. (p. 54).

'the chronic psychopath may be a tough therapeutic nut to crack but when treated with patience, imagination, skill and an unruffled understanding of his compulsive recidivism the outlook is much more favourable than is generally supposed', in many cases that come before the courts it is decided that little can be done to change them.

The diagnosis is often sweeping and, once accepted, inevitably conditions the probation officer's attitude and limits his efforts to rebuild his client's character. Such people do exist and so long as their condition is thought to be virtually incurable and the psychiatric services continue to be understaffed, many are likely to remain the responsibility of the probation service—provided the prognosis is not too serious. It is likely, too, that the record will conclude something like this : '. . . he still lies to perfection, though he is always ready with assurances of good behaviour and co-operation. He is quite prepared to take unfair advantage of any situation and twist things to suit himself. Beneath his façade of correctness, he is an individual without conscience; his only loyalty is to himself and if he keeps out of trouble in the future it will be because of his dislike of the possible consequences and not because of any improvement in his standards of honesty.' A bitter summary, but arrived at after two years' proffering of friendship and acceptance—without which perhaps the conclusion might have been even worse and included a long prison sentence.

Psychiatrists, as is true of doctors concerned with organic disease, cannot be expected to be infallible, but the harm that can come from a mistaken diagnosis of a severe psychopathic mentality can be disastrous; probably more so than one of, say, valvular heart disease. Probation officers are wise if they hesitate before confirming the diagnosis, as can be seen from the case of David described to me by Mr Compton who, according to one of his colleagues, 'genuflected to the holy trinity of Freud, Jung, and Pavlov every time he entered the office.'

'Read what they said about him.' Mr Compton handed me a

typed document headed with the name of a famous mental hospital. 'David was then fifteen and was remanded for inquiries after a series of minor larcenies.'

The key, most condemning passages said that David was '. . . a complicated character, very far from being as innocent as he first appears. In my opinion he is as cunning as any boy I have seen for a long while: I am told he is a model pupil at school, polite, helpful, hardworking, but under the surface he is probably a subversive influence among others. He has features that are typically psychopathic. He will be very successful. One can imagine him as a very successful business man—one who does not get on the wrong side of the law provided things go as he wishes. It is no accident that he has got himself into trouble. I cannot rule out a further outbreak if he should be subjected to any strong thwarting of his desires. The characteristic which impresses me most is his lack of any real feeling. This is concealed because he has charm and is such a facile talker, but his effort to please, to say what he thinks one wants is nauseating. . . .'

When I had finished reading, Mr Compton remarked that it was difficult not to be biased against a client after such a condemnation. 'I know they'd taken a lot of trouble with David, given him every type of test, but I'm still convinced they were wrong. He was temperamentally unstable maybe, rather apt to fawn and be ingratiating, but as we got to know each other better, this was something I became less aware of. He was very intelligent and I think he was really able to benefit from having someone outside the family to discuss his problems with—the usual sex worries, difficulties with some of his schoolmasters, and so on. He could never explain what made him steal, but that's true of plenty—and the fact is that he has kept out of further trouble. He finished his probation eighteen months ago, but I had a card from him at Christmas. Next year he takes his G.C.E.—advanced level.'

Various kinds of psychopaths and those of subnormal intelligence will be found among the 'inadequates' attached to every probation office. As explained earlier, these draw heavily on the officer's time and on his stores of patience and charity. But no degree of squalor can diminish the tragedy of an old man like Donald who was charged with loitering with intent and was put on probation merely because the bench felt he needed support. He has never learned to read, not even bus numbers, and supplements his old age pension by selling hot chestnuts—and *Old Moore's Almanacks* in the summer. The probation officer visits him at his pitch near a suburban station and usually gives him a few shillings from the court poor-box. All his life he has been in and out of mental hospitals and he now lives in a Salvation Army hostel. It is difficult to carry on a conversation: his mumbled answers to inquiries seem to exhaust him, though physically he appears quite fit for his years. Apart from a vaguely resentful set to his unshaved, grey old face, he is absolutely without vitality and seems to be drifting towards his grave.

Dulcie and her brother Godfrey would also qualify, I suppose, as psychopaths—the inadequate group; though both in their forties they have need of probation as a permanent crutch, and turn up at the office as often as three times a week asking for money or help in escaping from some tiresome confusion. Dulcie in particular finds it very difficult to keep her person clean—her face is usually smeared like a child's; she is regularly supplied with secondhand garments and shoes which she rapidly loses. She has bursts of drinking—draught cider mostly. Godfrey, a plump little man in a mauve cloth cap that pushes out his ears, is quite clean but he suffers from trench mouth and his breath is repellent; he does casual work helping on the stalls at a street market. Attempts have been made to settle them in various institutions and hostels but they never stay for long and after a few days are picked up by the police for sleeping on a vacant building plot or in a disused garage. They have been drifting downhill for the past three years, ever since their mother died. They quarrel fiercely with each other, especially after Dulcie has been on the cider, but Godfrey feels responsible for her and understands that her mind is too childish for her ever to manage on her own. His concern is perhaps mawkish but it is also touching; he is just about capable of looking after himself but so long as he is saddled with Dulcie he, too, is certain to deteriorate.

At one stage, after Dulcie had managed to burn a ten-inch hole in Godfrey's trouser leg and had been involved in a vituperative scene in a fish-and-chip shop after refusing to pay for two portions of rock salmon, the probation officer reports the full situation to the chairman of the bench and a warrant for her arrest is granted for failure to be of good behaviour. For this she is sent down for two months and meanwhile Godfrey is fixed up in a men's hostel and found a job working on the roads for the council. Very doubtfully, he agrees that it will be best if in future he keeps apart from his sister and he promises to remain in the hostel when Dulcie's two months are up. . . . For some weeks they do keep apart—she is found some hotel job at a seaside town—but with the winter she is back again. Both swear they are going to make a new start. They manage to rent a caravan and for a while little is heard of them, but then there is a quarrel with the people living in another caravan on the site. Dulcie falls and breaks her wrist, Godfrey loses a week's wages on the Lincoln, and the next day is sacked for bad time-keeping. . . .

Even though these kinds of cases occupy so much of the probation service's time, there is little value in recording further examples, and I must risk understating the inevitable familiarity of every officer with squalor, with the unwashed, with the tedious variations of sordid, feculent, crapulous, mucid corruption. This chapter, though, would be very incomplete without at least one alcoholic, one of those whose inner misery or fear or torment drives them to drink with pathological intensity—someone like old Madge. The origins of the probation service were linked with the temperance movement and, though many officers nowadays are no more teetotal than I am, it is difficult for anyone connected with the courts to avoid thinking of drink, so far as offenders are concerned, except as the traditional Victorian evil. Not only motoring offences, but a frightening proportion of thefts, physical assaults, and other crimes only happen because too much alcohol was flowing through the culprit's bloodstream, because it paralysed parts of the brain and thus removed the normal restraint, triggered-off the criminal impulse—I have heard the super-ego defined as that part of the human brain that is most readily soluble in alcohol! Not that it was like this with old Madge. For her and her friend Elsie, and several others I came across, drinking was a way of life. The day Madge was put on probation you could smell it in the courtroom. The gaoler told me they had to scrub out her cell: the stench of stale meths. was stronger even than the normal odours of sweat and urine. After the trial Mrs Oldfield discovered that Madge had only fivepence in her pocket—not enough to get home with—but she refused to give her anything from the court poor-box.

'She'd only have spent it on a little drop to "freshen herself up" as she calls it. I warned her not to drink even a glass of water till she got home. After a meths. bout like that any liquid is apt to make you squiffy again.'

Madge, getting on for sixty, managed, when feeling not too ill, to create an impression of a decrepit *bon viveur*. Her clothes were shabby but they had a certain style, that of the early nineteen-thirties—she always wore a large 'halo' hat; the ravaged puffiness of her face was grotesquely smothered with powder, much of which fell on her clothing. Her memory was hazy, even when she was sober: there was little she could recall of her husband, whom she had not heard of for years, or even of her three children all of whom were grown-up and, she thought, married. She lived on and off with her friend Elsie who, though a quiet, neat, shrivelled little person, drank with equal earnestness.

Madge's two years on probation is a complicated up-and-down story of relative sobriety and drinking bouts that sometimes lasted as long as four days, of new starts and promises, of jobs begun and lost, of quarrels with Elsie, of endless 'accidents'—bruised legs, cut lips, black eyes. Once again, lest I be thought to be exaggerating, I had better quote direct from the notes kept by

Mrs Oldfield: '. . . called at the house, door opened by Elsie bearing a candle and looking very scruffy. Madge said they were using candles as Elsie said the gas cost too much. Madge had obviously just woken up and I suspect had slept all night in her clothes—hair hanging all over her face, and beneath her chair three empty bottles of red biddy . . .' On another visit the room '. . . had a smell reminiscent of Tomcats and meths. Both were in bed and I fancy had been celebrating. Madge hailed me with warmth, explained that she had to lie up because she had fallen and hurt her hip. Before long she became very sentimental, talked about her vanished husband, and both of them cried. Elsie wanted to know if Madge would receive a Christmas present—presumably money from the court poor-box. When I told them that a Christmas pudding was in the post, they looked very crestfallen. . . .' Later, hooligans threw stones and broke most of the windows; they had no coal and still no gas, and Mrs Oldfield had to use her torch. This time Madge was eventually found 'under the bed, a bottle of red biddy clasped between her legs, an empty one lying beside her. Her words were very fogged but it seems that a strange man had climbed into the bed between her and Elsie, and she got pushed out . . .'

At this stage Mrs Oldfield arranged for Madge to be taken into hospital where she underwent a course of treatment for alcoholism. They cut her stimulants down to a daily bottle of stout and occasional pinches of snuff. Her health improved and she was, as Brendan Behan puts it, 'dried out', but not many weeks after her discharge she was brought back insensible to the police station.

There are, of course, plenty of alcoholics who can be treated successfully and in these cases the probation officer can supplement the work of the doctors with encouragement and help in reordering the client's practical affairs, suggesting new interests, and so on. Sometimes the reason for the craving can be discovered, brought to the surface, discussed and thereby eased, though with chronic alcoholics deeper therapy by a specialist is usually necessary.

III

Occasionally it is possible to recognize a direct connection between the offence and some mental or emotional disturbance that has been brought about by physical illness or disability. Mr Compton had a young man whose dare-devil escapades on a motor-bike and violent tempers were tragically and clearly connected with recurring epileptic fits and his determination to prove that, despite them, he was as virile as normal youths. A parallel defence mechanism could be detected in another boy of seventeen who was grotesquely obese. For him, stealing did something to relieve the tension and lonely unhappiness that arose from years of being followed by jeers and giggling whispers. Physical illness, e.g. chronically infected tonsils, may well lower a client's ability to cope with life and therefore make him more susceptible to crime; encouraging him to undergo treatment may be as important as urging him to find work.

A familiar physiological upset, if not actual illness, was also the main reason why someone like Harriet found herself in the dock. In her case this was directly related to an emotional disturbance and the connection of both with the offence is easy to establish. Few offenders are as respectable and well-established in life as Harriet. Forty-seven, the wife of a successful furniture dealer with two grown-up married daughters, a pleasant suburban house with a rockery and greenhouse, a Rover saloon in the garage, a daily woman to do the heavy work—she had no obvious economic problems. Yet she confessed to stealing, from a local shop where she was well known, a jumper priced at £1 17s. 6d.

Interviewed before the hearing, she was quite unable to explain why she did it, though she described the theft in horrified detail—how she took the jumper while the counter assistant's attention was distracted, how she hid it among the groceries in her shopping-basket, her puzzled dismay at being approached by the shop-walker as she reached the exit.

'I knew at the time it was wrong, but somehow I *had* to do it . . . That's all I can tell you . . . it was something I just had to do. . . .'

The psychological explanation of her irrational act will be familiar to anyone connected with a magistrates' court: she was remanded on bail for a medical report and this stated that, although she was neither insane nor mentally defective, she had reached her menopause, a condition well known to cause psychological distress and lead some women to behave irrationally. Harriet told the doctor that, as well as suffering from sudden flushes, she had been having 'strange thoughts'. The shock of her arrest, the shame, the contrition that was without doubt genuine, were said by the chairman of the bench to be punishment enough, but he also placed her on probation for a year with the requirement that she should undergo treatment by her own doctor. Her probation officer's contribution was limited to giving general reassurance and helping her to see the episode in perspective, to win back self-respect and the courage to face the neighbours. It was very unlikely that Harriet would ever get into trouble again.

The growing understanding of the subtle interrelationship between mind and body has shown that much physical illness is 'psychomatic': likewise the study of the reverse connection, the effect of organic processes on the mind and emotions, is beginning to reveal a tantalizing new field of knowledge (e.g. the discovery that the absence of a single enzyme in the brain can cause mental deficiency; the use of drugs, the tranquillizers and energizers, in the treatment of mental illness). It is tempting to think that it will not be long before it is discovered that an increasing number of criminal characteristics, including some of the features of the psychopath, have an organic basis; or more probably that the manner and the extent to which the offender's personality matures is affected by organic factors—these may or may not be hereditary, but genetics complicates the question even further.

All this sounds like a cautious return to the theories of Lombroso at a higher level! But as yet nothing is certain. Whatever new importance is eventually attached to the effect of organic factors, the importance of the offender's environment and upbringing must never be overlooked. The need for caution is also shown by a carefully conducted survey in America of several hundred boys over some years: one of its conclusions was that such things as difficulties at birth, general health, glandular abnormalities, body deformities, were not significantly related to crime; only boys with definite neurological handicaps (brain damage, epilepsy, and so forth) or suffering from severe acne were found to be more likely to become criminals. Apart from these two exceptions, the investigators decided that 'there seems little basis for attributing criminality to physical causes'.[1]

IV

With clients who are mentally subnormal, psychotic, severely neurasthenic, or are upset by the menopause, the likelihood of a connection between the offence and mental instability is not in dispute. But once you start to consider apparently 'normal' clients, those who cannot be readily classified as psychologically sick, the extent of the influence of some disturbance in the mind or emotions becomes much more questionable and there will be some who will even doubt the possibility. Different interpretations lead to different attitudes and methods of treatment. The frontier between psychological disturbance and individual responsibility becomes increasingly blurred and will be variously placed by different officers; for some it tends to vanish altogether.

A surprisingly large percentage of the offences that appear to have no motive are inexplicable except in terms of mental or

[1] *Origins of Crime,* A New Evaluation of the Cambridge-Somerville Youth Study. William and Joan McCord, Columbia University Press, 1959 (pp. 66–67).

emotional disturbance. It is said that relief from depression, for example, or from tension resulting from sexual frustration is sometimes sought in an act of stealing—not that the offender is aware of the origin of the impulse, as the process occurs in the subconscious: a strong impulse is suppressed and another takes its place. The choice of object stolen may be determined by its sexual symbolism. Neurosis is sometimes described as an alternative to delinquency, and I have heard it said that neurotics usually lack the guts to be criminals, but many offences would appear to have a neurotic basis. With neurotic stealing, it is more accurate to speak of an instinctual force *and* a segment of the super-ego being repressed and lost to consciousness, but for my purpose it is perhaps sufficient to say that forces of which the client is unaware reach the conscious mind in the form of compulsive urges that he may recognize as being abnormal but are very hard to resist; they probably promote a sense of excitement or release, though this is usually short-lived. Probationers who are normally very well behaved and with a tendency to be obsessional and narrow-minded often come in this category, though they are not the only ones who feel under the necessity to commit an offence. A comparison can be made with sexual exhibitionists, those who display their persons (the official euphemism for genitals). These men are very clearly under the influence of an irrational force, though it may seem rational to them at the time: if human beings are driven to perform such an apparently pointless and self-harmful act—and exhibitionists feature on the daily charge sheets of most busy magistrates' courts—how much easier it is to accept the idea that other human beings feel themselves driven to commit a larceny.

Alec, a young man who had been a regular thief since the age of seven, was described by the consultant psychiatrist as someone who 'wanted to stop stealing, but had very little chance to do so without a great deal of help'. The report went on: 'I feel quite sure that the stealing in this case is neurotic and is bound up with certain personality problems. There is a certain flat quality about his make-up which does give rise for concern, while on the other hand it may well be a veneer to cover his real feelings.' His probation officer told me that from the start Alec was able to talk quite freely about his thefts, though he did not feel able to come and volunteer information—he had to be specifically asked.

'He worked as a radio assembler and he admitted that sometimes he found it desperately difficult to resist the temptation to take small parts home—not because he wanted to sell them but merely because he felt he must have them. The parents made it difficult for anyone to help him—not that they weren't well-meaning, even if a bit cold emotionally. I used to explain to Alec's father that my purpose was to try and placate the reasons for his stealing and he would then accuse me of finding excuses for the boy.' Alec was quite intelligent enough to be assisted to see that there were possibly reasons in his past, apart from greed, that made him want to steal; that this knowledge might strengthen his understanding of right and wrong '. . . but his parents couldn't see it and I think they believed I was a little bit unbalanced myself!'

However, Alec was helped, the repressed conflict was eased and there were no more offences; it meant, though, nursing him through several emotional crises and, if the officer had relied on more old-fashioned methods, on discipline and common sense, I suspect the outcome might have been very different.

A more obvious and dramatic example of someone who felt driven to steal is Clive. He had stolen money on numerous occasions, had spent periods in mental hospitals, and was one of those passed back by the psychiatrist as a hopeless psychopath. Not very helpfully the psychiatrist's report suggested that for his own protection as well as society's Clive should not be allowed to take any job where he was likely to handle other people's money or property: the only other recommendation was that everything should be done to impress upon him the futility of trying to use his medical record in order to escape the consequences of his actions. Clive's family were middle-class and he had been sent to a minor public school; he talked lucidly about himself, of his recurring feelings of persecution, and it was not difficult to suppose that he was having to cope with a great emotional turbulence—his haggard young face would continually twitch and smirk ironically: it reflected the violence of his feelings as distinctly as the rattling lid of a boiling kettle. His offences, he admitted, were foolish and made him remorseful; he was always aware of doing wrong but he declared he could never resist the impulse.

Clive's probation history is like a picaresque, angry-young-man novel. He had various jobs as waiter, garage mechanic, door-to-door salesman, window-cleaner. None of them lasted more than a few weeks. Once he got so drunk that he found himself in Tunbridge Wells with no idea how he'd travelled there. Another time he impulsively stole £11 and spent a month in a West Country gaol. Five months later he threw up quite a good job in an office, taking the contents of the till, and hitch-hiked to Scotland. Picked up by the police, he was brought south again; while awaiting trial in prison he was asked by the probation officer how long it had taken him to decide to run off with the money:

'Three minutes—probably less, though it's not the kind of thing you make decisions about. It just happens.'

Hidden in many such impulsive offenders is said to be an unconscious wish for self-punishment. This is a difficult conception for most of us to accept, and one must beware of wrong and facile conclusions, as shown in the case of Simon (Chapter 4), but I have learned enough of irrational behaviour and come across too many cases for which other possible explanations appear even more fanciful, for most of my disbelief to be scattered. Unconscious guilt, or fear that some intense forbidden desire has been inadequately suppressed, can lead to such demanding anxiety and uneasiness that 'nothing less than a token act of expiation can put things right'.[1] Some clients seem able to realize this need, but not its cause, quite consciously.

'In a way I hoped I'd get caught and be punished,' said one

[1] J. D. W. Pearce. *Juvenile Delinquency*, Cassell, 1960 (p. 117).

young man who had just left school and was found guilty of making obscene telephone calls. He admitted to being worried about masturbation.

'Supposing I'd been given the birch, or a long stretch perhaps—it'd been better that way. Made me feel easier, as you might say'.

One girl on probation to Mrs Grieves even went so far as to confess at an interview to having stolen a pair of shoes from a shop, and then, after long questioning, to make a second confession that she had invented the whole story. Everything in her life was going wrong, she sobbed, she was no good and only fit to be locked up.

Some indeed seem to crave prison as a means of expiation, as well as a source of security. Unhappily, not every old lag reacts as well to probation as Chris, the offender with twenty-eight previous convictions introduced in Chapter 5. Many, I suspect, are too severely scarred, or too violently driven by subconscious guilt, or find the demands of normal living too taxing, for them to be still within reach of the kind of help probation can supply. This was the tragedy of someone like Keith who, despite seven previous offences, for the last of which he had served two years' imprisonment, was also given a final chance on probation. A quiet, melancholy man of thirty-four with an underhung jaw, his withdrawn manner camouflaged a good deal of intelligence—he, too, had amassed an almost specialized knowledge of a few unlikely subjects, among them numismatics, comparative religion, and Atlantis, which he would occasionally talk about with the dogmatism sometimes met with among people who have educated themselves without guidance or system. But it was difficult to form any relationship with him: he always called Mr Young 'Sir' and, so to speak, stood mentally at attention throughout his interviews. He would take Mr Young's advice, but it was the passive obedience of those used to years of being ordered about by prison officers: there was never any sense that Keith was co-operating, that he did things because it was for his own good.

For a few months he seemed to be doing all right. He found himself quite a well-paid job with a firm of food processors and Mr Young fixed him up at a small hostel. Yet he must have been very lonely and spent most of his spare time reading books on the occult in the public library; he found it almost impossible to turn an acquaintance into a friend. On two occasions he went through very tense patches, during one of which he disappeared from the hostel and later admitted to a three-day drinking bout in Soho pubs and sleeping with several prostitutes—it was not in character and it appeared that he had driven himself to break out like this. He was ashamed and aware of having behaved stupidly, though he also seemed a little cocky as a result of his bravado, of what he probably considered to be defiance of the hostel warden and the probation officer. Mr Young was careful only to censure him mildly, because he realized that it was a departure, if a despairing one, from his usual habit of unhealthily passive obedience. Yet at a deeper level Keith was humiliated. Those wild dissolute four days filled him with guilt, were a betrayal of all he had read in the public library. He was failing as he had failed so many times before, he could not escape the prison of his loneliness, except for a drunken half-hour in the bed of a prostitute. He became more morose. Segments of his personality wrestled destructively with other segments.

'I tried everything', Mr Young told me, 'but I couldn't get through to him. Except at a superficial level we couldn't communicate. Keith was driven by forces that neither he nor I could have understood. Another disaster seemed inevitable. I tried to warn him but the only effect was to make him call me "Sir" rather more often.'

His next crisis did not release itself in Soho but in an ill-managed robbery of a suburban house. On the day before he did it he rang the office three times but unhappily Mr Young was away all day escorting a client to a mental hospital in the country. Before there was a chance to contact him Keith was in the cells at the police station.

'Keith tried. So did I. But in the end crime must have appeared as the only escape from his personality problems. I cannot define it more closely than that. I doubt if any psychiatrist could put an accurate label to the conflict going on inside him, but I hope someone will try and treat him while he is serving his sentence. There's plenty of time—he's there for seven years.'

Mr Young handed me several sheets of prison notepaper covered with scratchy copperplate. It seems that on paper Keith found it less frightening to express himself.

'In the Encyclopaedia I once came across the old Greek saying "know thyself". You know, sir, that is something I have never learned to do. Often as I lie in my cell I have an object in my mind at a point above me and look down on myself and ask myself what sort of man is that lying there, and I have no idea, none at all.' Another extract: 'The more I think about it, the more life seems to be meaningless and useless. Is it important to God or anyone else that we must live out to the full our time on earth, when the future is all blank? Surely, surely, sir, there must be something on the other side that makes death worth while. If this is true, why should one suffer existence?' In a later letter he wrote: 'Now there is nothing but darkness waiting to be illuminated by the flash of the hydrogen bomb. You see, sir, they don't even fight like men these days. Yes, sir, I have faced death myself and I have seen some good men die. For what? For nothing, absolutely nothing. There it is again, sir, meaningless . . . Have you ever been walking along a road, sir, and suddenly started to cry? That's me, sir. I have never told anyone before, because I was so ashamed. It is true, sir, I often break into tears. Sometimes it is like crying inside. I hope you understand me, sir. It seems there is something inside of me that just wants to burst; and if it would burst I am sure I would be much better for it.'

Keith's pessimistic nihilism may not be very original, but I do not find it difficult to accept that it throws some light on his futile housebreaking. His crimes were surely offsprings of his despair.

V

Some, instead of escaping into prison, invent their own fantasy worlds. Thus another of Mr Young's clients, a young man with a very ordinary background and a very ordinary job, liked to imply that he was really engaged on top secret work, something to do with nuclear energy; he also fancied himself as a writer and explained his offence by saying he needed to mingle with the underworld, to experience their lives in person, for the purposes of his next novel. Perhaps there was some truth in this: it was impossible to tell.

Most of us know how easy it is to start believing in our own untruths. This tendency seems to be exaggerated in many who find themselves in court, quite apart from schizophrenics. They confuse their day-dream world with the real one. Probation officers have to be on the watch for this, though it is sometimes difficult to distinguish it from mundane lying. Alice, one of Miss Lane's clients, was an attractive, likeable example of someone who is frequently difficult to believe yet is not what we normally mean by a liar.

'She once told a girl-friend that I was her half-sister.' Miss Lane gave one of her nostalgic smiles that appeared when she was remembering certain clients. 'Another time I was introduced as the manageress of an employment agency: I was on my way to a home visit when by chance I bumped into Alice and one of her friends. Apparently, not wishing to say who I was, she had impulsively explained that I ran an employment agency and might get the friend a job as a secretary. In the weeks that followed she invented more and more stories about me; naturally the friend wanted to meet me and so poor Alice had to think up a further complex of excuses—I was ill, I'd gone to Newcastle, I was called away to my sick mother . . . She even sent a Christmas card to the girl which was one I'd sent to Alice herself.

'I was always helping to extricate her from this kind of mess. Once when she was short of money, she gave me an elaborately detailed account of how she was knocked over in a bus queue and someone had stolen her purse: there was no truth in it, yet she wasn't trying to get the money for nothing as she had every intention of paying it back, and actually did so. Making up a story like that, and half believing it herself, appeared easier to her than having to admit she had miscalculated her wages.

'Once when she failed to report, she made the familiar excuse about not feeling well but overdid it to the extent of claiming to suffer from a grumbling appendix; to prove this she even went so far as to meet me at the entrance to a hospital where I was given to understand she'd just been examined by a specialist—later I happened to discover she'd been visiting her sister who was in the maternity ward.'

Fantasies, to varying extents, can provide the background against which crimes are committed. Nearly always they disguise emotional insecurity and acute feelings of inadequacy and inferiority. A young man like Peter, who took and drove the Daimler (Chapter 4), was 'living' a fantasy of the world he felt he had a right to belong to. The adolescent delinquent who in a mask and clutching a toy pistol threatens the local tobacconist and demands the contents of the till, for the moment lives his dream of being a ruthless, masculine gangster and thereby reassures himself that he is not as puny as he fears he is—or his father is always telling him he is. The need to do something to overcome the unbearable anxiety that one is inferior to others is the dominant factor behind so many offences—the mechanism is similar to that of the he-man husband in Robert Anderson's *Tea and Sympathy* whose football-loving braggadocio concealed his own unconscious fear that he might be homosexual.

I have seen cases where this particular fear became very conscious and led to an offence intended to offset it. Maurice, for example, who tried to rape a woman he had met through a marriage bureau, confessed to very serious doubts about his own masculinity. In the factory his workmates started to call him 'Pansy' because of his wavy hair and lack of stubble on his chin and, though he had never noticed any homosexual tendencies himself, his lonely misery and panic burst out at the expense of the good lady who was anxious to find a spouse—and, typically, he even bungled the rape.

Looking through my lists of cases and remembering the numerous sullen, aggressive faces I have watched in the courtroom, I realize that self-aggrandisement, over-compensation for self-doubt, is common to many different kinds of crime. The glamour of the tough, male world of crooks as portrayed by films and TV feeds this tendency: what balm to a secret terror of one's own inferiority to be admitted to the local gang of thuggish delinquents, even to mix with people who have done time, which they call 'porridge', to talk big about plans for carrying out bank-raids with the aid of transistor radios and the latest thing in plastic explosives. Here are a few almost random jottings from my notebooks: 'His mother says he likes to show off and look big; she mentions his habit of wearing several sweaters to swell his chest out. Client himself reveals the fact that he is mostly guided in his choice of friends by what they think of him rather than what he thinks of them; he agrees it would be better if he thought more about what kind of person they are and less about what impression he is creating. According to Compton, this young man is putting up a front all the time in order to hide his insecurity; when his guard is lowered he falls back on rationalizing mixed with despair.' Another client 'frequently gets involved in fights. Usual story is that he is insulted and decides to make an issue of it. Admits to a very quick temper. When he suspects anyone is whispering about him or he hears that someone has said a word against him, he has to attack them. Luckily he has the sense not to carry a knife or knuckleduster—says he knows he couldn't resist using it.' The same day I made notes about a first offender who 'attaches much importance to weight-lifting which is probably significant and seems to offset his feelings of inadequacy. He was not the prime instigator of the offence, but due to his self-doubt he is the sort of person who responds too readily to a challenge. He remarks: "Well, I am a failure, aren't I? I was no good at school, I've not found myself a trade, my girl's given me the run-around—that's me all over. Never been anything different. . . ."' A more extreme example, one who might more readily be labelled as clinically pathological, boasted that his father, who was dead, 'came of better stock than his mother. That's why, he says, when they go to the cinema together she always sits in a cheaper seat than he does, why he drinks coffee at Lyons and she drinks tea! He is always talking about what a big guy he is going to be one day. The owner of the ironmonger's shop where he works has just died and he says he wouldn't be surprised if he was left the business under the employer's will.' Fantasy again—in which his mother appeared as an aggravating intrusion.

As well as continuous reassurance and reminders of the real nature of things, I am told it does help, particularly with more intelligent clients, to reveal to them a little of the mechanisms of their behaviour. Unless the forces motivating the client are too deeply submerged in the unconscious, to suggest reasons why they steal or lie can sometimes prevent them from going on doing it—though their intellectual awareness has always to be bolstered with friendship and 'good feeling'. The insecure and self-doubters have in particular to be helped to realize that probation is not intended to punish them, even if it is a nuisance. Ideally, the probation officer holds out to the client the possibility of creating a new self, a more positive identity. The personal, anti-social, negative revolt can be assisted to take more constructive directions—the delinquent and the social reformer are both iconoclasts. The anger of young delinquents and of young Red-brick intellectuals is, one might say, directed against not dissimilar targets in the Establishment; the narrowness of the gulf between the person who chooses stealing to prove himself to himself or make people notice him and the person who finds satisfaction as a progressive and respected borough councillor is one of the more hopeful paradoxes. 'Delinquency lies between a state of being cowed and confident, so that a rebellious lad who is seeking reasonable self-expression against unnatural circumstances at home, unless he is to become a chronic rebel, must either win through to a degree of independence or else capitulate and resign himself to injustice, which may be a less healthy state than rebellion.'[1]

Feelings of inferiority are of course not always over-compensated. Some, as we have seen, avoid close human relations altogether and perhaps find a substitute as did one offender whom I remember for his passionate affection for and understanding of dogs—he even made friends with the police dog who tracked him down! But with every variety of self-doubter the humiliation of the arrest and trial is apt to aggravate their condition. They not only need reassurance: they demand it. On top of their earlier anxieties they now feel called on to make reparation for the offence and this results in a continual seeking of approval—a symptom that can be very trying at the end of a long reporting session. This can be bound up with its apparent opposite—'testing', which was discussed earlier. The show of temper at an interview, the insolent bragging about doubtful associates or exploits with girls, even repeated failures to report, can be interpreted as a desperate wish to be accepted and liked, because in a twisted way it is a compliment to a probation officer to show that you do not fear him; testing is usually a healthier sign than cowed, over-respectful obedience.

[1] Dr Peter Scott, who is in charge of the clinics for offenders, at the Maudsley Hospital; quoted in *Psychological Disorder and Crime* by W. Lindesay Neustatter. Christopher Johnson, 1953 (p. 239).

VI

Most of the characteristics discussed in the last few pages are, of course, symptoms and, more often than the doctor, a probation officer is limited, one must admit, to palliating these; he helps his clients counteract them, to recognize them and adjust themselves in a positive way to their basic inner disturbance. It is not practicable to think in terms of a complete rebuilding of a personality. The more limited process, though, can be very effective, though even this is helped by seeking the forces that have caused the personality to be disturbed. With others, particularly juveniles and adolescents, there can be a greater hope of promoting basic changes. Far more probationers can be described as maladjusted rather than psychotic or severely neurotic, and so once again emphasis is on learning about the offender's early background, his relationships with parents, brothers, sisters, and other relatives.

It may be coupled with other factors, but emotional deprivation as a child rears up like a relentless spectre at every turn in the argument. My selection of cases has not been weighted scientifically and those placed on probation are not necessarily typical of offenders as a whole, but I have scarcely come across a case where there is not, in some degree or other, an unhappy family history: it may be a divorce or continuous quarrelling between the parents, or the death of one or other parent, or an unsympathetic stepfather or stepmother, or separation as an infant from the mother—if some such element is lacking, you notice it. All this may be very obvious, even laboured—and I need hardly add that to be deprived in some way as a child does not necessarily lead to delinquency—but the study and understanding of the effects on the personality caused by deprivation (to use the word generically) and the social maladjustment it can lead to provides the basis for many successful techniques of psychological treatment. It has already had and is still having a radical influence on the technique of probation, and we must therefore take up the dangling threads left at the end of the last chapter and examine it more thoroughly.

Following the teaching of August Aichhorn, Käthe Friedlander, J. Bowlby, and many others, an extensive literature has grown up on this subject, to which the reader is referred, and I shall limit myself to describing what seem to me a few of the commonest features of maladjustment as I have observed them in actual cases. One of the effects of deprivation in childhood—it can also be true of its opposite, over-indulgence—is to thwart the development of some of the elements in the personality. If a boy, for example, loses his father or has a stepfather whom he dislikes and who dislikes him, his moral sense, his code of behaviour (the super-ego), is likely to be retarded. (This is the opposite to George [Chapter 3] whose super-ego was not retarded, but whose parents provided him with a super-ego of the wrong type.) The growth of an understanding and belief in right and wrong is best nourished by strong emotional relationships. A retardation of one element in the personality can distort the whole structure—like missing bricks in a wall. This is another way of saying that the person fails to mature. The extent to which this can happen varies—he may be too self-centred, unrealistic, aggressively cocksure, unable to grow out of his childhood tantrums, or show some of the other symptoms mentioned earlier; immaturity can be said to make the individual more susceptible to delinquency. With the immature personality the assaults, stealings, and anti-social behaviour expected and to some extent condoned in the nursery are apt to persist in adulthood.

The psychological mechanisms of delinquency are, however, more complicated than this: the deprivation (or over-indulgence) in childhood, or maybe it is merely a faulty child-parent relationship, is thought also to result in a deep, unsatisfied need and to set up a conflict, a pattern of unhappiness and dissatisfaction in the child's mind that eventually—usually in adolescence—can no longer be borne. The 'child ends the difficulty by resolving, as it were, to forget the need, to do without the gratification, to disown the whole thing; he does not want it any more. He shuts it "out of his mind", but this is a misleading phrase as one cannot shut anything out of mind. One can only shut it in. So what he does is to banish it from his awareness; in other words, he shuts it out of consciousness.'[1] The repression is not always complete and is only maintained by the waking personality adopting a contrary attitude of mind—instead of wanting to be loved or to love, he becomes tough, hostile, anti-social. 'The usual history is that when he was younger, the child's need for love, appreciation and valuation was hopelessly and constantly unsatisfied. He may have been the illegitimate son of his mother, whom some man other than his father later married. There is a row of half-siblings. He remains the object of his stepfather's hatred and the ever-present reminder of his mother's lapse from virtue. Year in and year out, being persevering and of a robust temperament, he does his utmost to please, to win favour, to gain some token of affection: but throughout he fails and his unhappiness is intense. The situation eventually becomes intolerable and he realizes the hopelessness of his struggle. Rather than admit defeat, as these youngsters never do, he decides that he does not want the parental love, or indeed any love from anybody. He will no longer be dependent, he is self-sufficient. He will show them. So he represses the whole need for love and appreciation and tenderness, and he becomes independent, anti-social, hostile to his parents and to all authority. His personality undergoes a profound reversal. From being a sensitive child, seeking affection, trying to find acceptance as a member of the family group, he changes into a hard, self-contained callous delinquent.'[2]

Crime in this kind of case represents an attempt by the offender to relieve inner tension, to reach adjustment—with his own inner

[1] J. D. W. Pearce, ibid. (p. 183).
[2] ibid. (p. 184).

dissatisfaction and misery and, very often, with his home circumstances. Conversely, to refrain from crime, to give up being tough and unpleasant, means recognizing once again the need for affection and the misery associated with its absence. Often it is the strong intelligent temperament that reacts by turning delinquent; others with less robustness remain cowed and meekly depressed. This short account of a complex theory must not conceal the possible variations either of the faulty child-parent relationship or of its results : thus the 'teenager with a dominating, over-protective mother forgets his oppressive feelings of inferiority in outbursts of self-assertion that may be difficult to control; another compensates for his lack of affection by stealing.

Money, in particular, appears as a symbol of love. Sometimes the person from whom the money or object is stolen is significant: it can be a wish to punish or revenge, or maybe it is a subjective desire to own something belonging to someone admired or loved. One of Mr Young's clients, who had spent most of his childhood in orphanages, was twelve when he discovered that his mother was still alive. He was elated when he first went to live with her, but she was more interested in gentlemen friends and Babychams than an illegitimate son, and failed to hide that she considered him a nuisance. Disillusioned, he left home as soon as he was old enough. His offence was to steal four £5 notes and a gold-plated clock. It was not difficult to believe him when he said he was horrified by the theft and that he was at a loss to understand what made him do it, but it was probably not without significance that the lady he stole from was not unlike his mother in age and habits.

As is to be expected, 'institutionalized' children often provide the clearest examples of the effects of deprivation. Later this same young man committed another offence and wrote pathetically to Mr Young from prison : '. . . When I go to court I am going to ask them to send me to a home. I did not like to say it to you before, or to anyone, but I feel I must now. I am overcome with lonesomeness. All my life has been in institutions. I am not able to face the outside world. . . . I want your help but I don't know how to ask for it. You understand what it is to be brought up and loved by a Mum and Dad. I don't and will never know . . .'

Stealing in order to punish someone came out very distinctly in the case of sixteen-year-old Humphrey Evans, on probation to Mr Compton: 'He even put it into words. I noted them verbatim on his record: "Well, sir, I wanted to hurt her." When I suggested to Humphrey that perhaps he felt a need to punish his mother for his feeling that she had let him down by remarrying, he nodded.'

The theft and Humphrey's difficult behaviour generally could only be interpreted as a reaction to his feelings of emotional insecurity, which had originated when he was very much younger, and as an attempt to stifle his worry about his own illegitimacy and his dissatisfaction with his stepfather—the latter feeling could be interpreted as a mixture both of rational dislike and a reversal of his need to be wanted and loved.

'When I served the probation order, I went through some of the information contained in the report to the court, so that he should get an idea of what I knew about him. I ended the interview, as I usually do when they come for the first time, by asking if he had any questions. "Yes," he replied immediately. "You can tell me why I'm called Evans and not Johnson." I explained what he knew already, that his father had been drowned at sea—his ship was torpedoed on convoy duties across the Atlantic—and that as the tragedy happened before he was born, it was understandable, when his mother remarried, he should take the name of his stepfather, Evans. His reply to this was: "I never asked her to marry him, did I." He then pulled out a very worn photograph of a man in merchant seaman's uniform. "Can you see the likeness?" he wanted to know anxiously. "I think we have the same kind of mouth. His eyes were brown like mine. He was good at metalwork, too. Always making things, Mother once told me. Model ships and things like that . . ."

'The next day I visited his mother. She confirmed that things had never been easy between Humphrey and her husband. She was ready to agree, too, that it was largely the stepfather's fault and that Mr Evans was also apt to be jealous of their own two little girls—Humphrey's stepsisters. On the other hand she was unable to accept any criticism of herself. She said she was puzzled why Humphrey should want to know more about his past. Though his birth certificate bore the name Johnson, she had thought it best to call him Evans, because of the neighbours, because she didn't want people to talk . . . because she and Humphrey's father had not been properly married—not in the eyes of the law. I had obviously touched some pretty sensitive spots as, telling me all this, she became tearfully angry and accused me of being unkind to stir up unhappy memories. She blamed Humphrey's father for having deserted her—almost, I felt, for getting himself drowned—but was quick to resent my suggestion that she might, without knowing it, resent Humphrey's existence.

'She refused to recognize that there could be any connection between Humphrey's behaviour and her own, that it was the result of his home experiences. It was very difficult to get her to see that he had an idealized picture of the father he had never seen, with which Mr Evans, the unprepossessing stepfather, could only be compared very unfavourably; that what Humphrey was doing was to say: "I don't want to be Evans, I want to be Johnson." '

Mr Compton did his best to relieve some of the tension in the home and to get the boy to recognize his true feelings of anger against his stepfather; bottled up, they would always be liable to express themselves in temper or some form of bad behaviour. But the question of the name was still the magnetic pole for Humphrey's resentment.

'One afternoon Mrs Evans, Humphrey's mother, complained that one of his friends, a boy she'd never met before, had spoken to her as Mrs Johnson. Evidently Humphrey had started to call himself by his real name. I seized the opportunity of saying that just as she didn't like being called Johnson, so did Humphrey dislike being Evans. She said nothing much at the time, but the point had gone home. On my next visit she told me that she and her husband had talked the whole thing over and they were prepared to agree to Humphrey having his own way over the name. It would take some living-down with the neighbours and they couldn't see why he made such a fuss over it, but it was worth a try—"anything to keep him out of more trouble with the police." '

In the circumstances and for such a family it must have been an audacious decision. It was also a successful one, because from then onwards Humphrey became unmistakably happier, less bitter and more tolerant of his stepfather.

'As is so often the way, the improvement first showed itself by his reporting becoming less regular. To begin with he had needed me as an ally. He would come to the office at least once a week and took no notice when I suggested that a fortnightly visit would be sufficient. Now he could do without me. Forgetfulness about reporting, remember, can be an indication of reform, of growing self-reliance.'

Few cases, unfortunately, offer the possibility of such a dramatically simple cure and even in this instance, in order to make my point, I have understated the quantity of sympathy, insight, and patience Mr Compton expended on this family. Humans, unlike machines, do not automatically restart functioning properly when the disrupting spanner is removed. The damage to the personality is, at best, only slowly overcome.

The concern and significance which the individual—and society—usually attaches to his or her parental origin may be extravagant but it is very real. A sudden, unexpected discovery of one's own illegitimacy, for example, can upset a relatively mature personality. I know of one very persistent offender, a middle-aged lady with plenty of the right sort of 'background', whose habit of petty pilfering dated back to the age of nineteen, when she was informed during a quarrel with her stepmother that her real mother had not been married. Up to that moment her conduct had been more or less normal. It seems that the shock was so severe and damaging that at times she could only find comfort by secretly hoarding small items like toothbrushes, ash-trays, inkstands, and paper-knives belonging to other people. Mr Young told me of a similar case, a young man whose stealing dated back two years when he discovered by accident that he had been adopted: the offence for which he was arrested—a clumsy attempt to rob a prostitute—occurred the night before his foster parents emigrated to New Zealand. Was this an attempt to punish them by causing them shame, an effort to gain their pity, merely an act of despair—or none of these things? Emotional, traumatic, shock was an element in both these offenders, but there may well also have been an earlier history of unsatisfactory parent–child relationships which up to the moment of distressing revelation had been insufficient to generate an offence, though it made them, so to speak, susceptible to delinquency.

Impoverishing early relationships, capable of preventing the growth of a realistic acceptance of the demands of civilized living and the needs of others, can occur—though this is almost too obvious to need saying—with parents who are one's own, who are not divorced, or who do not quarrel overtly; just as step-parents, foster-parents, widowed or deserted parents are able to bring up children who show no signs of maladjustment. Whether or not the home set-up is overtly normal, an adolescent's sense of deprivation and rejection is apt to be effectively suppressed and masked—over-compensated—by rebellious independence, by an attitude of 'don't care' defiance. It can amount to a recognizable, psychological disorder—though this does not necessarily mean that the client will receive professional psychiatric treatment—and is a condition that is apt to worsen under harshness and discipline; in extreme cases the individual may degenerate into a difficult recidivist, boastful of being a public enemy. On the other hand, it must be again stressed that plenty of adolescent rebellion is normal, is merely a striving after independence, and is certainly not pathological, and that a good proportion of juvenile delinquency comes within this category. The frontier between what are in the main misguided reactions to difficulties at home or resulting from the ordinary strains of growing-up, and the behaviour due to psychological disorder and maladjustment is, however, very blurred. In everyday practice it is impossible in many cases for a probation officer to decide on which side of this frontier they fall, and anyway such a subtle diagnosis is likely to be academic, because at the level at which probation is able to work, even in the hands of the most psychologically inclined officers, the treatment of both categories is not likely to differ greatly.

VII

Though modern probation casework is imbued with psychological concepts, though its officers can be said to apply what are generally termed 'mild' psychotherapeutic techniques, it is not their job to operate full-scale psychotherapy, let alone psychoanalysis. They are not qualified to go this far and it could be very dangerous if they attempted to do so. Full-scale psychotherapy is likely to involve bringing to the surface deeply repressed hatreds, fears, jealousies, and, if the unravelling takes place too rapidly and without very expert guidance, severe harm can be done to the patient. A frequent procedure in psychotherapy is to encourage the patient to 'regress', in other words to retrace his emotional development to the point where things started to go wrong, and only when he has made some contact with his unconscious conflicts, does the reintegration process begin. This summary of a galaxy of complex techniques is grossly oversimplified, but it is sufficient to show that, quite apart from being as potentially dangerous as a dentist's drill in untrained hands, psychotherapy can run directly counter, at any rate in its early stages, to probation. Psychotherapy, as practised for example in some special schools for disturbed children, is a method that makes them worse before it can make them better; the process of releasing unconscious conflicts is only too likely *temporarily* to lead to outbursts of acute 'testing', actually to increase delinquency. Probation, on the other hand, is essentially a technique of re-education, of inculcating self-discipline, of helping the offender to master or at least control his irrational drives—unravelling them is beyond the scope of its ambitions—even though, as will be explained later, further offences, provided they are not too serious, are frequently condoned if the probation officer judges that there has been an over-all improvement in behaviour and attitude.

Despite this fundamental contradiction, probation and psychotherapy do have much in common. Like the psychotherapist, the probation officer makes use of various methods of persuasion and suggestion, he helps people to understand themselves better, to mobilize the healthy elements in their personalities, and he 'accepts' the negative elements. Even with clients who do not merit treatment by a psychiatrist—at any rate by present-day standards—his own attitude and technique rest on the assumption that crime can be some form of escape from emotional distress, a compensation for anxiety, a reflection of inner despair.

Owing partly to the paucity of psychiatric facilities available to the service, partly to different attitudes among magistrates, and partly to different standards of diagnosis, a proportion only of maladjusted, deprived cases receive professional psychiatric treatment, usually at an out-patient centre—the proportion among delinquent children and adolescents is apt to be much higher. The results are encouraging. The Portman Clinic, for example, attached to the Institute for the Study and Treatment of Delinquency 'carries an annual case-load of over 900, of whom 500 are new cases. Every variety of psychological treatment, either of individuals or groups, is employed and, although complete psycho-analysis is rarely carried out, an analytic approach is commonly applied in short treatment. The average duration of treatment necessary to bring about satisfactory changes is surprisingly short, running to about twelve sessions spread over a few weeks or months and ranging from a few advisory interviews to courses of about 150 sessions. The results as checked by after-histories are very satisfactory and the treatment of young psychopaths, at one time the bogey of the psychotherapist, is undertaken with considerable confidence.'[1] The methods of group therapy pioneered by the social rehabilitation unit at Belmont hospital are also very hopeful.

But many offenders remain the sole responsibility of the probation officer, and even with those attending clinics he carries most of the day-to-day burden: I think it would be quite misleading to talk of the probation officer as supplementing the work of the psychiatrist, though they do have affinities with psychiatric social workers. An analysis of the psychological health of a large, typical sample of probation cases, if such a thing were possible, would be likely to show the paradoxical result that probation officers have sole responsibility both for those clients whose degree of mental disturbance is not sufficiently severe to merit psychiatric treatment (or who refuse to co-operate with the psychiatrist) and for those whose disturbance is too severe to benefit from it.

It follows that many officers believe there is a need not only to enlarge the psychiatric facilities available to the service but also for more officers with psychological training. This at once raises the question of what brand of psychology? But the answer would appear to be that 'modern psychology has moved away from the position of different "schools" towards the direction of an accepted body of knowledge, supported by experimental evidence, which includes the hypotheses of psycho-analysis';[2] to which one might add W. H. Auden's lines on Freud:[3]

> 'To us he is no more a person
> 'Now but a climate of opinion . . .'

[1] Edward Glover, ibid. (p. 21).

[2] D. R. Price-Williams. 'The Place of Psychology in Social Work', *Case Conference*, September 1956.

[3] 'In Memory of Sigmund Freud,' in *Another Time*, Faber & Faber, 1940 (p. 118).

Undoubtedly danger must lie in any approach to psychology that is too eclectic and Freud's theory, for example, is all too easily blunted and 'cosily' oversimplified—that this should happen is presumably inherent in its disturbing implications? It is worth recalling, too, the warning of the late Professor Alexander Kennedy[1] that: 'As Appleton has said, a theory is only an hypothesis that has become respectable. No one has put this better than Sigmund Freud (1949) who was well aware of the purely empirical purpose of his constructs: "The future may teach us how to exercise a direct influence by means of particular chemical substances upon the amounts of energy and their distribution in the apparatus of the mind. It may be that there are other undreamt-of possibilities of therapy. But for the moment we have nothing better at our disposal than the technique of psycho-analysis, and for that reason, in spite of its limitations, it is not to be despised." ' There are dangers, certainly, in ill-digested, over-enthusiastic acceptance of psycho-analytical theory, but at the level of watered-down application aimed at in probation case-work there are likely to be few disagreements over doctrine.

Most probation officers are, as already described, in touch with psychiatrists who, in addition to making diagnoses and treating certain clients, are available with advice and support in the handling of more disturbed clients. Some groups of officers meet regularly together with a psychiatrist to discuss certain cases and, equally important, their own attitudes towards them. I attended one of these group discussions which took place at fortnightly intervals under the guidance of a resident psychiatrist at a near-by mental hospital. A woman of perhaps fifty, she wore a flowered chiffon dress, her grey hair beautifully set, herself an object lesson in reassurance, yet she presided with shrewdly watching eyes and her questions, though seemingly casual, were as pointed and barbed as a bullfighter's *banderilla*.

'Why, I wonder, didn't you bring this case up with us before?' she asked with soft insistence. 'You've told us that it was too big a

[1] *The Lancet*, 11 June 1960.

thing for you to manage by yourself. Your reason could be important.'

The procedure was for one of the six officers present to outline in some detail a case which was causing him particular difficulty and for the others to criticize his handling of it and to make helpful suggestions. The main item that day was a peculiarly nauseating case of sexual perversion involving a child; the client had just been sent to prison for a further offence. It was complicated by the case having been transferred from another area and by an administrative muddle over records which had led the probation officer who had taken it over to underestimate the potential danger to the child. Personally I could not see how he could have done any more than he did, because until the second arrest there were plenty of reasons for thinking that further trouble was unlikely, but the psychiatrist was now implying that there might be an unconscious weakness in the probation officer; she spent a long time probing him, forcing him to re-examine his own attitude towards the case, to take the measure of his own revulsion, to explain to us and to himself any reasons for hesitating to assess the client accurately. The session ended with intelligible, but tactfully cautious, suggestions for how such a case ought to be handled.

This kind of group session can be very helpful, not only because it is a channel for expert advice, but also because it supplements in a deeper, more systematic way the sharing of difficulties and the support most officers obtain when talking shop over office cups of tea or waiting outside court between cases. But the experience can be very unpleasant, almost as gruelling and demanding as psycho-analysis, if it means getting into touch with one's own repressed anxieties.

VIII

Though a psychiatrist may investigate much deeper levels of the client's personality, his range is by no means as wide as that of the probation officer who is also concerned with a spouse or parents, the client's job, sparetime interests, his friends, the house and street he lives in. The psychiatrist may take cognizance of these factors, but his main concern is the client's unconscious and the structure of his psyche; the probation officer as well as helping to ease the client's feelings of guilt, tenseness, and anxiety, is able, as we have seen, to help him to change his circumstances, to ward off external as well as internal causes of stress. In a much wider sense his function is prophylactic—particularly if the client has children of his own. For me the most depressing feature of so many cases is that the client repeats the very pattern—or one very similar—which caused his own maladjustment. The Wilson family are one of the many examples I have collected of this ominous chain-reaction:

Clive, aged eleven, was under supervision for stealing four packets of potato crisps, 'borrowing' a school-friend's satchel, and because of his persistent truanting. He had a very lively, comical little face and an intelligence quotient above average, but his teachers reported that he had frightening outbursts of temper and you noticed at once the pallor and indefinable appearance of muscular flaccidity seen in many deprived children. It was not difficult to find reasons for his delinquency, because his father was also on probation for some petty larceny complicated by a threatened assault on a couple who lived in a neighbouring council flat. There were two other children: Wendy (5) and Patricia (3). As Mrs Wilson was keen on 'gadding to the pictures', it very often fell to Mr Wilson to give the three children their tea and see them into bed.

'As soon as I get home, she's off. Says she's fed-up with being stuck all day in the flat. More often than not she leaves me nothing . . . nobbut a bit of bread and cheese—maybe a kipper if I'm lucky. I'm nothing but a skivvy, the way she treats me . . .'

Mr Wilson, a heavy, lumbering builder's labourer, was slow in speech and had to be allowed to follow his thought through to the end. It came out that he had an additional reason for resentment, because as a child himself he had been expected to look after his younger stepbrothers and stepsisters: his own father had died and when his mother remarried he often felt himself to be rejected, the odd one out, the scapegoat for everything that went wrong. Being expected to do so much as a husband reactivated his childhood unhappiness and frustration. He admitted that his own temper sometimes frightened him and said nothing when Mrs Wilson complained that he often struck her.

It was difficult to decide who was the most inadequate: he was always accusing her—with every reason—of letting the flat get filthy and of not washing or feeding the children properly; she—with equal reason—grumbled that he was always being laid off work because he refused to get up in the mornings. He would accuse her of allowing other men 'mess her about' and of always 'wanting it', while she grumbled that whenever she was pregnant he brought 'some bitch or other back to the flat'. Their hatred for each other was horrifying yet you felt they were locked together by some primitive sense of dependence which, I suppose, might be called 'affection'. Mr Wilson was perhaps the weaker of the two and was jealous of the children's claims on his wife, neglected though they were.

Having failed themselves to mature, having known little love from their own parents, they did not understand how to give it to their children. The fears, tempers, jealousies, defiance implanted in them during their own upbringing were now projected on to Clive, Wendy, and Patricia. Mrs Wilson was always threatening to have Clive sent off to 'one of those approved schools' and the only paternal guidance the boy could expect was a slap across the head.

In the end the children's officer had to be brought in. On the evening he called, Mrs Wilson was as usual at the pictures; Mr Wilson was asleep half-dressed in a bed with a saturated mattress —he had never overcome his enuresis—while Clive read a comic and the two little girls played on the floor. Their game, Wendy said, was called 'mothers and fathers'. They were both filthy. Patricia's dress was damp, her eyes looked sore, her hair was matted and appeared verminous. Wendy was only wearing a vest and knickers and a red mark on her leg looked like a recent burn. Neither would stop crying. . . .

Wendy and Patricia were placed in a residential nursery and Clive went to a special boarding-school. For a while their physical needs would be better supplied and they would, one hopes, be treated with understanding and receive a substitute brand of parental love. Perhaps it was not too late, but I find myself trying to imagine what *their* children, the grandchildren, will be like.

Children even of families like the Wilsons can be remarkably resilient and, as Lady Wootton has pointed out, 'the self-perpetuating quality of the problem family still remains to be proved or disproved',[1] yet there can be no doubt that the absence of love in childhood, or faults in its quality, is the greatest single cause of crime, for it can be detected in many of the offences where the dominant factor lies in the client's circumstances or in other people. To the child love is as essential as sunlight. Its lack is felt in families that are better ordered than the Wilsons and with parents who themselves appear well adjusted. They must not only provide love but be able to communicate it.

I have given much of this chapter to adolescents because with them the connection between crime and maladjustment, crime and mental or emotional disturbance can be demonstrated more clearly and immediately than in adult cases, because the cause of the trouble within themselves is less deeply overlaid. With children the frontier is even more difficult to detect: truancy and bed-wetting, thieving and anxiety and nightmares, playground

[1] *Social Science and Social Pathology* (p. 60).

assaults and temper tantrums and immaturity, are inseparably joined—the same thing reflected in different mirrors. It follows that the earlier that maladjustment can be discovered and treated, the greater are the chances that criminal tendencies will be diverted: with adolescence the personality has already started to become less malleable.

Probation officers in effect try to stifle the early growths of crime in two different, but closely related ways: by their work in the juvenile courts and as marriage counsellors. A sizable part of the Service is always occupied in these two branches. In England and Wales it handles something like 70,000 new matrimonial cases a year, the majority of which have no connection with any criminal offence. In most juvenile court areas the probation officer features in a high proportion of cases, including those concerning children in need of care and protection; children who have committed no offence but who are placed under the probation officer's supervision because they are beyond their parents' control. A special section carries out investigations into which parent should be given custody of the children on behalf of judges in the divorce courts . . . the field is too large and too important and the techniques used with children—though in essence similar to those I have described for adolescents—are too specialized to be fitted comfortably in the space left to me. The same is even truer of marriage reconciliation which, even though it is related so closely to my central argument, lies outside the scope of this book.

8

Yardsticks for Success—and Failure

*

TO reach any conclusions about the general effectiveness of probation, either in isolation or compared with other forms of penal disposal, such as Borstal, corrective training, or preventive detention, is very much more difficult than at first may appear. The figures available are surprisingly meagre and in any case require complex analysis and qualification. They have to be related to the curative purpose of probation, to the tolerance extended to many probationers in deciding what amounts to a breach of the order, to the probation officer's dual function as caseworker and court official, to differing conceptions of morality and individual responsibility. But to start with, here are the essential statistics.

The most recent and most illuminating survey to date is that carried out by the Department of Criminal Science at Cambridge University under the leadership of Professor L. Radzinowicz. To avoid complication and too many figures I shall on the whole confine myself to its findings. Their report, published in 1958, surveyed 9,336 probationers in London and Middlesex whose orders terminated in 1948, 1949, and 1950. Two stages in the probationers' progress were distinguished: the first covered the actual period of the probation order, the second covered a follow-up period of three years, starting with the order's termination. The cases were divided into adults and juveniles, males and females, and the information collected enabled a variety of

[1] *The Results of Probation*, Macmillan, 1958.

aspects of probation to be studied which provides interesting comparisons, e.g. the success achieved with first offenders and those who had previous convictions. Though the figures are some ten years out of date and relate only to a small part of the country, the sample was sufficiently large to be statistically significant and the general findings are almost certainly still valid. I shall reproduce only a few of the key percentages here but the reader who wishes to pursue the subject more deeply is warmly recommended to study the full report. Of great interest also is the report prepared for the United Nations by Dr Max Grünhut which contains a valuable comparison of the results of probation in different countries.[1]

The first major conclusion brought to light by the Cambridge inquiry was that as many as 79 per cent of the adults and 73 per cent of the juveniles, under seventeen years old, completed their probation successfully. This means that none of these was brought again before a court for a breach of the order for a further offence during the period of supervision. This lasted anything between one and three years. When the more rigorous criterion of the three-year follow-up period was added, the success rate, as one might expect, fell slightly, but for 70 per cent of the adults and 57 per cent of the juveniles probation proved to be successful 'in the strictest sense of the term'. When the figures are broken down further, the chances of success are shown to improve with increasing age (58 to 74 per cent for males; 73 to 88 per cent for females) and that the general success rate for females turns out to be quite considerably higher than that for males (83 as against 64 per cent). The better results for females, according to Dr Grünhut, '. . . is not entirely a reflection of the well-known fact that women figure low in any criminal statistics based on court cases. It seems as if the deeper cause of much of the criminality of women has to be sought in personal conflicts and

[1] *Practical Results and Financial Aspects of Probation in Selected Countries*, United Nations, New York, 1954.

social difficulties which make women particularly susceptible to the probation officer's help.'[1]

Though the general success rate falls rapidly depending upon the number of previous convictions (72·4 per cent for first offenders; 60·3 per cent for those with one previous conviction; 49·0 per cent for those with two or more), the findings of the Cambridge report are, I believe, reasonably encouraging, particularly when it is recalled that a certain minimum percentage of failures is implied in the risk taken with every offender who is put on probation. To those unfamiliar with the discouraging reality of criminal statistics these percentages may appear alarming, but it is necessary to compare them with the reconviction rates recorded for other forms of disposal. To make the comparisons valid they need to be broken down into age-groups. When this is done, the similarity in the different reconviction rates is at once evident and startling:

RECONVICTION RATES (PER CENT) FOR FIRST OFFENDERS IN ENGLAND AND WALES

Age	*Imprisonment*	*Supervision by probation officer*	*Dismissed or bound over without supervision*	*Fined*
16–17	24·7	35·5	26·3	21·7
18–20	29·4	29·8	24·2	23·9
21–24	28·8	29·3	22·1	19·8
25–29	22·4	28·2	19·8	20·1
30–39	16·4	22·3	13·7	14·7
40 & over	9·6	11·8	9·9	10·8

These figures were published[2] by the Home Office as long ago as 1938, but a similar (unpublished) comparative survey for Scottish offenders in 1947 showed remarkably parallel results. A more up-to-date and accurate confirmation of this tendency has also been provided by the Home Office's statistical research unit. Advantage was taken of the large variations in the sentencing

[1] ibid. (p. 19).
[2] *Criminal Statistics, England and Wales, 1938.* Cmd. 6167 (p. xxvi).

policy of different courts to compare ninety-seven cases sentenced in 1952 at a court of quarter sessions which made frequent use of probation (in 52 per cent of its cases) with cases from a control area whose use of it (in 18 per cent of the cases) was closer to the national average.[1] As far as possible each of the ninety-seven cases was 'matched' by an identical case from the central area and, as in the Cambridge report, the cases were followed-up for three or more years. The findings were that the frequency of reconviction was almost identical; in other words similar cases show similar results irrespective of the sentence, whether it be probation or prison or Borstal.[2]

This fits in with the theory that many people grow out of crime, just as they grow out of other bad habits, regardless of the treatment they are given. A parallel can also be drawn with Professor H. J. Eysenck's[3] suggestion that whether or not treated by psychotherapy similar proportions of patients grow out of or adjust themselves to their neuroses. If further authority is needed, one can turn to Dr Grünhut who, writing of first offenders, remarks: '. . . the outstanding majority of first offenders become law-abiding citizens again. Crime and punishment remain one unrepeated experience in their lives. This fact seems to be established with regard to whatever treatment has been awarded for the offender's first crime. Whether the absence of further offences is due to the treatment, occurs independently of the treatment or even in spite of the treatment, no statistics can tell. If one compares the reconviction rates of the various modes of penal and

[1] Leslie T. Wilkins. 'A Small Comparative Study of the Results of Probation', *British Journal of Delinquency*, January 1958.

[2] It is very possible that the further conviction of ex-probationers is more frequently for petty offences compared with those committed by ex-prisoners; also that there tends to be a longer interval before the ex-probationer commits the further offence. The exact importance to be attached to these qualifications must depend on further research.

[3] Does Psychotherapy Cure Neurotic Disorders?' *New Scientist*, 16 May 1957 (pp. 12–14).

correctional treatment with one another, the results seem not too favourable to probation.'[1]

All these rather damping conclusions and findings can be interpreted in two ways. On the one hand they suggest that probation is no better than prison or Borstal when it comes to assessing the long-term result, its rates of eventual success and failure as a means of reform; on the other hand they suggest that the use of probation for a large proportion of offenders whom many courts send to prison would not entail any greater risk to society, in that there is likely to be no increase in the risk of reconviction. When considered merely in terms of national economics, the advantages of using probation instead of adding another inmate to a chronically overcrowded prison or Borstal institution are impressive: the average cost to the nation of keeping an offender on probation for one year has never been worked out, but in one area it has been calculated that this comes to about £26; this compares with an average annual figure of £400[2] for prisons, Borstals, and detention centres—a difference of fifteen to one is thought to be conservative and a very 'safe' estimate with the information available. This takes no account of the cost of maintaining a prisoner's family at public expense, or of a probationer's contribution to the community in terms of production or services, which is likely to be considerably higher than the value of his work in prison, sewing mail-bags, etc. When assessed also in human terms, the advantages of probation are overwhelming: the offender is reformed without the unhappiness and degradation of gaol; his future and that of his dependents are free from the taint inseparable from a prison record.

[1] ibid. (p. 13).

[2] The average annual cost per inmate (excluding the cost of new buildings, building maintenance, etc.) is: prisons, £368. 2s. 11d; Borstals, £574. 9s. 4d; detention centres, £562. 9s. 1d; all establishments, £399. 19s. 7d. *Report of the Commissioners of Prisons, 1959*. Cmd. 1117 (p. 174).

II

Probation, then, would seem to be not only as effective as prison or Borstal but also cheaper and more humane. Though at first sight the Home Office's findings may be disappointing, they do amount to an argument in favour of a great increase in the use of probation that only the most revengeful are likely to wish to refute. Statistical rates of success and failure, however, even when subjected to painstaking qualification and analysis, can only provide us with very incomplete answers. No criminal statistics have yet been devised which reflect adequately human idiosyncrasies—or human irrationality. To say this, is not the same as adopting the comforting, all too prevalent, Philistine viewpoint that 'statistics can be made to prove anything', or to dismiss them when they point to results that are not as satisfactory as one might have hoped. The crucial reckoning, as with the elucidation of the causes of a crime, must be made in terms of each individual. The very words 'success' and 'failure' need precise clarification—in fact a different one each time. Statistical success, the mere absence of a further charge, does not necessarily mean that the client has been reformed. Every probation officer knows of clients who, he is convinced, notwithstanding their own assurances, a lack of direct evidence, and their non-reappearance in court, are still entangled in crime; or are living and behaving in such a way that proves the treatment is having no effect, and that at the termination of the order they will be no better equipped to cope with their difficulties than they were at its start; that the second chance is not being taken. Miss Lane, I remember, had a girl who on her reporting visits could scarcely resist flaunting her dishonestly gotten clothes and furs. A casual call-girl, originally convicted of decoying men into a 'club' where they were systematically robbed and threatened by her male partner (who got four years), she now spoke of a wealthy fiancé who was something in the City—'to do with money and shares and things like that.' Miss Lane who had once spotted this fiancé from the office window, escorting her probationer at the conclusion of an interview, had a different opinion of his profession. Yet, statistically, this girl went down as one of probation's successes.

It would be misleading and wrong to imply that many of the successes are phoney, because sooner rather than later a high percentage of the probationers who continue to offend are likely to get caught. Much more important than the phoney success is its corollary: the partial failure—not only because these are more numerous but because a reappearance in court, even the revocation of the order, does not necessarily mean that probation was a mistake. The Cambridge research team made this very clear[1] '. . . nearly 8 per cent of the total had been found guilty of a breach of the order or the commission of a further offence and yet were kept on probation by a continuation or extension of the period of supervision.' As might be expected '. . . among those whose initial response to probation was unfavourable, a greater proportion continued to commit offences, and for them the rate of success dropped to 73 per cent'—compared with 81 per cent for all adult first offenders put on probation. For juveniles and recidivists comparable success rates are lower, but are nevertheless 48 per cent and 57 per cent respectively.

With quite a few clients further offences can mask a basic reform and even be an inevitable step in the process of coming to terms with themselves. A positive, overall trend of improvement in the case-record can outweigh in importance the lapse or even a succession of lapses. An experienced probation officer can interpret a case-record with a facility not all that dissimilar from that with which a chartered accountant 'reads' a series of balance sheets or a meteorologist interprets a barometric chart, though the troughs of depression and peaks of high pressure are apt to appear more frequently during the first six months or so and represent

[1] ibid. (pp. 9–10).

the client's struggle both with himself and with the probation officer. Once these struggles have been resolved the case-record usually becomes uneventful. Sometimes a breach of the order can be forecast with the certainty of an approaching insolvency or typhoon and the battle to forestall it is a cardinal element in the treatment. Even the reversion to crime may in itself present an opportunity to win more of the client's confidence and be the setting for his recovery, the turning-point when he finally chooses between readjustment to reality and lifelong recidivism.

This kind of crisis could be seen to occur with another of Miss Lane's clients. Here was a case that is included in the statistics as an uninterrupted success but at one stage it was certainly eligible to be added to the total of failures—and in less sympathetic hands would have been. Hilda's feelings about Authority were so confused that they led her to mix a normal class consciousness and disapproval of 'capitalists and toffs—you know the lot I mean: them that go holidays in the Bahamas and have swish cars with one-letter number plates'—with the belief that, provided the victims were rich, she was entitled to recompense herself for her inferior station in life by pilfering. With misgiving the bench placed her on probation; it was understood that she would train as a hospital nurse.

For some months she seemed to do well and the sister tutor, who knew Hilda's history, spoke encouragingly of her progress, but Miss Lane herself was less sanguine. Though their relationship was close Hilda seemed to have difficulty in facing minor difficulties and by means of a slight lie or some venial dishonesty would evade rather than resolve them. After some six months her reporting became irregular. Then one afternoon, following two broken appointments, she arrived looking unhappy and, as Miss Lane described it, 'wearing her unease on her cuff'. When asked what was up Hilda eventually confessed to having stolen £3 from the bedside of a patient in a private ward—'so rich that I doubt if she as much as noticed.'

Miss Lane grimaced distastefully at the memory. 'A confession like that can be unpleasantly tricky. After all we are not father confessors, but officials of the court. On the other hand we are not usually sneaks. We do respect things told us in confidence.

'The fact that she had told me was in itself an advance, even though I think she was expecting me, there and then, to turn her in. When I suggested that the best course would be to return the money and confess the whole thing to the sister tutor, all she could do was shake her head despairingly and burst into tears. She said she no longer had the money, so I offered to lend it to her.

'Eventually after a long talk about mistaken ideas over losing face and the probable and partly unconscious motives behind the theft, plus some stiff injections of wheedling, she agreed to my plan—provided I went with her. Before she could change her mind, and though the waiting-room was full, I whisked her on to a bus. At the hospital we marched straight into the sister tutor's office.

'Luckily she was in and also very understanding. So was the robbed patient, and no more was said. But for Hilda, who normally shirked the smallest unpleasantness, it was probably a decisive experience. It showed her that facing a situation squarely, doing something about it, was not so terrifying or impossible as she had feared. By not sending for the police we were able to make Authority appear less like the enemy.'

The remainder of Hilda's probation was uneventful and she can be rated as one of the genuine successes. There are quite a few cases in which progress is even more erratic and which reflect vicissitudes that are infinitely more serious and prolonged. A client of Mr Young's provides a good example of a case in which a second offence could not be kept out of the statistics as a breach of the order, but which was eventually converted, thanks to the skilful and understanding way in which it was handled, into a genuine as well as a statistical success.

The decisive, critical phase opened with a telephone call from a detective who informed Mr Young that he was looking for one of his probationers: he was suspected of having stolen an expensive wrist-watch, as he had been actually seen to leave a hotel bedroom from which it was missing. The next day this probationer reported wearing what must have been the stolen watch.

'He could never have afforded it out of his wages. While we chatted he even kept admiring it and fiddling with the winder. It might have been a scene from *Crime and Punishment*, with me taking the part of the policeman, except that when I warned that the real police were after him, he broke down at once and admitted having pinched it.

'He saw readily enough that I had no alternative. The best I could do was to help him give himself up rather than be arrested in the street but I made it clear he must do it of his own free will. I told him truthfully that I had no idea what the magistrates would do but that he couldn't count on escaping a sentence. As I'd hoped, he agreed to walk round with me to the police station and fortunately, when he appeared in court next morning, we were lucky with the bench chairman. If the other chairman had been there, he'd have gone down, but he was given a final chance. The breach was recorded and the order was extended for a further year. That extra year made all the difference.'

An appreciation of the lengths that some clients, but not all, are permitted to go before a breach of the order is reported to the court is necessary to an understanding of what is meant by failure on probation. The total of failures would add up very differently if every breach, those of substance let alone merely technical ones, were reported to the courts—but so would the total of eventual, genuine successes. To grasp this, to understand that probation frequently needs a continuation of tolerance, that it can be a very long process, in which success has the habit of growing out of the skilful handling of failure, also explains why probation's achievements can only be measured superficially by statistics; why to rely on them solely is even less meaningful than reaching conclusions about a child's future on the basis of his end-of-term marks.

For my last example I have chosen a young man called Sydney

because the fluctuations of his case demonstrate all this more strikingly than any other I have discovered, why the statistics must always be qualified, and because it portrays the long duel between the officer and his client which is at the heart of probation. Sydney, too, has so far been a statistical failure and he may very well fail again, but even if he does, his time on probation will, I think, prove to have been justified. Like an antibiotic, but much more slowly and less dramatically, probation has begun to change Sydney, to help him realize in himself the majesty of being human.

The first of his two years on probation was certainly more than usually tempestuous and rancorous. At one interview he would appear willing, if not eager, to co-operate, to find himself a better job than his present one as a builders' labourer, to discuss his problems with what, compared with many, was refreshing intelligence. At the next, for no immediately clear reason, he would be sour and aggressive, his insolence curdling his insight and distorting his intelligence with bogus cynicism.

'Why should I want your help? I don't need help from no one. What can you do for me anyway? You're like all the rest except that you wear a sort of disguise. All nice and kind outside but underneath . . . underneath you're nothing but a copper.'

Another time he would complain that his probation officer was too soft and should be stricter with him.

'I wish I'd gone inside and got it over with, like what happened to my mates. Four-and-a-half months and they're as free as sparrows.'

When it was suggested that perhaps he said this because part of him hankered to return to the security of the children's home where he had been brought up, unpleasant and regimented though it was, he fell silent and bit morosely at the skin round his little finger-nail.

His inner loneliness could also be discerned in his attachment to a gang, the kind of outfit that provokes brawls at the local dance hall and goes on cushion-slashing and lamp-smashing rides on the

Southern Region. Some of the members were known by the police to have gravitated to a fairly well organized series of gas-meter raids. On his good days Sydney would talk very frankly about the gang and once he even admitted to having acted as look-out during a stick-up at a dairy depot—it ended in fiasco as the cashier had gone home before they got there. Then, the day following an ugly gang fight round the back of a pin-table arcade, in which two men were left with fractured arms and a girl was concussed, Sydney, whose own cheek was bruised, said he was thinking of breaking away, that things were getting too hot for him. But he was frightened.

'They'd mark me for life if I scarpered. I seen it done to others. Once you're in, you're in, see! You know too much and that makes you special. Like them, you're different. That's something you can't change.'

As well as by fear, Sydney was shackled to the gang by strongly felt loyalties, and these could be seen in conflict with his desire to go straight. Once he telephoned to ask if he could come up to the office immediately. He wanted advice. It was urgent. But when he arrived he appeared to have thought better of it. He agreed he was worried, that he was in what he termed 'a spot of bother', but would say no more. After ten minutes of this he stood up abruptly and walked through the door. An hour later he rang up from a call-box to apologize and then it came out. The gang had done a plant on him, made him hide a tape-recorder they had stolen from the leader of a youth club. Together with a rope and a set of tools, it was in the chest-of-drawers at his lodgings. He had only taken it on the understanding that they would fetch it next evening but no one had turned up.

'They're scared. Wetting their pants. The dicks know all right —they picked up Len for questioning. I'd nothing to do with it—honest I didn't. Didn't even know it was happening till they come round with the stuff.'

The probation officer replied that Sydney could do one of two things: return the tape-recorder to its owner or take it round to the police.

'I knew you'd say that.'

'What else can I say? You tell me?'

'I might have known you'd want me to split.' His angry breath hissed into the receiver's earpiece. 'What's the bloody point when you'll be telling the dicks yourself?'

The retort was that squealing was not a function of a probation officer who in this instance could only point out what he considered to be the right course. If Sydney chose not to follow his advice, that, as far as the two of them were concerned, ended the matter.

Nothing more was indeed said, though weeks later Sydney let slip that the gang had come back for the tape-recorder and he had no idea what they had done with it. It would be pleasant to be able to write that the probation officer's display of forbearance led to a rapid reconciliation between Sydney and Authority. Almost certainly it helped by fashioning a new, especially private bond between officer and client, yet it was but one of many incidents in a complex struggle to prise Sydney away from the gang, a struggle reminiscent of Dantesque forces of Good and Evil. Before it ended the probation officer was forced to have Sydney brought in on a summons, not for any crime but for repeated failures to come to interviews and to keep at work. In reporting the breach to the bench the probation officer ended with a plea that the order might be extended for a further period. This was agreed and, otherwise, Sydney escaped with a £2 fine.

For a long time afterwards Sydney was very bitter. A letter, angrily scribbled in pencil, arrived at the office the next day: 'I should have thought that by now you'd have stopped being surprised at anything I do, especially when it's coming to see you. I have not forgiven you for putting out that summons. You know damn well where you could find me. You're not the only one that can play tough. I am used to that game as well. I could not come Tuesday as something else turned up—more important. Please go easy with those summonses. You may need them for some other unfortunate victim of yours. . . .' Despite its accusations and frustration, this letter conveys, I cannot help thinking, a sense of fundamental trust: it is a communication between two people who understand each other well—it is like the quick anger a child turns against a parent with whom it really knows it can feel safe. Perhaps this is a romantic view, yet, as I write this, Sydney's probation order is still in force and no further trouble has occurred. There will perhaps be further lapses but the tie between Sydney and his probation officer is, I believe, now sufficiently strong to help his eventually discover a happier, less menacing alternative to the security he found in his amateur but vicious gang.

III

A relationship that often is not very apparent, but which is compounded of trust and liking and respect, which is growing and organic, is, we are told, the quintessence of probation . . . It may be healthily rooted even in those who continue to offend and, if so, there is still hope. . . . One step backward is sometimes the necessary prelude to two steps forward. . . . All this, I am convinced, is true enough, and not rationalization or mawkish casuistry and self-delusion, yet there is a limit to which one can qualify statistics. We are still faced with a reconviction rate of 27·6 per cent for first offenders on probation and with much higher rates for juveniles and recidivists. The reasons why many throw away their second chance are, it can be presumed, generally similar to those that made them commit the original offence—one must look for the particular complex of personal and social factors that influence each offender. We have also seen that there are undoubtedly plenty of cases where, because the bench failed to consult the probation officer, or the preliminary inquiries were insufficient, a probation order should never have been made. Yet, even permitting these allowances, one still has to ask to what extent are failures also the result of weaknesses in the service itself. How many of the 30 per cent (overall) of adults and 43 per cent of juveniles continue to go wrong because they were handled in the wrong way, because they were not given enough of the probation officer's time, because he asked the wrong kinds of questions or gave the wrong kinds of advice, because of faults in the technique of casework, or even because of an exaggerated, mistaken belief in its efficacy?

These and other charges could, I have no doubt, be substantiated in relation to specific cases. There are officers who seem blind to the advances in knowledge of human behaviour; who, in some instances, despite a brave psychiatric show, rely too readily on common sense and tickings-off; who fail to resist the relief afforded by sarcasm and even humiliation of the clients. There must indeed be those who have become probation officers for some very wrong reasons—even if they do not realize it themselves. Clearly the calibre of the service varies from officer to officer, from court to court, yet it is as elusive of general assessment as, say, the calibre of the medical profession—only more so. Before criticizing one must remember that probation is still, relatively, a new penal method; that it is still feeling its way, its techniques are not easily codified, they are changing and developing fast; that—as I have indicated—the Service is in the midst of controversy and self-examination which are likely to result in new patterns of thinking and work. To make generalized criticisms is more than usually risky. One is on surer ground in urging stricter standards of entry to the profession, in suggesting the desirability of separating after-care or matrimonial reconciliation from the main stream of probation work, in arguing that rates of pay could be raised without destroying the sense of vocation; much more could—and probably should—be spent on the Service and it would still be relatively more economical than imprisonment; but these matters, though they are very relevant, are outside the plan of this book and in any case, together with other aspects of the Service, are subject to detailed examination by a Government Departmental Committee set up in 1959. For a long time to come any attempt to assess the extent of probation's success or failure must be qualified by doubts as to whether the service is provided with the means, the premises, the facilities, organization, and manpower to meet the demands made of it. Even some of these doubts have to be enmeshed in further reservations. For example, the apparently indisputable assertion that in many areas case-loads are too heavy may need qualification, though this will depend on the importance one attaches to a survey carried out in California which indicated that the success rate of parole agents (similar to after-care supervisors) who looked after ninety cases was statistically no different from that of parole agents with only thirty cases.[1]

Despite his rich diet of human relationships and his daily contact with life at its rawest, the probation officer can in fact all too easily become walled-in by the small, closed world of the court, the office, and the cells: the isolation is in part self-protective and is intensified by long hours and evening visits that leave little time for normal leisure and friendships. There is always a risk, too, that the casework technique, combined with the mantle of the court's authority, gives the probation officer a false sense of omniscience and invincibility. Despite the new ideas and the cross-fertilization with other disciplines, is there perhaps a danger of a new orthodoxy, a casework academicism? Its assumptions are certainly not to be accepted uncritically—indeed the pretentious language in which they are explained makes them suspect, and for this reason I have, as far as possible, discussed them as they are applied to actual cases. Throughout the writing of this book, I have tried not to forget the twin pitfalls of over-enthusiasm and complacency. At times I have been so aware of

[1] *Special Intensive Parole Unit—Phase II: Thirty-man Caseload Study.* Division of Adult Paroles, Department of Corrections, State of California, U.S.A., 1958.

them that I have experienced a fear of near-paranoic quality that I, together with most probation officers, had become bewitched and lulled into a lazy acceptance of the merits and efficacy of probation that was far from justified. Had I not perhaps absorbed too much of the official point-of-view? Had I done enough to find out how probation appeared from the standpoint of the probationer himself or herself? I knew that frequently the probation officer was not as ignorant as some of his clients might imagine of their contempt for his efforts—this contempt is inherent in what he sets out to change—but how many of the apparently co-operative clients, the successes, enjoyed a good laugh at their probation officer's expense? How many officers kidded themselves that they were getting results in order merely to stave-off a nervous breakdown? I found that to pass through a waiting-room full of brash, cocky delinquents with their 'duck's-arse' haircuts and covert solidarity, would sometimes be enough to make me feel a foolish, middle-aged sucker.

A confidential questionnaire, allied with skilful independent interviews of a representative and sufficiently large sample of probationers, might produce some interesting conclusions. Yet what allowance would one have to make for their own inevitable and very natural bias? When talking to men who had broken their probation and thus served prison sentences, I found it difficult to know how to assess their criticisms of the Service? So as to be free from the taint of the Establishment, I approached a few of these 'failed' probationers without official help and I was convinced they spoke very frankly. Yet I could never be sure to what extent their opinions were unconsciously affected by their desire to rationalize their own failure. Even those who had favourable things to say, were, I suspected, types who were neurotically in need of continued reassurance and thus likely to relish their interviews at the probation office. In contrast there were others who even made probation a scapegoat for their having got into trouble again. Often, though, what these men had to say of the Service's weaknesses and mistaken methods had the ring of accuracy:

'So far as I was concerned, it was a waste of time. My bloke meant well, I suppose, but all he did was lose me my job.' The speaker had worked at an hotel and the probation officer, happening to call when he was out, was recognized by another employee who told the manager. The result was the sack, difficulty in finding another job he liked, and this was blamed for the further offence.

'It's the long waits that got me down. An hour, usually more. It's enough to make anyone brassed-off, at the end of a day's work.'

'Keeping the rules isn't all that difficult, but they treat you like a kid. Never do anything really helpful.'

'You should see the waiting-room. "Give up hope all ye who enter here!" ought to be the motto over the fireplace—not that it's often lit.'

'The best he could offer was Rowton House. He never lifted a finger to find me proper diggings.'

'My lot was too stuck-up. Been in the Navy and made you feel you'd pissed on the quarter-deck. Could never understand what he was driving at.'

Another man complained that his probation officer had not been strict enough. 'If he'd given me a right good telling-off, it might have been different. I'd have pulled myself together like. Even when I'd been up for a breach he still gave me the old syrup—seemed to be sorry for me. After that, probation seemed a farce.'

'I don't mind admitting it's the only thing to keep me straight. Coming up to the office each week acts as a reminder. You don't say to yourself: "Here goes! I'm now going to commit a breach!" You only think about it afterwards. I must say I enjoy the long talks we have.'

'I had three different officers in eighteen months. You never knew where you were with them.'

'One day he'd ask me all sorts of silly questions—about my Dad and girls I'd had and all that lark. Never wanted to know anything useful.'

'Soon as I heard him say "hostel" I scarpered. I never want no more of them. Just to hear him suggest one of them places made everything seem hopeless.'

'My bloke was always on his holiday, or gone off on what he called a "course", the only times I really wanted help.'

'What can anyone do to help you anyway? You can only help yourself.'

'We used to sit a full minute just staring at each other. Then, all of a sudden, he'd ask: "Well and what shall we have a talk about today?" That's enough to shut anyone up.'

These conversations confirmed, once again, the most essential truth: that success or failure depends to an even greater degree than I had already realized on the calibre of the individual probation officer, on his personality, tone, quality—call it what you will. It is not being obscurantist to assert that the most correctly trained officers, those who are versed in psychology, sociology, and in every refinement of casework, will turn out to be flops when faced with the scowling Terrys and Carolines, unless in addition they possess that very special, indefinable compound of sympathy and insight and ease of communication. More than technique or the application of scientific knowledge, vital as these are, probation is an art.

IV

To record a success for probation means of course more than making sure that the client merely avoids further trouble with the police, than keeping within the law. Success, to be complete, implies many things: a re-ordered way of life, the maturing of a self-reliant citizen, and the husbanding of other social virtues. It also suggests the acceptance of a recognizable system of moral values. At a certain, elementary level these will be shared by and inculcated by all probation officers, though like the British constitution they are not codified and written down. They are the unspoken values accepted by the community and imparted to well-brought-up children by parents, clergy, and school-teachers. It might be described as a morality that is practical rather than lofty. The probation officer is almost by definition society's personified conscience but, at another level, when advising on the more complex moral decisions posed by their probationers' lives, each officer will colour his recommendations according to his own personal system of values, to his own attitude towards the Establishment, his political views, and so on; though he will also modify his advice to suit the stamina of his client's personality and the magnitude of the difficulties he is up against—as we have seen, experience implants in most probation officers an approach to moral judgements that is far from rigid or orthodox.

An officer's personal beliefs, whether he is, say, a Roman Catholic or a humanist agnostic, are bound to affect his attitude towards certain features of his clients' lives (e.g. birth-control). With many officers their personal beliefs are likely to be reflected only in the emphases and nuances they superimpose on the general body of agreed morality, but when the religious, political, or social outlook of the officer is more consciously held, it inevitably has a more distinctive influence, particularly on the more receptive client. One officer will urge his clients to conform and accept the established order; another will also urge them to conform, yet be far more ready to sympathize if they reject and criticize its standards. (I am making a distinction here between the moral outlook inculcated by probation officers and their attitude towards the clients: the latter is likely to be equally strongly determined by their opinions of, and understanding of, psychology, not to mention their own personalities.)

Except for the mentally subnormal, the insane, and the grossly inadequate, my own feeling is that most offenders are well aware of what society considers to be right and wrong. Even those brought up by professionally criminal parents appreciate this—

after a certain age their understanding is indeed apt to be more profound than the average. Ignorance of basic morality is relatively rare among offenders. To talk merely of 'moral inadequacy', as some do, betrays a very shallow understanding of the nature of crime. Much more important is, like the criminologist, to ask what has caused it. Some offenders certainly have inadequate feelings of guilt, in others they are exaggerated, others act impulsively or compulsively, yet it is probably safe to say that nearly all know when they are doing wrong and what 'wrong' means in the circumstances—even if they 'don't know why they did it'. You might say that the 'wrongness' is often part of the reason they do it. The task of probation is usually not to teach what is right and wrong, but to make the knowledge of right and wrong effective.

To separate moral awareness from moral responsibility, as I am doing, is convenient but also artificial, as the two are closely, dynamically interrelated: a strongly inculcated conscience, or super-ego, can overcome a diminished responsibility (though maybe the price will be exacted in another form!). The separation is nevertheless inherent in the issue that now exercises penologists, moralists, and all concerned in any way with offenders: viz., will our increasing knowledge of the motivation of human behaviour lead to the complete withering of the concept of individual criminal responsibility? (Responsibility in this sense should not be confused with guilt: it refers to the offender's responsibility for a crime of which he has been proved guilty.)

Lady Wootton and others suggest that the conception of criminal responsibility must inevitably become discredited. Their contention is hard to refute. The number and types of crimes that can be explained 'pathologically' rather than in terms merely of moral weakness or wickedness is almost certain to increase. Does this mean then the collapse of morality? The surrender to a hopeless, mechanical determinism? I know that some believe that this may happen but their fears are unnecessary. On the contrary, an acceptance of the new understanding of the nature of crime is likely eventually to reveal how the individual's amorality can be vanquished. The degree of the offender's responsibility, as opposed to the factors that may explain his crime, can only create confusion when deciding the sentence. As Lady Wootton has pointed out, if responsibility is considered relevant by the bench, those who are entirely irresponsible should be given an absolute discharge! Subject to the needs of deterrence—and this is a weighty qualification—society ought to be more concerned with his reform, with curing him, preventing a further offence, than with calculating the price he must pay for his guilt. The latter is a sterile occupation. Propositions like 'An eye for an eye, and a tooth for a tooth'; 'Let the punishment fit the crime'; 'According to their deserts'; are no longer tenable: nor are they practicable or helpful. An acceptance of the idea that the extent of the offender's responsibility when the offence occurred, in the past, can be disregarded is not incompatible with the need to nurture responsibility in the present and future. Psychology and other disciplines, it is true, have turned our conceptions of the offender's individual responsibility for the crime upside-down, but they also provide the means by which the influences that have weakened it can be dispersed.

Probation, it would seem, is ideally fitted to resolve the confusion and public fear that has arisen over this question of criminal responsibility—though a radically new approach to the treatment of those in prison could serve the same purpose. Probation is designed precisely to make the offender become more responsible for his behaviour; it does in fact protect society, as well as offer practical and tolerant help to the offender, thus showing that in many cases the interests of the offender and society need not be in conflict. It offers a workable, intelligent reconciliation between the interests of both. Though it means overlooking the Home Office research unit's 'matched' comparison, I find it very difficult, too, not to believe that for the majority of offenders probation is more likely to boost responsibility and independence than does a stretch in prison. Probation, being founded on faith in the individual, is positive and avoids the sense of hopelessness that pervades most of our prisons and the special difficulties faced by the ex-prisoner in re-establishing himself—these erode the texture of responsibility as certainly as atomic radiation destroys the marrow in our bones.

Probation cannot be assessed accurately without taking account of the resistances it meets with among the community. It does not function in isolation. The probationers themselves are not immune to the opinion in which it is held by the people they live amongst. Though most of us nowadays are prepared to accept the existence of probation and are ready to be convinced that, like medicine, it is a good thing—just as modern surgery and drugs are an advance on blood-letting and clysters—it still faces enough opposition and cynicism to affect its results adversely. Its achievements will be hampered until it is backed with a more positive degree of goodwill. Though, with exceptions, magistrates and judges accept probation as a normal method of dealing with offenders, though it is undeniable that over the last twenty years the Higher Courts have awarded probation orders more frequently and the grand total of probationers, like offences, has gone up, the fact remains that it is used in a smaller proportion of cases. The following table[1] compares the total numbers of people

OFFENDERS PLACED ON PROBATION IN ENGLAND AND WALES

	1938				1959			
Age group	Males	%	Females	%	Males	%	Females	%
Aged 8 and under 14	7,406	50	470	56	9,193	35	873	44
,, 14 ,, ,, 17	5,952	51	524	57	8,013	35	1,055	46
,, 17 ,, ,, 21	4,254	42	826	63	5,565	25	1,059	47
,, 21 ,, ,, 30	2,552	18	799	39	3,742	12	925	31
,, 30 and over	1,656	9	906	20	3,108	9	1,338	17
	21,820		3,525		29,621		5,250	

[1] Extracted from larger table in *Criminal Statistics, England and Wales. 1959*. Cmd. 1100, (p. xxv).

placed on probation after being found guilty of indictable offences at both higher and magistrates' courts in England and Wales in 1938 and 1959 : the figures for each age-group are also expressed as percentages of the total numbers found guilty.

When the 1959 figures are compared with those for the two previous years, the percentages suggest a continuing decline. Perhaps this was caused by a desire not to add to the work of a service that is already overburdened? Perhaps fines are considered more suitable for an 'affluent' society? Perhaps the proportion of hardened professional criminals who are unsuitable for probation has increased? Perhaps courts nowadays select probationers with more care? The drop in the percentages is surely too great for these explanations. Despite the relative cheapness of probation, its—at worst—equal efficiency to prison or Borstal, it is difficult not to conclude that over the country as a whole the courts rely less than they once did on the kind of positive reform that probation is able to offer.

The benches reflect, on the whole, the attitudes towards crime and punishment of the society they represent. This is also true of the police : as far as I can gather, their opinion of probation can vary between helpful support through various grades of tolerance to veiled obstruction and undisguised, scornful disapproval. It is perhaps understandable that beneath the stress of coping with a virulent local outbreak of crime, and hampered by inadequate numbers, that some police officers complain that 'we use all our skill, and indeed risk our lives, tracking criminals down, and all that happens to them is a nice holiday on probation. It makes us look soft—not to say ridiculous. A good giggle at our expense, that's what it often amounts to.'

That the police tend to have a different idea of who is a success or failure on probation has to be appreciated. Though public alertness to protect the citizen's rights *vis-à-vis* the police is essential and admirable, the eagerness with which many sections of the Press score off the police and appear to assume that the police must be wrong in any dispute over the handling of a criminal is, to my mind, irresponsible and antisocial. To say this, is a necessary preface to the conclusion that on occasion the failure of the police or rather of individual police officers to co-operate with probation officers can be unfortunate, to put it at its mildest. I have stumbled across two cases at least where probationers would appear to have been recruited as stool-pigeons or informers: in other words they were encouraged to continue associating with doubtful company, something which was diametrically in conflict with the advice given by the probation officer. In another case the mother of a probationer complained that the police had criticized her son for having discussed his questioning about a further charge, which he denied, with his probation officer. The mother was also told at the police station to get her son to admit the offence, otherwise at the end of seven days a warrant would be taken out for his arrest. Such accusations by a client must always be suspect and it was pleasing to hear of the readiness with which senior police officers are prepared to investigate complaints from probation officers, and to prevent this kind of thing from happening, but these instances are symptomatic of a lack of understanding of probation and of modern penal methods and aims generally. This lack is not limited to the police, many of whose members have a mature understanding and compassion for the people they have to deal with.

V

Unless one's view of social organization is entirely utilitarian, probation has not merely to be assessed in terms of its success with the individual or as an efficient method of ridding society of criminals, but also as a measure of human progress. Even to write down such a phrase smacks of a naïve Victorian belief in the inevitability of progress, but in an age familiar with genocide, in which mankind is separated from self-annihilation by the push of a button, it is all the more important to recognize and welcome social advances whenever they are genuine. Our attitudes towards the criminal are always to be mistrusted; it is said that crime stirs up in us, both as individuals and members of a group, long-buried feelings of aggression and guilt and arouses obdurate emotional prejudices; public opinion sways confusedly between the wish to understand and to inflict revengeful punishment, to be merciful and to flog; there is even a tendency, I believe, to wax sentimental over the awarding of probation to some as a means of assuaging the guilt felt at inflicting long prison sentences on others. None the less probation, as used today, has to be seen as part of a heartening revolution in human relations; as the complement, indeed the advance-guard, of other penal reforms and of the responsibility nowadays recognized by the community for the aged and very young, for people who are either physically or mentally sick. Like most revolutions, the progress in penal reform and ideas of punishment is very uneven, but probation represents an advance as fundamental as was the jury system compared with the ducking-stool. It must be remembered, too, that the scientific knowledge of individual behaviour and social forces from which probation draws its strength and gains its impetus is very recent; further discoveries are certain and are likely not only to improve the technique of probation but also to extend the types of offenders to which it can be applied.

The newness of probation historically, as well as the innovations and variations in its methods, makes any tabulated summing-up as unwise as is generalized criticism. Inevitably this attempt to assess probation's results is inconclusive. It is also incomplete. Throughout the book, to make my investigation more manageable, I have designedly limited it to factors that can be under the probation officer's direct influence or which affect their clients most directly, and I have omitted what are perhaps some of the most fundamental, if imprecise, considerations. Probation may be easy to recognize as a social advance but society itself presents it with its most refractory problems, imposes the most hampering limitations. Underlying the complexes of factors that influence each offender, overshadowing the personal morality inculcated by each probation officer, are society's own values, and the varying stresses it inflicts on its members. Crimes are not committed in a vacuum. As well as being departures from moral normality, they also reflect it. As Edward Glover puts it, '. . . each community produces the criminals it deserves. . . .' The probation officer not only calls upon society's positive values but has to combat its negative ones, though different officers will have different interpretations of what these are.

To a small extent I have touched on these social forces and values in the chapter 'In Trouble with Circumstances'. If this were a study merely in criminology, that chapter would be immensely longer and require many sub-divisions. It would have to discuss and explore deeply the effects on offenders of such factors as the decline in the influence of religion and the failure of many to adopt a substitute; the influence of television, films, the Press, comics, including the vogue for entertainment exploiting brutality and horror—in fact most of the issues examined by Richard Hoggart in the *Uses of Literacy*.[1] Similarly, one cannot isolate crimes of violence from the legitimized violence of two world wars, nor the floating anxiety evident in so many probationers from the ever-present fear of the H-bomb, germ warfare, and the propaganda of double-think and cold war. Strain that expresses itself in crime is undoubtedly also the result of changing patterns in society—the weakening of the security provided by the family circle (though this is perhaps two-edged!), the early sense of failure brought about by a muffed 11-plus exam, the daily battering of the rush hour and our choked, blood-spattered roads. . . . One has to ask also to what extent are adolescent

[1] Chatto & Windus, 1957.

gangs a reaction to the anonymity of the great city, and anti-social behaviour the result of fewer personal restraints compared with those met with in a smaller, tighter community? Can the increase in crime be entirely separated from the pressures of modern advertising—and also from its dishonesty; from the continual exhortations to succeed, the tendency of cash values to usurp all others; from the frustration of the dead-end job, inevitable in a society in which only one in three boys and one in eight girls are given any sort of specialized training; from the gossip columnists' arch reports of the private lives of the very rich, from the comparison of tax-free stock exchange gains with the inexorable deductions of P.A.Y.E.? There has been a very real narrowing of economic differences but can one say that it has lessened the urge for possessions, or has it opened up material ambitions that were hitherto dormant? Does not this narrowing disguise that inequality remains the greatest incentive to crime?

Probation is concerned only with the individual. These larger, amorphous factors are but the setting in which probation works—and what might be described as the penumbra to this book. An awareness of them can help the probation officer be more percipient, to understand the offender more thoroughly, but he can do no more than palliate their effects. Probation officers can prevent crimes from being committed but they must never be judged by the current height of the crime wave. The cure for this lies deeper, for it is a symptom of society's own sickness, and only as such can it be treated with hope.

Short Bibliography

*

AICHHORN, August. *Wayward Youth.* Imago, London, 1951.

BOWLBY, John. *Maternal Care and Mental Health.* World Health Organization, Geneva, 1952.

BOVET, Lucien. *Psychiatric Aspects of Juvenile Delinquency.* World Health Organization, Geneva, 1951.

British Journal of Criminology (formerly *British Journal of Delinquency*); edited by Edward Glover, Hermann Mannheim, and Emanuel Miller. Published for The Institute for the Study and Treatment of Delinquency by Stevens, London, quarterly.

BURT, Sir Cyril. *The Young Delinquent.* University of London Press, Bickley, 1944.

Criminal Statistics, England and Wales. Home Office, annually.

DAVIES, A. B. Lloyd. *The Boundaries of Casework.* Association of Psychiatric Social Workers, London, 1957.

EAST, Sir William Norwood. *Society and The Criminal.* Home Office, London, 1949.

FERGUSON, Thomas. *The Young Delinquent in his Social Setting: a Glasgow Study.* Oxford University Press, 1952.

FRIEDLANDER, Käthe. *The Psycho-analytical Approach to Juvenile Delinquency.* Kegan Paul, Trench, Trubner, London, 1947.
Delinquency. Kegan Paul, Trench, Trubner, London, 1947.

GLOVER, Edward. *The Psychopathology of Prostitution.* Institute for the Scientific Treatment of Delinquency, London, 1957.

GLOVER, Edward. *The Roots of Crime.* Imago, London, 1960.

GLOVER, Elizabeth. *Probation and Re-education.* Routledge & Kegan Paul, London, 1949.

GLUECK, S. S. and E. T. *Delinquents in the Making: Paths to Prevention.* Harper and Brothers, New York, 1952.

GLUECK, S. S. and E. T. *One Thousand Juvenile Delinquents: their Treatment by Court and Clinic.* Harvard University Press, Cambridge, Massachusetts, 1934.

GRÜNHUT, Max. *Practical Results and Financial Aspects of Adult Probation in Selected Countries.* U.N.O., New York, 1954.

JONES, Howard. *Crime and the Penal System.* University Tutorial Press, London, 1956.

KING, Joan (editor). *The Probation Service.* Butterworth, London, 1958.

McCORD, William and Joan. *Origins of Crime.* Columbia University Press, New York, 1959.

MANNHEIM, Hermann (editor). *Pioneers in Criminology.* Stevens, London, 1960.

MANNHEIM, Hermann, and WILKINS, Leslie T. *Prediction Methods in Relation to Borstal Training.* Home Office, 1955.

MORRIS, Terence. *The Criminal Area: a Study in Social Ecology.* Routledge & Kegan Paul, London, 1957.

MULLINS, Claud. *Crime and Psychology.* Methuen, London, 1943.

NEUSTATTER, W. Lindesay. *Psychological Disorder and Crime.* Christopher Johnson, London, 1953.

PAGE, Sir Leo. *The Young Lag: a Study in Crime.* Faber & Faber, London, 1950.

PAKENHAM, Lord Frank (assisted by Roger Opie). *Causes of Crime.* Weidenfeld & Nicolson, London, 1958.

PEARCE, J. D. W. *Juvenile Delinquency.* Cassell, London, 1952.

Probation. Official organ of The National Association of Probation Officers, London, quarterly.

RADZINOWICZ, L. *The Results of Probation.* A report of the Cambridge Department of Criminal Science. Macmillan, London, 1958.

RADZINOWICZ, L. *Sexual Offences.* A report of the Cambridge Department of Criminal Science. Macmillan, London, 1957.

ROLPH, C. H. (editor). *Women of the Streets.* Secker & Warburg, London, 1955.

STOKES, Sewell. *Court Circular.* Michael Joseph, London, 1950.

UNITED NATIONS. *European Seminar on Probation* (October 1952, London). U.N.O., New York, 1954.

UNITED NATIONS. *Probation and Related Measures*. U.N.O., New York, 1951.

WOOTTON, Lady Barbara (assisted by Vera G. Seal and Rosalind Chambers). *Social Science and Social Pathology*. Allen & Unwin, London, 1959.

ZILBOORG, Gregory. *The Psychology of the Criminal Act and Punishment*. Hogarth Press, London, 1955.

Index

INDEX